THE UNIVF GHA

Social Policy in Germany

Social Policy in Germany

Edited by

Jochen Clasen and
Richard Freeman

HARVESTER
WHEATSHEAF

New York   London   Toronto   Sydney   Tokyo   Singapore

First published 1994 by
Harvester Wheatsheaf
Campus 400, Maylands Avenue
Hemel Hempstead
Hertfordshire, HP2 7EZ
A division of
Simon & Schuster International Group

Typeset in 10/12 pt Times
by The Midlands Book Typesetting Company, Loughborough

Printed and bound in Great Britain by
T.J. Press (Padstow) Ltd

British Library Cataloguing in Publication Data

A catalogue record for this book is available from
the British Library

ISBN 0 7450 1548 4 (pbk)

1 2 3 4 5   98 97 96 95 94

Contents

List of tables and figures

Tables

Figure

Notes on contributors

Prue Chamberlayne is Principal Lecturer at the University of East London and subject area leader for European Studies. Her ESRC-funded research on 'Cultures of Care', conducted with Annette King, is based on narrative interviews with home-carers in Bremen and Leipzig, and uses methods of interpretative textual analysis. This East–West comparison is an initial attempt to extend comparative social policy to the informal sphere. Recent work for publication includes 'Transitions in the private sphere in East Germany', in W. R. Lee and Eve Rosenhaft (eds), *The State and Social Change in Germany 1880–1980* (2nd edn, Berg, forthcoming), and articles on developments in post-war welfare systems in Western Europe in *Policy and Politics* (1992) and in *Critical Social Policy* (1991/2).

Jochen Clasen studied Sociology and Economics at the Free University Berlin and received his PhD from Edinburgh University. He is currently Lecturer in Social Policy in the Department of Social Sciences at Loughborough University. He is a co-editor of *The Sociology of Social Security* (Edinburgh University Press, 1991) and the author of *Paying the Jobless: A comparison of unemployment benefit policies in Great Britain and Germany* (Avebury, 1994).

Richard Freeman studied History and German in Oxford and then Social Policy in Manchester. Postgraduate research in health politics and in policy responses to HIV and AIDS took him to Cologne, Bonn and Berlin in 1990. He is currently Lecturer in European Policy in the Department of Politics at the University of Edinburgh, and is working on a book, *The Politics of Health in Europe* (Manchester University Press, forthcoming).

Norman Ginsburg is Reader in Social Policy at South Bank University. He has recently published papers on aspects of housing policy in Britain, particularly in relation to race and housing, and also a book, *Divisions of*

Welfare (Sage, 1992). This is a critical introduction to cross-national policy analysis covering social security, family and health care policies in Sweden, Britain, the United States and West Germany, based on library research of primary and secondary sources.

Mark Kleinman is currently Lecturer in the Department of Social Policy and Administration at the London School of Economics. For the last eleven years he has carried out research into housing and urban issues at the LSE and at the University of Cambridge. He is an active member of the European Network for Housing Research, and is co-author of *European Economic Monetary and Political Union: Consequences for national housing policies* (Delft University Press, 1993).

Walter Lorenz is Senior Lecturer in Social Work at University College, Cork. His research fields include comparative issues in social work education and practice in Europe, and his recent monograph, *Social Work in a Changing Europe* (Routledge, 1994), explores historical and political factors that account for diverse forms of social work and social pedagogy. He maintains teaching and research links with many social work schools in Europe, in particular now with departments in Central and Eastern Europe.

Steen Mangen is Lecturer in European Social Policy in the Department of Social Policy and Administration at the London School of Economics. He has been researching (West) German social policy for over ten years, initially in the area of mental health reform. Later he specialised in German health and social security with particular reference to Helmut Kohl's *Wendepolitik*. He is currently completing a study of the politics of urban renewal in inner-city Europe, an investigation which includes a case study of Hamburg.

Michael Moran is a graduate of the Universities of Lancaster and of Essex, and has researched on comparative public policy for over twenty-five years. He is presently Professor of Government at the University of Manchester. His publications include *Politics and Society in Britain* (Macmillan, 1989), *The Politics of the Financial Services Revolution* (Macmillan, 1991) and, with Bruce Wood, *States, Regulation and the Medical Profession* (Open University Press, 1993).

Eve Rosenhaft received her BA from McGill University and her PhD in History from Cambridge, where she was a fellow of King's College. She is presently Senior Lecturer in the Department of German at the University of Liverpool. She has done research on the history of the labour movement, juvenile delinquency, youth culture and youth policy in twentieth-century Germany. Her publications include *Beating the Fascists? German communism and political violence 1929–33* (Cambridge University

Press, 1983), *The State and Social Change in Germany, 1880–1980* (co-edited with W.R. Lee, Berg, 1990, 2nd edn forthcoming) and *Rationale Beziehungen? Geschlechterverhältnisse im Rationalisierungsprozeß* (co-edited with D. Reese, C. Sachße and T. Wiegel, Suhrkamp, 1993).

Claire Wallace is Lecturer in Applied Social Science at the University of Lancaster and is currently seconded to the Central European University in Prague, where she is Head of the Department of Sociology. She has worked on a number of Anglo-German studies of young people, their life transitions, education and employment, and is currently doing similar comparative work in Poland and the Ukraine. Her most recent books include *Youth, Family and Citizenship* (Open University Press, 1992), with Gill Jones, and a series of volumes with Stein Ringen on comparative social policy in Eastern and Central Europe called *Prague Papers on Social Transition* (Avebury).

Preface

The social policy of European countries is a relatively new but now rapidly growing interest in the social sciences. This enthusiasm is in part an effect of topicality, as teachers of politics, sociology and social welfare, like others, respond to the development of European integration. In part, too, it is led by more academic exploration of cross-national comparative method, in which the historical and political experience of other states is used to test hypotheses generated by our own. The study of Germany, frequently acknowledged as a leader or model in welfare development and, of course, part of the heartland of the European Union, is central to this emerging field.

A major purpose of this book is to fill a gap in the literature. The gap was, simply, that there was no single introductory text in English available to those wishing to find out more about social policy in Germany. Either Germany has formed a single chapter in introductory comparative texts on social policy (Heinze *et al*, 1986; Zapf, 1986; Ford, 1987a; Muller, 1989; Ginsburg, 1992; Wilson, 1993), or social policy has formed a single chapter in texts on German politics and public policy (Michalsky, 1985; Katzenstein, 1987; Mangen, 1989, 1992). Meanwhile, unification and other recent developments in Germany have served only to increase a sense of uncertainty and lack of information among students and teachers alike.

The second reason relates to the recently rekindled tradition of comparative method, which distinguishes types of welfare states with the aim of capturing some of the differences in the way in which countries provide social services and benefits (e.g. Esping-Andersen, 1990; Langan and Ostner, 1991; Leibfried, 1992). Different structures of welfare provision (emphasising markets, families or the state) imply differences with respect to employment and social stratification. In most of these classifications, Germany is thought of as a prototype of a 'corporatist-statist' or conservative regime (Esping-Andersen, 1990). It is taken to represent a 'third way' (Schmidt, 1988) between countries with predominantly liberal, market-oriented policy programmes, on the one hand, and egalitarian, citizenship-oriented welfare states, on the other. Vertical redistribution of welfare is negligible, the role of market or occupational benefits is marginal, and traditional family relations are manifested in the exclusion of non-working wives from social insurance. The latter, largely financed by contributors rather than by taxation, provides benefit levels strictly determined by earnings. Rather than the avoidance of poverty, as conventionally assumed, the key principles here are the preservation of income and status. But what does this classification mean, exactly? If the characterisation is accurate, how far do its major traits apply to social policy fields other than to income maintenance, which has so often been the primary focus in comparative books on 'welfare states'? These and similar questions prompted the idea for a more detailed text on social policy in Germany. We hope that it will contribute to an increasingly sophisticated understanding of the different facets of social policy in Germany and so prove to be a valuable source for further comparative studies on the nature and development of welfare states in different countries.

The book is organised in three sections, the first describing the political, economic, legal, ideological and historical context of social policy in Germany. The second is concerned with five main areas of social policy delivery in turn. The third discusses the relationship between social policy and the major social divisions of race and gender. As in other fields of public policy, the social policy model of the former West Germany has been extended to the territory of the former GDR, albeit in some cases allowing for a transition period. When concerned with developments before unification, therefore, the book refers for the most part to policies, organisational characteristics and institutions of the former West Germany as a guide to understanding current policy-making. Reflecting their illustrative and informative purpose, each chapter closes with a guide to further reading, listing primarily other work in English but pointing also to important German sources, both primary and secondary. The book's contributing authors are all academics working in the United Kingdom and Ireland whose research has taken them into the field of German social policy and who therefore combine an understanding of their respective research fields with an awareness of the needs of students.

This project was born of a study day on Social Policy in Germany which was held in London in February 1992, under the auspices of the Social Policy Association's Comparative Social Policy Group. The editors would like to thank both the Association and members of the Group for their continuing support.

Jochen Clasen
Richard Freeman

March 1994

The German social state: an introduction

Richard Freeman and Jochen Clasen

To the rest of the world, Germany presents an image of modernity, efficiency and reasoned order; its social policy is an essential part of that order. Germany is thought of as a social policy leader, in perhaps two senses. First, as the first industrial country to introduce social policy legislation in the 1880s, it represented a model for other welfare states. Britain's Liberal reforms of 1908–11, for example, owed something to Lloyd George's visit to Germany in 1908 (see Hennock, 1987). Second, as a key player in the world economy, West Germany has shown an envied ability to match social spending with economic competitiveness, successfully combining 'Anglo-Saxon liberalism with continental statism and corporatism in a modern social welfare state' (Katzenstein, 1987, p. 3). This book aims in part to account for Germany's social policy success, describing the characteristic institutions and principles on which it is based. In part, too, however, it will point to the superficiality of stereotypes: social policy in Germany, as elsewhere, displays weaknesses and problems, failures and conflict. The purpose of this introduction is to provide background and context for the more detailed studies which follow. It begins by asking, simply, what sort of a welfare state is Germany?

In Titmuss's famous scheme, Germany would fit best with the 'industrial achievement-performance' model of social policy, in which welfare functions as an adjunct to the economy and which holds that 'social needs should be met on the basis of merit, work performance and productivity' (Titmuss, 1974, p. 31). Mishra (1984) thinks of Germany as a corporatist or 'integrated welfare state', and more specifically as one in which the interdependence between social and economic policy is recognised and institutionalised. For Esping-Andersen (1990), too, Germany is typical of the 'corporatist' welfare states, like Austria, France and Italy. Classifications and descriptions of this

1

kind are necessarily brief. As answers to our initial question, they seem unsatisfactory and incomplete. They suggest that a fuller understanding will depend on exploring other questions first. What sort of a state is Germany? What kinds of legal, political and economic organisation shape its social policy-making? What are the ideological principles according to which welfare is provided? By which institutions is it led? These are the questions which structure this introduction, and which imply a particular mix of principles and practice in the provision of welfare which it is the purpose of the book as a whole to explore.

The modern German state

Germany has been described as a 'semisovereign' state (Katzenstein, 1987), a characteristic which reflects both the internal and the external conditions of German politics. The post-war settlement in Europe prescribed an unusual degree of control over German foreign and defence policy for foreign powers. With integration into the European Community, of course, this may or may not become true of economic policy also (see Kirchner, 1992). Meanwhile, large areas of public life are governed independently of the state by a heterogeneous set of parapublic institutions which merge public and private bureaucracies (Katzenstein, 1987), such as the Federal Bank, works councils, social insurance funds and independent social services organisations. All of these, and the concept of subsidiarity which underpins their activities, are considered in the course of this introduction.

As well as being 'semisovereign', Germany has also been described as a 'state without a centre' (Smith, 1992a). It is a federal republic, in which power is shared between the national government, the *Bund* or collectivity, and the individual states or *Länder*. The government is responsible to parliament, the *Bundestag*, while the states are represented in its other chamber, the *Bundesrat*. The states hold considerable power not only because, in legislative terms, the *Bundesrat* approves the federal budget and has the right of veto over law-making which directly affects *Länder* interests, but also because the federal government depends largely on the states for the implementation of policy (Smith, 1992a). The *Länder* hold primary responsibility for education and health as well as for policing, broadcasting and cultural affairs. In the field of social policy, the states control planning, they either own or contribute to the capital costs of some services such as hospitals, and they fund means-tested social assistance. To some extent, responsibilities are shared with the municipalities (*Kommunen*), though the constitution is less clear about the demarcation between state and local governments than about that between the states and the centre. Public spending is shared between the three tiers of government: most federal spending is taken up by defence and social security transfer payments, most state spending by salary payments for staff in education and the police, and the greater part of local government spending is represented by public investment in health care, welfare, education, sewage and roads (Katzenstein, 1987).

While federal and state governments work to different electoral calendars, the states differ in terms of their political composition. They differ also in terms of their economic organisation, their wealth as measured in tax revenues, and their levels of unemployment. The integrative, coordinating function of federal administration is limited, in respect both of states and of areas of administrative interest, though a degree of inter-regional coordination is provided by Standing Conferences of ministers of culture (responsible for education) and of health. Public policy in Germany, that is to say, is the product of differences not only between political parties but also between federal and regional tiers of government and between states. Such complicated political bargaining tends to result in high levels of spending on existing programmes, rather than in conceptual innovation and the introduction of new policies. The impact of West German federalism on public policy is perhaps best described as paradoxical. 'It . . . discourages radical policy initiatives, and yet at the same time it tends to favour the further extension of the interventionist role of the state' (Schmidt, 1989, p. 80).

Unification may contribute to a process of centralisation in the German state, insofar as the weakness of the new *Länder* in the East makes them more dependent on the federal government both for economic support and for administrative expertise than their counterparts in the West (Smith, 1992a). At bottom, it is the addition of the five relatively poor eastern *Länder* to the original (and richer) eleven which is the source of problems. Not only has the number of states increased; so have the differences between them in terms of wealth and resources. This, in turn, introduces a new logic to the relationships between the states and the federal government (Sturm, 1992). The six eastern *Länder*, including Berlin, tend to operate as a bloc in seeking financial aid from the federal government and are much less sensitive than those in the West to the extension of federal jurisdiction over state affairs which such intervention implies (Sturm, 1992).

Public policy-making in Germany can be understood as a process of law: the constitution or Basic Law (the *Grundgesetz*) describes the German state as a 'legal state' (or *Rechtsstaat*). One aspect of this is the way in which the *Bundestag* is a working rather than a debating parliament, as indicated by its high legislative output (von Beyme, 1985; Smith, 1992a). More important, however, is the protection of the provisions of the Basic Law by the Constitutional Court, which is charged with its interpretation. The Court is autonomous and wholly independent both of parliament and of the Ministry of Justice. Its function is not only to uphold the basic constitutional freedoms of the individual but also to arbitrate in disputes between different parts of the state and between federal and regional governments. It rules on the constitutionality of parliamentary legislation and, in giving reasons for its decisions, holds a *de facto* power of amendment (Smith, 1992a). In this sense, effective policy-making in Germany is the result of judicial interpretation of federal and regional legislation.

Politics

German party politics is based on a system of proportional representation and coalition governments. Parties' access to parliament was restricted in 1961, since when 5 per cent of the vote or the direct election of three candidates has been required for a party to be represented in the *Bundestag*. Since the 1950s, the political landscape has been dominated by two mass or people's parties (*Volksparteien*), the Christian Democrats and Social Democrats. In practice, the major parties are forced by the consistent balance of electoral support into forming governing coalitions with a third party, invariably the much smaller Free Democrats, or Liberals. It is notable that this triangular stability has been largely unaffected either by the emergence of the Greens in the early 1980s or by the process of unification (Smith, 1992b).

The CDU (Christian Democratic Union) united disparate interests in the centre and on the right of German politics which before the war had been organised separately: conservatives, nationalists, liberals, Catholic social reformers, conservative Protestants, entrepreneurs and Catholic workers (Katzenstein, 1987). It has both labour and business wings as well as representing, in different ways, small business, the churches and women. The party successfully assimilated refugee parties and regionalist movements in the 1960s, although one remaining regional party, the Bavarian CSU (Christian Social Union), in effect constitutes the CDU's Bavarian wing. Importantly, the CDU is a Christian party as well as a conservative one, traditionally committed to the defence of religious values (Gallagher *et al.*, 1992). This, as well as the role of 'social committees' in the party's organisation, makes for a less controversial pattern of welfare politics than in the United Kingdom (von Beyme, 1985).

Since the Second World War, the SPD (Social Democratic Party of Germany) has moved from being a committedly class-based Marxist party to one seeking mass support. The party's 1959 conference in Bad Godesberg agreed the renunciation of what would be termed 'Clause 4' socialism in relation to the Labour Party in Britain, accepting the economic framework of the market at home and a commitment to NATO abroad. The trade unions passed a similar resolution in Düsseldorf in 1963.

The FDP (Free Democratic Party) are positioned between the CDU/CSU and the SPD, being both secular and non-union. They are a small party, claiming between 5 per cent and 12 per cent of the national vote. This is just enough to gain them seats in parliament, but also enough for their support to be crucial in enabling either of the major parties to govern. This kingmaker function makes the FDP almost a permanent party of government (Schmidt, 1989). This, in turn, makes FDP policy positions inordinately important: its interest lies in economic efficiency rather than equality, in the market rather than the state, in price stability rather than employment. While its economic liberalism makes it an acceptable coalition partner for the CDU, its commitment to civil rights and interest in socio-legal issues makes for common ground with the SPD. However, the FDP does not share the links which both major parties have to the labour movement and to substantial welfare clienteles; the tolerance it shows towards the German welfare system is contingent upon economic growth (Schmidt, 1989). Indeed, while both the CDU and the SPD can be described as ardent defenders of established patterns of social provision, the FDP, supported by many of those exempt from compulsory contributions to statutory social insurance funds (such as the self-employed, tenured civil servants and some professionals), frequently stresses the need for reduced state involvement in social policy and the introduction of more private sector options.

The combination of interests expressed by these three parties makes for a triangular system of alliances based on class (CDU and FDP versus SPD) and religion (CDU/CSU versus FDP and SPD) (Pappi, quoted in Gallagher *et al.*, 1992). Where the CDU and the FDP together tend to promote the interests of industrial capital, the Catholic reformism of the CDU generates alliances with the SPD in social policy, and the secular interests of the SPD and FDP combine to resist Catholic intrusions into public policy on specific issues such as abortion. Each of the two main parties is in competition for the electoral middle ground at the centre of the triangle, making for what has been termed a centripetal system (Smith, 1992b). In this search for consensus, political issues tend to be articulated not according to opposed ideological standpoints of right and left but as the product of expert analysis. Policy formulation in both main parties is legitimised by a process of public hearings and consultation with independent advisers (Kolinsky, 1991). Often, changes of government make for relatively small changes in policy (von Beyme, 1985).

The Greens (*Die Grünen*) first won parliamentary representation at federal level in 1983. The party is an expression of a new politics of mass action and of new issues such as environmentalism and sexual equality (Smith, 1992b). The arrival of the Greens might have made possible a new red–green alignment on the left of German politics, the Social Democrats becoming less dependent on the liberal centre, though they also threatened to draw support away from the SPD, particularly that of younger voters. The emergence of the far-right *Republikaner* (REP) in the late 1980s, echoing the NPD in the late 1960s, posed similar strategic problems for the CDU (Smith, 1992b). While the FDP is rooted in a culture of political consensus and system support established in the immediate post-war period, these new parties reflect a shift towards participation, conflict and dissent characteristic of the 1970s and 1980s. This radicalisation on both left and right may be interpreted as a response to the increased uncertainty of employment and social integration among younger Germans (Kolinsky, 1991). At the same time, the emergence of the smaller parties points to the way in which the decentralised fragmentation of its political system gives protest movements greater leverage in Germany than in other similar countries (von Beyme, 1985).

The first post-unification general election, which was held in December 1990, confirmed the governing mandate which the conservative–liberal coalition had held in former West Germany since 1983 (Smith, 1992b). The SPD's negativism with regard to the process and potential costs of unification left it trailing badly, especially in the East, while the West German Greens' inability to construct any sort of platform with regard to the dominant issue meant that they failed to clear the 5 per cent hurdle and so lost representation in the new *Bundestag*. They nevertheless continue to hold considerable strength at regional state level. The PDS (the reformed socialist–communist SED which governed the former GDR), meanwhile, having gained over 10 per cent of the vote in the East but less than 3 per cent overall, seems unlikely to survive in federal politics, though it may continue to hold a presence in some of the former East German *Länder*.

Länder politics have become increasingly complex since 1990, giving rise to a number of different coalition patterns between these four parties. What is important is that the parties which form the federal government currently make up a minority of those coalitions and therefore command a minority of seats in the *Bundesrat* (Smith, 1992b; Sturm, 1992). However, a record number of *Länder* elections during 1994 and the general election which comes at the end of the same year may change the political landscape significantly.

Economic organisation

Though a romantic attachment to the land persists in German culture, the orientation of the economy has continued to move away from agriculture and towards industry in the post-war period. The proportion of agricultural labour in the workforce fell from 25 per cent to 5 per cent between 1950 and 1981, while agriculture represented 12 per cent of GNP in 1949 and less than 2 per cent in 1985 (Conradt, 1993). German economic strengths now lie in chemicals (Bayer, Hoechst), car manufacturing (Volkswagen-Audi, BMW, Daimler-Benz) and machine tools (Bosch).

An economy of private ownership affords the state an unusually small steering capacity (von Beyme, 1985). In Germany, industrial competition is protected not through rigorous regulation but through limitations on the scope of government intervention (Gilbert, 1986). Just as importantly, the regulation of the money supply remains formally independent of government.

The Federal Bank (the *Bundesbank*) has a statutory responsibility to safeguard currency stability, controlling inflation by regulating both the money supply and the availability of credit to the economy (Padgett, 1992).

German economic interests are organised along corporatist lines. Most firms belong to at least one of the main employers' federations, the Confederation of German Employers' Associations (BDA) or the Federation of German Industry (BDI). These reflect a German tradition of organisation by cartel, and constitute unofficial forums of industrial and social and economic policy-making respectively (Gilbert, 1986; Katzenstein, 1987). The coherence of policy development is further enhanced by the active role of major banks on company boards. Small businesses are legally obliged to affiliate to the Association of German Chambers of Industry and Commerce (DIHT) (Gallagher *et al.*, 1992). German labour, on the other hand, is organised by industry rather than by craft, which makes it possible to engage in industry-wide collective bargaining. Seventeen industrial unions, the most influential of which represents the metal-workers (*IG Metall*), make up the German Confederation of Trade Unions (DGB); other union members belong to the German Civil Service Union (DBB) (Gilbert, 1986; Katzenstein, 1987). The Co-determination Acts of 1951 and 1976 which applied to the coal and steel industries and the Works Constitution Acts of 1952 and 1972 secured workers' rights to representation and consultation in the workplace by means of complex legal and institutional structures for partnership in industry (Gilbert, 1986).

The division of the employers' organisations, as well as the fact that individual unions are not bound by the negotiations of the DGB, means that economic organisation in Germany can be described as a pattern of 'medium corporatism' (Gallagher *et al.*, 1992), or perhaps of 'concertation' in policy-making (von Beyme, 1985). The two sides of industry are not bound with government into a formal process of decision-making in the way that they are in Austria, for example, though they tend to be oriented towards negotiation and cooperation rather than conflict and confrontation (Gallagher *et al.*, 1992). Comparative research suggests that welfare spending and provision in the context of a corporate culture of this kind is a competitive asset (Pfaller *et al.*, 1991). Elsewhere, it has been described as a 'circle of virtue':

> The structure of industrial relations at the workplace has permitted high
> productivity, high productivity has allowed for high real wages and elaborate
> social insurance provisions, and the latter have contributed to union moderation
> in general and union acceptance of the industrial relations system in particular.
> (Streeck, quoted in Gilbert, 1986, p. 144)

This integration of economic and social policy is also expressed in the term and philosophy of the social market (*soziale Marktwirtschaft*). The concept was developed by Ludwig Erhard, Germany's Minister of Economic Affairs between 1949 and 1963 and subsequently Chancellor until 1966. The root assumption of the social market is that employers and employees are partners in an interdependent but essentially private activity. They are thought to share a sense of mutual obligation, a cultural adherence to a greater good which is higher than any individual or sectional interest (Gilbert, 1986). In social policy terms, it echoes a paternalist tradition of employers' responsibility for workers' welfare. At the same time, however, it is seen to be vital that core economic relationships remain undisturbed by social policy. The social insurance system, for example, seeks to compensate for the failures of the market rather than to disrupt its incentive structure (Alber, 1986a). It is geared to income maintenance rather than redistribution (see Chapter 3).

Yet it can also be argued that the German industrial relations system is protected by the weakness of organised labour as much as by social benefits. Labour is weakened by a low level of unionisation (35 per cent) and by the influx of migrant labour. Strike legislation is restrictive, and union organisations have been excluded from the workplace in favour of the works councils. The participatory institutions of German corporatism have been designed for labour rather than by it (Gilbert, 1986).

There is a further question to be raised about the validity of this 'partnership' of capital and labour in German economic and social policy: it is crucial to recognise that the respective 'social partners' are employers and *German* employees (Lawson, 1980). This partnership is supported from below by a third party, that of immigrant labour. 'Guestworkers' have been a permanent feature of the German economy since the 1960s. They have come predominantly from Turkey and Southern Europe and constitute 9 per cent of the labour force. They tend to be clustered in low-paid, menial jobs, and few have German citizenship (see Chapter 9).

The economic development of the new Germany remains uncertain. German unification is as much an issue of political economy as of state-building. Parallels have been pointed out between the economic condition of the new eastern *Länder* and that of the newly founded Federal Republic in the immediate post-war period, between the economic division of Germany into East and West and that of Italy between North and South, and between the position of the new *Länder* and that of former West Berlin (Padgett, 1992). The post-war conditions which fuelled the West German economic miracle, however, have not been repeated for the new Germany. West Germany was then competing with other European countries similarly trying to rebuild their economies in a climate of general growth; the East German economy, by contrast, quickly deprived of exchange rate protection by currency unification in 1990, has been unable to match the productive efficiency of mature western economies. At the same time, however, the location of the eastern *Länder* at the crossroads of Eastern and Western Europe at a time of considerable economic change and development further East, when coupled to the locomotive impetus of the old *Länder* to the West, makes prospects seem more hopeful than comparison with the Italian *Mezzogiorno* would suggest. The experience of West Berlin points to something in-between. There, economic activity has continued to progress but continues to be dependent on external support. The future development of the East German economy may institutionalise some of those measures which were conceived as short-term features of the unification process; meanwhile, the burden already assumed has affected the economic stability of the Federal Republic (Padgett, 1992).

The direct costs of unification accounted for almost a quarter of estimated federal government spending for 1991 (DM 93 billion of DM 412 billion) (Padgett, 1992). The need to finance so much spending, in combination with the impact of the recent economic recession, has created new dilemmas for German economic policy. The government is reluctant to increase taxation, which would be politically unpopular and which may dampen the economic activity in the West which is needed to drive the development of the unified economy. Increased borrowing, however, is being resisted by the Federal Bank because of the inflationary threat it represents. A third option is to reduce government spending in the West, especially in the field of social policy. Yet this is to bring new distributional conflicts between East and West and between capital and labour into the open. By the end of 1992, such conflicts of interest were being expressed in growing labour unrest, indicating the extent to which the 'democratic corporatism' of German industrial relations, on which its economic success was seen to have been built but which had begun to be undermined during the 1980s, was further threatened by unification (Padgett, 1992). The continuation of the political and distributional consensus on which the stability and success of the former West Germany had been based now seems less than certain; social policy, as always, seems likely to become an instrument both of present and future distributional conflicts and of their resolution (see Chapter 2).

The social state and social policy

Social policy principles in Germany are based on ideas both about individual contract and about collective response to need. They express a conceptual fusion of legalism, which draws on the bourgeois constitutional liberalism described earlier in this introduction; of solidarity, which reflects the influence of organised labour on social policy; and of the idea of subsidiarity articulated in Catholic social thought. In part, too, they can be understood as a reaction against the National Socialist state which preceded the Federal Republic as well as to the continuing goad of East German communism (Alber, 1986a).

The term welfare state (*Wohlfahrtsstaat*) had negative, paternalistic connotations in Germany at least until the 1950s (Ritter, 1991). This is one of the reasons why the term 'social state' (*Sozialstaat*) has come to be applied to the provision of statutory benefits and services. Indeed, one of the most significant legal constructions of its constitution characterises Germany both as a democratic *Rechtsstaat* and as a *Sozialstaat*. Where the idea of the *Rechtsstaat* expresses liberal principles such as the protection of individual freedoms and the rule of law, that of the *Sozialstaat* upholds both Christian Democratic understandings of the social responsibility of the state and the Social Democratic commitment to social justice (Smith, 1992a).

Furthermore, the term *Sozialstaat* embodies a normative commitment to social justice and to reducing inequality and guarantees the legally codified claims of individuals versus the state. It goes beyond the notion of a welfare state in countries such as Great Britain, for example, where the scope for politically motivated change in social policy is much larger than in the German *Sozialstaat* (Schulte, 1991). The principal significance of the idea of the 'social state' is not only that it entitles public authorities to intervene in markets but also that, within certain limits, the government is actually obliged to address social inequalities and to pursue social welfare goals which are enforceable by the courts (Ogus, 1990; Lampert, 1991). At the same time, it gives coherence to legislative action, as expressed in the Social Code (the *Sozialgesetzbuch*). The means by which public authorities are committed to creating 'an equitable social order' (Kittner, 1989, p. 673) and to improving 'life chances' (Schmidt, 1988, p. 15) include income maintenance, help for large families, health care and housing, as well as the attempt to create greater equality of opportunity, for example through education. While the *Sozialstaat* principle provides some legitimation of state activity in these areas, it is also, and perhaps inevitably, the source of considerable policy-making rhetoric (Ogus, 1990). Nevertheless, the strong legal codification of conditions for and entitlements to social insurance rights in particular has to be acknowledged as an important feature which distinguishes Germany from other welfare states (Braun and Niehaus, 1990).

A central aspect of the social state is the system of social insurance which embodies a particular type of solidarity. The insurance contributions of those in work support the benefits of those who no longer work because of their age, because of sickness or disability, or simply because they are unemployed. The system works because those who contribute now expect to become the future recipients of others' contributions. In this way, solidarity is expressed across generations (in the form of pensions) and between the sick and the well (through sickness insurance payments). However, this solidarity extends only to employed contributors to social insurance schemes: access to forms of social security more adequate than means-tested social assistance is granted on the basis of employment rather than citizenship. Furthermore, both contributions and benefits are earnings-related: benefit levels are contingent upon contributions, which in turn reflect the earnings status of the insured person. This proportional relationship between contributions and benefits is designed to promote equivalence rather than redistribution, replicating differentials in earnings and preserving those of status between blue-collar, white-collar and civil service labour (see Chapter 3).

The idea of subsidiarity is much stronger than that of solidarity. Subsidiarity is the broad principle according to which social, political and economic activity is to be undertaken at the lowest appropriate level of social organisation. It is a cornerstone of Catholic social teaching, and in Europe – in Belgium and the Netherlands as well as in Germany – it has generally been promoted by political parties associated with Catholicism (Spicker, 1991). In the social policy context, it means that primary responsibility for welfare is held to lie with individuals and their families. Secondary responsibilities lie with local communities, the organisations of which they are composed and the private sector; the role of the state remains subsidiary. By the same token, central government should not take action for which municipal and local authorities may be better suited. In effect, the principle of subsidiarity means that much of the responsibility for welfare in Germany tends to be provided on the basis of earned right (according to a contribution record) rather than of perceived need. Welfare benefits are awarded in cash rather than kind, taking the form of social transfer payments made to individuals, while services are provided by independent and non-statutory organisations.

The dominance of the principle of subsidiarity is reflected in the segmented institutional structure of the German welfare system. For its part, the federal state is 'not itself a universal provider but, rather, the guarantor and overseer of certain social rights mostly fulfilled by other agencies' (Mangen, 1989, p. 169). These include the *Länder* and communes or municipalities, the social partners (who control the social insurance funds), as well as independent social service agencies. Social insurance, for example, is administered by independent funds financed by employers and employees through what is effectively a system of payroll taxation. Insurance schemes are organised according to contingency: there are different funds for sickness, unemployment, old age and disability compensation.

In terms of the provision of services the subsidiarity principle accords a 'conditional priority' to the non-governmental, non-profit-making or voluntary sector (Jarré, 1991; see Chapter 7). Both the Federal Social Welfare Act and the Social Code refer to a relationship of collaboration between statutory authorities and voluntary bodies: while local, *Land* and federal authorities bear ultimate responsibility for ensuring that social service needs are met, they do so by supporting and promoting voluntary organisations. In the former West Germany, these agencies employed three-quarters of a million staff supported by one and a half million volunteers. In 1987–8, 35 per cent of hospital beds, 70 per cent of institutions caring for children and young people and 65 per cent of those caring for the elderly were in the voluntary sector (Jarré, 1991). The more than sixty thousand *freie Träger* (or 'free bearers') of social services are grouped into six associations: two are denominational, Protestant and Catholic; one is union-sponsored; one is organised through the Red Cross; one is organised by the German Jewish community; while the sixth is a federation of small agencies. Their work is financed by municipal grants, or by negotiating operating fees with insurance funds. As charities, some have independent resources; Protestant and Catholic organisations receive money from the churches derived from their tax income. The plurality of providers can result in a lack of overall strategy in the provision of services, although some coordination and brokerage is provided by the German Association (the *Deutscher Verein*).

All of this suggests that the organisation of social policy in Germany is complex and sophisticated, but also fragmented and disjointed. Its structure makes for significant limitations on policy-making. In the first place, it is difficult to innovate or reform when consensus must be established across so many organisations, both service agencies and insurance funds. There is little incentive for individual agencies to make concessions in the interests of overall efficiency (Mangen, 1989). Second, and as this introduction has tried to outline in a more general way, the administrative fragmentation of the federal system, the broad constellations of interests represented by the major political parties, the effective necessity of government by coalition, the independent existence and authority of parapublic agencies and the process of judicial review in the Constitutional Court all impede innovation and make for a pattern of incremental policy development (von Beyme, 1985; Katzenstein, 1987; Mangen 1989, 1991b).

For these reasons, expressive of the way in which social policy is embedded in its polity, welfare cutbacks in Germany during the 1970s and 1980s remained limited (Mangen, 1991a). In the context of declining economic growth in the period after 1975 social spending was called into question in Germany as in other western countries. The election of a Christian Democrat and Liberal government under Kohl in 1983 was presented as heralding a sea-change or turning-point (*Wende*) in the patterns of politics which had dominated the 1960s and early 1970s. As in Britain and the United States, and to some extent in France and Spain, neo-liberal economic policy was to be combined with neo-conservative social policy (Mangen, 1991b). Reductions in entitlements and levels of benefit in the areas of health, pensions and social security, begun in an *ad hoc* way under Chancellor Helmut Schmidt in the second half of the 1970s, were intensified between 1982 and 1985 but then halted by the CDU's poor performance in regional elections and by the government's concern for its prospects in the general election of early 1987. The absence of any significant revision of institutional arrangements means that the period of so-called 'crisis' in the welfare state in Germany is better described as one of consolidation rather than retrenchment (Alber, 1986b; Mangen 1989, 1991b; see also individual chapters in this volume).

What has begun to change in the last decade or so, and partly but not wholly as a result of *die Wende*, is the vocabulary of social policy in Germany: the right makes much of a 'new subsidiarity' and a renewed commitment to the family, while the red–green left is developing a new communitarianism based in 'social ecology' (Mangen, 1989, 1991a). The common denominator of these different strands of thought is an interest in self-help, albeit variously conceived. For some, it represents a liberal–conservative reassertion of individual responsibility, while for others it holds up the possibility of more progressive, communal social action. The emergence of these 'new' forms of citizens' initiative in health and welfare dates from the beginning of the 1970s, many originating in the women's, green and peace movements (Trojan *et al.*, 1986). By the mid-1980s, there were an estimated 5,000 self-help groups in the health field alone, with a membership of between 300,000 and 500,000 (Murswieck, 1985).

To an extent, the growth of self-help reflects a multi-faceted dissatisfaction with the German welfare system. What is in principle a system of pluralist decentralisation, organised through many local agencies and insurance funds, comes to be in practice one of corporatist centralisation, in which arrangements are in fact negotiated between representatives of enormous associations of organisations. Furthermore, the formulation of policy tends to be determined by those who pay for the system through their contributions, that is, by the interests of employees rather than those of users or beneficiaries. The emphasis on cash transfers, too, rather than services in kind, is seen to be highly impersonal. Continuing problems of this type, as well as the relatively limited nature of recent changes and the impact of unification, make further social policy reform in Germany more rather than less likely. These are some of the organisational and political issues that are dealt with in detail in later parts of this book.

An outline of the book

The book is divided into three parts. Part I places German social policy in its historical context, looking as far back as the origins of welfare administration in the seventeeth and eighteenth centuries, tracing its development through periods of industrialisation, war, recession and renewal, and offering a detailed assessment of the recent impact of unification on social policy. In Chapter 1, Eve Rosenhaft describes and explains the development of social policy in Germany in the context of broader social, political and economic change. She points to the significance of evolving conceptualisations of the appropriate role of the state in the provision of welfare, showing how these have shaped, and in turn been shaped by, a distinctive political and institutional history. In Chapter 2, Steen Mangen considers the extent to which unification of the two Germanies in 1990 imposed an agenda for social policy unparalleled in Western Europe since the period immediately following the Second World War. He describes the assimilation of the eastern *Länder* into the model set by the social state in the former West Germany, discussing the particular problems of administrative reorganisation and of funding social provision in the context of high unemployment.

The second part of the book provides more detailed and specific information about patterns of organisation and service delivery in each of five major fields of social policy. Individual chapters assess inputs and outcomes, examine issues and problems and interpret policy developments in relation to social security, health care, housing, education and training and the personal social services in turn. Because unification implied no more or less than an extension of former West German social policy into the territory of the former GDR, these discussions of current provision are located in the context of developments over the past two decades in West Germany. While this replication of the West in the East in itself has been by no means a straightforward process (see Schmähl, 1992b), it is attention to the achievements and shortcomings of social policy programmes in the West rather than the East which will allow a better understanding of current structures, principles, institutions and problems. By way of additional illustration, each author draws comparison and contrast with arrangements in other countries, and with the United Kingdom in particular. Each also gives a guide to further reading in English, as well as to important sources of empirical information.

It is the characteristics of its system of income maintenance in particular, perhaps, which distinguish the German social state from other types of welfare capitalism. The way in which benefit entitlements are closely related to previous earnings, and the emphasis on restitution and status preservation rather than redistribution or the alleviation of poverty, have displayed a remarkable historical continuity since their institution in the 1880s. Having developed in a mainly uncontroversial fashion, and having become more universal in its coverage after the Second World War, social insurance continues to dominate income maintenance in Germany today. However, as Jochen Clasen demonstrates in Chapter 3, economic and labour market changes as well as social and demographic developments during the past two decades have widened gaps in the system. As a result, dependence on generally much lower, means-tested assistance benefits has soared in the 1980s and early 1990s. The recent economic recession which has reinforced this trend has led critics to demand substantial reform of this system; for its part, the government has responded with a series of cutbacks in social security programmes.

The funding of sickness insurance is based similarly on earnings-related contributions, as are other social insurance schemes. In Chapter 4, Michael Moran discusses organisational principles, achievements and shortcomings of German health care. Among the successes of health insurance are certainly its universal coverage and its capacity to deliver a high standard of care while allowing some freedom of choice to the patient seeking specialist consultation, although the system has recently been forced to address problems of effectiveness, equity and cost. However, its institutional fragmentation has made for a control deficit which, in turn, has made reform very difficult. Unification, meanwhile, has both magnified existing difficulties and added new ones, not least since the introduction of the former West German model in the new *Länder* seems to require a level of financial support and political control as yet unseen in the Federal Republic.

In Chapter 5, Mark Kleinman considers housing policies in Germany before and after unification. In comparison with other European countries Germany stands out by the importance given to market conditions within a framework of law. Rather than relying on direct local authority housing, the emphasis in social housing is on subsidies in conjunction with regulations about the allocation of tenancies, rent levels and standards. Kleinman demonstrates the considerable difference between Great Britain, where the private rented sector has declined over the last decades, and Germany, where owner-occupation is comparatively low and private renting has been retained as a large and diverse sector, providing accommodation for all income levels. However, housing in Germany is undergoing change due to pressures such as an imbalance between demand and supply in the market, access difficulties and homelessness and the need for modernisation of the housing stock in the new *Länder*.

The degree of public intervention in the areas of education and training has certainly been far greater. In Chapter 6, Claire Wallace describes the organisation of Germany's educational system, and the way in which it allows a considerable degree of flexibility in the routes by which students attain degrees. The 'dual system' of employment training, frequently identified as a major reason for West Germany's economic success, is also described in detail. It brings together employers and the state, the former responsible for providing practical training for apprentices, and the latter for their theoretical training in vocational schools. As a result, a larger proportion of 16- to 19-year-olds in Germany are involved in education and training than in many other countries. However, the chapter also points to problems of gender stratification and the relative under-achievement of children from ethnic groups. Here, too, problems have been exacerbated by the combined impact of recession and unification.

In Chapter 7, Walter Lorenz describes how social work in Germany is derived in part from a nineteenth-century conception of social education. Today, the particular administrative complexity of personal social services in Germany may be explained in part by their less than established status, and in part by the degree to which the prevailing interpretation of subsidiarity limits the capacity of the state to impose order. As social work activity has become professionalised, however, and as the relationship of voluntary and private sector organinsations with the state has become increasingly corporatised, they are seen to have become as remote as public bureaucracies. Both now face challenges represented by self-help initiatives and the emergence of social problems in the new *Länder*.

The final section of the book, Part III, addresses two important social divisions within the German social state. In Chapter 8 Prue Chamberlayne considers the position of women in East and West Germany over the past two decades in respect of employment, family structures and entitlements to social provision. She shows that social policies, even when aimed at creating better opportunities for women, have tended to reflect and even reinforce the arrangements of 'private patriarchy' in the West and the operation of 'public patriarchy' in the East. Furthermore, it is women who have borne the brunt of unification by being harder hit by unemployment than men (female labour force participation in the old GDR was very much higher than in West Germany), by the loss of social rights such as the provision of public childcare, and by changes in attitudes and behaviour with regard to family and social life. Women's responses to policy change, meanwhile, have been complicated by strategic divisions over the relative values of the achievement of 'equality' and the recognition of 'difference'.

In the book's final chapter, Norman Ginsburg examines the situation of ethnic minorities in Germany. Until recently, West Germany had witnessed two phases of inward population movement, the first of which was the post-war migration from territory in the East which continued until the building of the Berlin Wall in 1961. A second phase saw the recruitment of 'guestworkers' from Southern Europe and especially Turkey in the 1960s until a ban was imposed in 1973 (although family members have continued to join already resident workers). Later, at the end of the 1980s, the number of East Germans as well as 'ethnic' Germans from East European countries seeking work and residency in West Germany increased considerably, adding to a continuous flow of asylum seekers. Germany's 'foreigners', numbering almost five million, are poorly integrated into the host society, deriving relatively low incomes from menial employment and living in housing of poor quality. Their access to social benefits and services is mediated by their relatively low legal and employment status. The chapter emphasises the apparent contradictions of a country which, though it has been more open than any other in Europe to people seeking asylum, continues to refuse full citizenship and permanent settlement rights even to most of what is now its third generation of migrants.

Guide to further reading

There are a number of basic introductions to policy and politics in the former West Germany, among them von Beyme and Schmidt (1985),

Edinger (1986), Smith (1986) and Conradt (1993). The recent one by Smith *et al.* (1992) is invaluable as a relatively detailed first assessment of the political system of the new Germany and of the more prominent public policy issues it faces. Derbyshire (1991) is a useful source of facts and figures of the political history of the Federal Republic and the process of unification. In the economic sphere, Gilbert (1986) writes about the organisation and operation of the social market. Krüger and Pfaller (1991) discuss the competitiveness of the German economy, and the relationship between it and the welfare state. Katzenstein (1987) develops the idea of the 'semisovereign state' in chapters relating to the management of the economy, industrial relations, social welfare, migrant workers, administrative reform and university reform.

Chapter-length introductions to social policy in the former West Germany, still of some value, include Heinze *et al.* (1986), Zapf (1986), Ford (1987a), Alber (1988a), Brauns and Kramer (1989) and Muller (1989). Wilson (1993) has the virtue of being the most recent. Alber (1986a) is a signal study, and Ginsburg (1992) includes a chapter on Germany. Ogus (1990) discusses legal-constitutional aspects of social policy in Germany, drawing helpful comparison and contrast with the United Kingdom. Helm (1981) and Anheier (1990) give useful accounts of the voluntary sector. For social policy in the former GDR, see Winkler (1989), in German, and, in English, Scharf (1984) and Ford (1987b). Schmähl (1992b), in German, discusses the social policy issues of unification. Perhaps the most important recent general work in German is Leisering (1992).

A number of English-language journals regularly publish material of interest to students of social policy in Germany, including *German Politics*, *Debatte*, *Journal of European Social Policy* and *Voluntas*. German journals include the *Zeitschrift für Sozialreform*, *Leviathan*, *Sozialer Fotschritt* and *Soziale Sicherheit*.

Part I

Social welfare in Germany – past and present

Chapter 1

The historical development of German social policy

Eve Rosenhaft

In the problems that it faces and the solutions it proposes, social policy in Germany today has much in common with that of other western welfare states. Indeed, at the end of the nineteenth century German social policy was widely regarded as a model for international emulation. It displays certain features, though, which set it apart and mark it as the result of a particular historical experience. We might begin with the German term for social policy itself: *Sozialpolitik* does not have the breadth of reference of the English term. Rather it refers to the range of policies directed specifically at workers as individuals and as a class. It includes worker protection at the workplace, wages policies, social insurance and the management of industrial relations. Its use is a marker of the way in which the articulation between these areas of policy, and particularly the last two, makes up the core of public provision against the effects of social inequality in twentieth-century Germany, a core to which all forms of direct benefit are subsidiary. It points back to the origins of contemporary institutions in the nineteenth century, when social policy emerged as a project for containing the political consequences of industrialisation. *Sozialpolitik* is *Arbeiterpolitik*, a class-oriented policy which in its turn has reinforced Germany's development into the model of a work-oriented society (*Arbeitsgesellschaft*), in which productive labour alone entitles. A further defining feature of German social policy, the reliance on private or voluntary agencies as providers of social services within a publicly administered system, reflects the way in which modern social policy developed in the field of tension between the historic example of a strong interventionist state and the values of an emerging liberal bourgeoisie. More specifically, the growth and consolidation of the voluntary sector represent one strategy for the collective self-assertion of groups which were excluded from national political power in nineteenth-century Germany, in this case the middle classes and particularly middle-class women. The growth of municipal administration as an alternative arena for progressive social policy is related to this. It took place, of course, within the general decentralisation of administration characteristic of a federal system with a long tradition of urban self-government. Finally, it is impossible to ignore the role that racial and reproductive policies have played in the development of welfare institutions and public health in Germany's past, or the extent to which ethnicity continues to function as an independent principle in the allocation of civic, social and economic rights. Here we can refer to the particular circumstances of Germany's late emergence as a nation-state, needing to define the terms of a common identity in an age when the discourse of nationality was already giving way to the language of race. At the same time, it seems clear that the recourse to medical and technological methods to solve social problems was facilitated in the German case by a relationship that predates the first German unification, namely the mutual dependency of state bureaucracies charged with the making of policy and professional or would-be professional experts.

Absolutism and *Polizeystaat*

In German-speaking Europe, a continuous practice of state intervention to regulate the sphere of social reproduction can be traced back to the absolutist states of the eighteenth century. To the mercantilist vision of the ruler's duty to increase the wealth and population of his (or her) territories, the philosophy of the Enlightenment added an imperative to guarantee the safety and well-being of each subject. This would be the state's contribution not only to the general moral and economic good, but also to the achievement of that state of rational happiness (*Glückseligkeit*) which each human being was inherently capable of attaining 'in the best of all possible worlds'. This assignment of vital functions to the state provided a new source of legitimacy for rulers who throughout the seventeenth and early eighteenth centuries were engaged in struggles to assert their own, or central, power against the historic claims of local and regional nobilities. Its role as an ideology of modern state-building is particularly clear in the case of the Hohenzollern rulers of Prussia, from the 'Great Elector' Friedrich Wilhelm (1640–88) to Friedrich II (Frederick the Great, 1740–86); over four generations they managed to neutralise the nobility's power to obstruct monarchical initiatives, create a standing army and a professional bureaucracy directly answerable to the Crown, and consolidate and extend Prussia's territories, so that by the end of the eighteenth century Prussia was a major power in Europe as well as a model for a well-ordered state.

At the same time, the idea of enlightened good government developed a force of its own, its principal bearers being the members of the service bourgeoisie, or educated middle classes trained for employment in the burgeoning state bureaucracy. The key term in the new bureaucratic ethos was good policy, or *Polizey*; the ideal was a state governed by rational and predictable principles of regulation rather than by the arbitrary exercise of power. It is in this sense that the term *Polizeystaat* was used by contemporaries to designate the kind of system that the absolutist state was or ought to be (Raeff, 1975; Pankoke, 1986); in theoretical and pragmatic discussions of state practice, *Polizey* meant the range of policies and institutions directed at regulating one or another area of social life, as in the eighteenth-century literature on the idea of a *Medizinalpolizey* (system for the enforcement of public health) (Göckenjan, 1985). Indeed, it was in measures designed to maintain the health of the population that the Prussian 'welfare state' (Dorwart, 1971) was most active, introducing inspectorates for food, instituting sewerage systems, regulating weights and measures, insisting that physicians be licensed, and promoting 'enlightened' practices such as breastfeeding through admonition and legislation. Implicitly, then, 'policy', 'police' or 'policing' had an enabling as well as a preventative or controlling aspect. The aspect of absolutist practice that best prefigures modern social policy understood as a network of services to the individual is compulsory primary education, which was introduced in Prussia in 1717 and was subject to extension, improvement and rationalisation throughout the eighteenth century. In most respects, though, absolutist policy was prophylactic rather than creative, its principal object being to guarantee public order by preventing the development of grievances or conflicts that might threaten it (*Gefahrenabwehr*). The title of one of Frederick the Great's early administrative initiatives, a Bureau for Security, Order and Commerce (1742), is a telling indicator of the extent to which the political interests of the state and the narrowly economic definition of the common good continued to be primary. From this point of view, the narrowing of the meaning of *Polizey* to its present-day sense – a state agency operating to prevent and punish breaches of order – was foreshadowed by the early bias of public policy. Conversely, powers of regulation and surveillance of everyday life have continued to be accepted in Germany as proper to the functions of the state and figure alongside the 'nightwatchman' duties of the uniformed police to this day.

The 'social question' and the beginnings of industrial society

From the 1780s on, in the wake of the French Revolution and the Napoleonic Wars, the German states experienced a phase of liberal reform, in which state bureaucracies took the initiative in removing what were perceived as obstacles to political and economic development. A bourgeois public, already in formation under the absolutist regimes, began to assert more confidently the values of free association and of a self-regulating (or self-policing) civil society (*policierte Gesellschaft*) (Pankoke, 1986). State policy was called upon only to remove the brakes to free development and to guarantee order – a precondition for freedom all the more urgently invoked in the light of the spectacle of France's revolutionary terror. Measures of direct intervention – the term *Gesundheitspolizei* was still current in the 1830s (Göckenjan, 1985) – were acceptable only in the exceptional case of individual incapacity to help oneself.

The flowering of liberal politics was frustrated by the era of political reaction that followed Napoleon's defeat in 1815, but economic and social change proceeded unchecked. The growth of the 'social question' (*sociale Frage*) gave a new impetus to the formation of social policy and prompted new measures, both state and voluntary. As in other parts of Europe, the 'social question' in Germany had a number of complementary aspects, most of them reflecting the first impact of the industrial revolution. The 1830s and 1840s created the infrastructure for the first phase of significant economic growth, with the lifting of customs barriers between the German states and the creation of a transport network. The building of railways from 1835 on both contributed to the mobility of goods and population and stimulated the growth of native extractive, metal-working and machine-building industries, and a concomitant of the growth of industry was urbanisation – the creation of new population centres and the expansion of old ones.

There was no aspect of this process of transformation that did not appear to pose a danger to social order and the public good. The 'social question' meant the novel spectacle of child and woman labour in the factories. It meant the problems of housing the urban poor and the dangers of contagion breeding in the new slums (fears for physical and social health clustered around the cholera epidemic of 1832). It meant the fact that the more people were working the less they seemed to earn; the borderline subsistence wages of workers in industry, the falling incomes in declining trades, the concentrated destitution of the urban unemployed and new kinds of poverty in the countryside combined to produce the phenomenon of generalised pauperism (*Pauperismus*). One widely canvassed explanation for endemic poverty was overpopulation, perceived as a problem both of the management of a biological economy and of declining moral standards (Matz, 1980). And behind all these lay the threat of social revolution, of 'communism', should the increasingly vocal theorists of new schemes for social justice and harmony manage to make common cause with those workers who were beginning to form associations of their own and to take collective action against employers (Tennstedt, 1981).

The two decades leading up to the revolution of 1848 were thus characterised by a number of social policy measures coming from various agencies, with various rationales, all aimed at containing the consequences of social change. The question of how to deal with poverty was the most urgent one. Under the old regime, the relief of poverty had been the responsibility of the municipalities (*Gemeinden*; the term's original sense was 'parish', but it is retained in contemporary German to refer both to religious communities and to local government). The destitute were supported by funds raised through local taxes and administered by officers of the municipality. Within their respective communities, the poor were often treated as members of a wider class of the marginal and deviant, so that measures for relief merged with coercive measures of social discipline, for example in the institution of the workhouse or reformatory (*Zuchthaus*). Public relief was necessarily complemented by private charity. In principle, the burden on the local economy was held in balance by the complementary rights of municipalities to determine who could claim relief by defining who had the rights of a legal resident. Outsiders who fell into poverty could simply be forced to move to another jurisdiction, and were, in increasing numbers (Tennstedt, 1981).

As the number of paupers increased in the early nineteenth century, the burden on the municipalities was compounded by falling tax income. In the first instance, then, the problem of poverty was approached by legislators as a problem of the definition of rights of residency, or more generally demarcating freedom of movement. In the south German states and Saxony, the restrictive rights of municipalities were reinforced and complemented by new powers to regulate marriage as a means of keeping the population in check. In Prussia, on the other hand, legislation of 1842 significantly reduced the powers of municipalities to deny civic rights to individuals who were already resident, and specifically confirmed and extended their duty of poor relief. The complement to this legislation, which manifestly increased the burden on public funds, was official encouragement for and patronage of organised private poor relief. The creation of a Prussian *Centralverein* (Central Association) for the 'relief of the physical and mental distress of artisans and factory workers', with the explicit approval of and a large subsidy from the Prussian Crown, is typical of a wave of middle-class activity in the formation of voluntary associations for poor relief (*Armenvereine*) in this period. Since the interests of the urban middle class lay equally in relieving the tax burden represented by the poor and enforcing the virtues of decency and hard work that would help people out of poverty, the work of these associations was particularly directed towards propaganda and schemes of self-help (Gladen, 1974). This period also saw new initiatives in the establishment of institutions for the education and training of the poor and for indoor relief; schools, hospitals, orphanages and poorhouses provided a focus particularly for the charitable activities of women, as individuals, in secular associations and in church-related societies like the newly founded Protestant 'orders' of deaconesses (Prelinger, 1986).

The 'Elberfeld System' of 1853 provided a model for the fusion of public and private initiatives in an aggressive and creative poor relief that was emulated in other German cities and abroad. Created to answer the needs of one of the new industrial towns of the Rhineland, the system instituted a new form of public outdoor relief based on voluntary social work. Poor families were allocated to volunteer visitors (*Armenpfleger*), on a geographical basis and on the principle that each visitor should be responsible for no more than four families. In fortnightly visits, the visitor would determine the need and eligibility of the household, identifying the idle and work-shy, who did not qualify for relief, and also any possible source of income, such as the property or earnings of relatives. What the visitor had to offer the deserving poor was money (provided from local taxes), exhortations to thrift and mutual support, and the possibility of employment either in public works or in the private economy (Tennstedt, 1981).

The pattern of mid-nineteenth-century legislation in Prussia, which was extended to the north German states with the creation of the North German Confederation in 1866 and to most of the rest of Germany after unification in 1871, established the abstention of central government from creative policy-making in the area of poor relief. State law fixed the obligations of the municipalities, but it implied neither an obligation on its own part nor a right to support on the part of the poor; indeed, those who were dependent on poor relief were deprived of most civil rights, including the franchise. Nineteenth-century poor law represented the minimum intervention necessary to protect public order against the threat posed by unrelieved hardship. By contrast, an area of policy in which the German states maintained and extended their powers of direct intervention and regulation was that of working conditions – *Arbeiterschutz*, or the protection of workers within the developing system of industrial wage-labour. The best-known example of this from the first half of the nineteenth century is the legislation to control child labour. In 1839 children under the age of 9 were prohibited by law from working in factories in Prussia – a law which came at the end of twenty years of official inquiry and debate about the effects of factory work on children's physical and mental development. The restrictions on child labour were extended in 1853 (Gladen, 1974). In the later part of the nineteenth century, the protection of the worker from the consequences of work would become the keystone in the whole edifice of what came to be known and admired as German social policy, but it took a new form.

Bismarckian social legislation

The combination of the rationalisation of poor relief and the expansion of the labour market with full-scale industrialisation meant that poverty as such ceased to be the central issue from the mid-nineteenth century. The concerns that underlay social policy from the 1860s onwards were those associated with the advent of the industrial working class as a significant group in society and the growth of an organised and oppositional labour movement. The rate of industrial growth increased steadily through the 1850s and 1860s, and accelerated rapidly after 1870, encouraged by political unification and the subsequent creation of national financial institutions. Within a generation, Germany became the premier industrial economy in Europe; in 1907, more than half the population depended for its livelihood on industry and the expanding tertiary sector (in both of which sectors about three-quarters of participants were in paid employment).

The immediate challenge posed by industrialisation was that of social revolution. The revolution of 1848 had failed to bring about the unified Germany under a liberal constitution which was the principal aim of its middle-class leaders, but it had succeeded (to their considerable chagrin) in mobilising artisanal and industrial workers, and generated the first national organisations of workers raising articulate political demands. In spite of a wave of repression in the wake of the revolution, an organised labour movement, self-consciously independent of bourgeois liberal tutelage and with a broadly socialist programme, emerged in the 1860s. The growth of trade unions was assisted by the lifting of legal restraints on the right of association in most of Germany in 1868–9. In 1875 two regional social democratic parties came together to form the Socialist Workers' Party (*Sozialistische Arbeiterpartei*, SAP), a party operating on a national basis with about 25,000 members at the time of its founding and firm links to the expanding international labour movement (Fricke, 1976).

The rise of a socialist labour movement was perhaps the greatest single threat to the political balancing act represented by the constitution of the German Reich of 1871. This was a political order in which the power of the Crown was guaranteed through the simultaneous mobilisation and containment of public opinion. Universal manhood suffrage as the basis for the election of deputies to the *Reichstag* served to neutralise the real influence of the liberal bourgeoisie while appearing to answer one of its historic demands, and at the same time the *Reichstag* itself was denied the right to initiate legislation or make and break governments. Even under the government of its chief begetter, Chancellor Otto von Bismarck, this system required constant tactical manoeuvring to maintain the intra- and extra-parliamentary alliances that kept a conservative regime in power. The Social Democrats, however, were beyond the pale of political accommodation, and the first approach to the challenge they posed was open repression. In 1878 the SAP, its press and all its organisations were banned, as were all publications and any public meetings in which socialism or communism were discussed. Even underground, however, the Social Democratic movement continued to gain strength and to garner votes; once the ban was lifted in 1890, membership and electoral support increased rapidly, so that following the elections of 1912 the renamed Social Democratic Party (SPD) had the largest single delegation in the *Reichstag*. The principal effects of twelve years' illegality had been to sever the formal links between the party and the free trade union movement and to push the party's intellectuals into the self-consciously Marxian revolutionary position represented by the Erfurt Programme.

It was as a complement to the policy of repression that Bismarck conceived an elaborate scheme of state-sponsored social insurance for workers. His explicit aim was to reduce the attractiveness of revolutionary programmes by providing benefits from above that would place workers in a relationship of direct dependency on the state and consolidate their allegiance to it. Bismarck's intention, then, was to go beyond the selective regulatory functions inherited from the absolutist state and to introduce a more organic and comprehensive kind of intervention; he actively opposed the legislation of 1878 that extended protective measures to young and female workers and introduced a system of factory inspection (Gladen, 1974). In a real sense, this kind of direct regulation had been overtaken by developments in any case: one of the earliest and continuing functions of the trade unions had been to provide against the vicissitudes of working life through mutual funds based on membership contributions. By the 1870s, major industrial employers, including representatives of the old heavy industries like Krupp and the leaders in the emerging 'second industrial revolution' like Siemens, were beginning to introduce pension schemes alongside other forms of direct provision – housing, recreation, education – for their workers. This was the beginning of a tradition of employer paternalism, or company-based social policy (*betriebliche Sozialpolitik*) which formed an important counterpart to public social policy well into the twentieth century. It was motivated in the first instance by three concerns: the need to maintain a stable workforce in a situation of high labour mobility; the desire to suppress socialist and trade union agitation; and the hope of pre-empting state intervention (Ullmann, 1981). By the 1880s, then, state policy was being formulated in a situation of general competition between established social actors for the allegiance of the working class. At the same time, the tendency among bourgeois social reformers was increasingly to look to the state for positive measures to deal with the pathological features of industrial society; the *Verein für Socialpolitik*, founded in 1872, devoted itself to the scientific study of social problems as the basis for informed public policy (vom Bruch, 1985).

In the event, both Bismarck's own policy aims and his hopes of a wider political resonance were frustrated in the social insurance legislation of the 1880s. The first measure to be placed before the *Reichstag*, in 1881, was a scheme for insurance against the consequences of industrial accidents. The original proposal, that the Reich government provide both the administrative machinery and substantial financial contributions to the scheme, was rejected on the grounds that it undermined the powers of the federal states. As a result, when accident insurance went into effect in 1884 it had an ambivalent character: the Reich made insurance obligatory, fixed the benefits (medical costs and compensation for loss of earnings) and provided adjudication in disputes or cases of appeal. It also required that commissions be established, on which representatives of workers and employers would sit, with the function of devising binding regulations for accident prevention for the respective areas of industry. The scheme was financed, however, entirely through employer contributions, and administered by associations of employers. Similar, though not identical, principles applied to the system of sickness insurance which was introduced in 1883; it was funded by worker and employer contributions, which were expected where possible to be administered by already existing medical insurance schemes (*Krankenkassen*). Where such schemes were inadequate or non-existent, the law required the creation of new ones, either on a geographical basis (*Ortskrankenkassen*) or, where a large number of workers worked for a single employer, at the level of the firm (*Betriebskrankenkassen*). The state, then, provided a framework of legal compulsion and administrative terms of reference, but not much more. By contrast, insurance against invalidity and old age, introduced in 1889, involved a fixed financial contribution on the part of the state to each pension, as well as contributions by employers and by workers (Gladen, 1974).

By and large, these measures failed to 'buy' the attachment of workers to the Wilhelmine state (Tampke, 1981). The benefits paid to workers and their dependants in case of old age or incapacity to work were deliberately set at the minimum necessary to keep them off the poor relief rolls; the old-age pension was regarded as an income supplement, since there was no assumption that workers would cease earning at any particular age. Invalidity and old-age insurance, moreover, presented themselves in the first instance as deductions from workers' take-home pay. On the other hand, the real improvements in quality of life implied and eventually achieved by the system should not be underestimated; the system of sickness insurance, in particular, with its guarantee of free medical care and drugs for workers and their families, both made life significantly easier for large numbers of people and drew them into a new relationship with the state and the medical profession. Over the long term, Bismarckian social policy can be seen as having an important effect in integrating the working class, providing guarantees against the worst consequences of work and the loss of earning capacity, introducing predictability and the concept of a legal claim to protection into the business of day-to-day survival, giving workers a financial stake in the system, and introducing them to the disciplines of a modern bureaucratised society. The political incorporation of workers as a collective status group (*Stand*) or interest group by way of social policy, which was to become a permanent feature of German public administration, was already present on a small scale in the role allotted to the representatives of the insured on the bodies that administered the social insurance funds (the principle of self-administration, or *Selbstverwaltung*). Beyond this, the early decision to counter the hazards of industrial society by compensating individuals retrospectively rather than developing a comprehensive programme for prevention 'taught' the insured to view themselves and others in terms of a quantifiable capacity for productive labour: the (masculine) individual was essentially worker, and all social entitlement flowed from that (Milles, 1990; cf. Quataert, 1984).

The 'new course' in social policy, 1890–1914

The specific, indeed the sole, object of Bismarckian social policy was the industrial worker. Between Bismarck's dismissal by the new Kaiser Wilhelm II in 1890 and the outbreak of the First World War, the provisions of social insurance were extended to other groups of manual workers, alongside new measures of protective legislation. A separate, and privileged, scheme for old-age and invalidity insurance was introduced for salaried employees (*Angestellte*) (Gladen, 1974; Hentschel, 1983). These reforms acknowledged the growing differentiation within the ranks of the economically dependent classes, at the same time as they served to reinforce it. The expansion of the terms of reference of state social policy was also associated with moves towards populist appeal and experimentation (in both domestic and foreign policy), with which successive governments attempted to answer the rise of mass politics across the political spectrum. Alongside the burgeoning SPD, the rise of new forms of political organisation and agitation and new parties and pressure groups on the right bespoke the disaffection of a wide range of social groups, and made the Bismarckian balancing-act obsolete. There was a shift, too, in the public discussion of social policy, which had begun to identify a wide range of problems and pathologies related only indirectly to the fact and conditions of industrial work (Sachße, 1986). By 1910, more than one-fifth of Germany's population lived in cities of 100,000 or more, and movements for social reform directed their attentions more and more towards the cities as sites of crime, poor housing, disease, pollution, prostitution and moral and physical degeneracy. The problems of women as workers and mothers, the moral and practical implications of prostitution and the sexual double standard in a social order that was both patriarchal and materialist were raised for general debate by women's organisations, which achieved a membership of nearly half a million before 1914 (Meyer-Renschhausen, 1989; Allen, 1991). Youth, too, was identified as a problem (Peukert, 1986; Linton, 1991; see also Chapters 6 and 7). All of these issues were increasingly seen as demanding organised social intervention.

The 1890s also witnessed the beginnings of a new approach to the relief of poverty. The social insurance system was designed to stabilise the position of workers in work. Those who had no work, or who fell into another form of social need, lay outside the purview of central government; they remained the responsibility of municipal poor relief. As the economy expanded and regular work under protected conditions could be seen as an achievable norm, poverty began to be redefined in terms of unemployment. A peak in the numbers of unemployed and homeless in the mid-1890s inspired the governments of Prussia, Bavaria and Württemberg to direct towns and cities to establish labour exchanges as an integral part of their poor relief operations; municipalities in other states followed suit. The poor were thus reduced to the unemployable and dependants of the unemployed. As far as cash benefits were concerned, the principle of subsidiarity prevailed: public support was available only after every other avenue, including private charity, had been exhausted. Such support was in any case always limited by the funds available, and the need to control outgoings contributed to a move towards the appointment of salaried staff to review and administer cases. This marks the beginning of a divide between social welfare administration and the practice of social work, where the former was carried out by employees of the municipality and the latter by volunteers (Sachße, 1986).

At the same time, there was a change in attitudes to social welfare. A new practice of 'social care' (*soziale Fürsorge*) could forestall poverty by changing the conditions and habits of life of the working class, without compulsion or discrimination. The municipalities took on new responsibilities (Steinmetz, 1993). They began to develop housing policies, involving variously the construction of public housing, public support for housing societies, measures for improving the quality of existing housing, and advice to households on how to make the best use of their living-space. This last was closely associated with increased activity in the area of public health, or rather in disease prevention. Here the focus was on diseases posing a particular threat to the public, including tuberculosis, venereal disease, alcoholism, mental illness and crippling conditions. Pregnant women, new mothers, infants and children were particular objects of care from the point of view of public health, with medical care and advice provided through a (still small) network of specialist clinics. By 1914, several cities had already established municipal child welfare bureaux (Sachße, 1986).

In all these areas of provision, the public authorities relied heavily on the work of a new kind of social worker, professionally self-conscious and schooled in a discourse that combined the languages of love or 'intellectual motherliness' and social prophylaxis, or hygiene (as in the expression *Sozial-hygiene*). In particular, social work provided an opportunity for women to transform traditional charity work into a socially acknowledged activity in the public sphere, and the women's movement played a significant role in its professionalisation. Social administration was one of the few areas in which women were employed in responsible positions in the public sector before 1914 (Sachße, 1986; Meyer-Renschhausen, 1989; Hong, 1990). Significantly, social work, both salaried and voluntary, continued to be organised largely by private agencies, which could be more comprehensive and better staffed and equipped than any public agency (Sachße, 1986). While the municipal social services often relied on their assistance, all of these agencies were jealous of their independence and suspicious of public claims to competence in the provision of social services.

The First World War and after: the birth of the modern welfare state

The First World War is regarded by many historians as marking the beginning of the welfare state in Germany. The emergency of a long war, which drained the human and material resources of the country and required the mobilisation of the whole of society, created the conditions in which the state could take unprecedented powers to coordinate social and economic activity and at the same time establish itself as final guarantor of the welfare of the nation. In many respects, what wartime policies did was to consolidate pre-war developments, but the result was a qualitatively new system.

One important consequence of the war was to reinforce the tendencies towards incorporation of the labour movement already implicit in the social insurance system. The war effort depended in the first instance on the acquiescence of the SPD and the trade unions, the so-called *Burgfrieden*, or civil truce. As the war dragged on, the need to coordinate the disposition of manpower so as to maintain both production on the home front and the effectiveness of the armed forces led to significant concessions towards the trade unions. Under the terms of the Auxiliary Service Law of December 1916, they were granted seats alongside representatives of employers and the military on local arbitration boards, and works councils were established to oversee working conditions in individual plants. Coming in the wake of earlier measures to bring representatives of private industry into the administrative machinery for coordinating the production of war supplies, this can be seen as a crucial move towards corporatism (Gladen, 1974; Preller, 1949).

At the same time, the state took on new functions of direct support. Maintaining the life and health of the population at home was now vital to the survival of the state itself. The state acted to guarantee the supply of food and to regulate its distribution (a crucial social and political issue since Germany was under blockade throughout the war). As a necessary complement to official efforts to recruit women to war-work, it also took overall responsibility for providing childcare and for the physical well-being of working mothers. By extension, maternal and infant health became a concern of the state. In practice, much of this provision continued to be carried by local authorities, whose pre-war activities continued and expanded to meet the intensification of problems of deprivation and delinquency occasioned by the stresses of war. But it was clearly central government, often in the form of the military authorities, that now set the imperatives for intervention. Moreover, the war created a new form of entitlement: financial support for the families of men at the front, for the survivors of fallen soldiers, for the masses of wounded and crippled, as well as the promise of veterans' pensions after the war, took on the character of an 'obligation to the nation's heroes' (cf. Hausen, 1987; see also Whalen, 1984; Wall and Winter, 1988; Bessel, 1990).

In order to meet its obligations, the wartime administration depended on a new kind of institutionalised cooperation between public and private agencies. The creation of the *Nationaler Frauendienst* (National Women's Service), through which women's associations of all political colours placed their organisations at the disposal of the government for deployment in social service, nursing and protection for women workers, is one example of the fusion of the public and voluntary sectors. In the day-to-day administration of social services, representatives of local authorities and voluntary agencies now sat together on the responsible bodies; agency social workers administered public policy and private agencies received public subsidies. The formal distinction between public and private thus remained, while the historic division of labour by which voluntary agencies stepped in to 'top-up' public poor relief effectively disappeared (Sachße, 1986; Hong, 1992).

All of these developments were consolidated and formalised after the war, in the legislation of the Weimar Republic. The roles of trade unions and organised employers as partners in a tendentially corporatist system were confirmed in private agreements between the two in 1918 and in the Weimar constitution. Legislation on compulsory state arbitration gave central government a new and critical function as guarantor of collective agreements in industry. The constitution stipulated the right and duty to work, and in 1927 the social insurance system was supplemented by the creation of a national system of unemployment insurance, again based on worker and employer contributions, as well as a statutory system of labour exchanges. Measures for workers' protection at the workplace, many of which had been allowed to lapse during the war, were reinstated and extended, and the eight-hour day formally established as a norm. The core of Weimar policy was thus a package of measures designed to integrate the workers as full social and political citizens in the new democracy, and to avoid the worst consequences of class conflict. It was to this package that the expression *Sozialpolitik* was normally applied in the 1920s (Preller, 1949; Abelshauser, 1987).

The other areas of public provision for social need came under the rubric of welfare; *Wohlfahrt* now became a part of the language of public administration, although the expression *Wohlfahrtsstaat* (welfare state) was used almost exclusively in a derogatory sense (Abelshauser, 1987). The Reich began to legislate in the fields of housing (rent control) and disease control, thus providing a new framework for local initiatives in housing provision and the expansion of the clinic system. More generally, during the 1920s, legislation confirmed the partnership of public and private agencies in a guaranteed system of locally based social provision. In response to new legislation on the duty of public assistance, most local authorities created central welfare bureaux (*Wohlfahrtsämter*) to coordinate social services, administered by boards on which the voluntary sector was represented (Sàchße and Tennstedt, 1988). In important areas of policy, the principle of subsidiarity left vital functions of prophylaxis and normative intervention to the private sector (see, for example, Harvey, 1993, pp. 168–72). Its persistence gave the voluntary agencies, increasingly centralised and bureaucratised in response to their new functions, a significant and lasting role in the making and executing of social policy within what has been variously described as a 'welfare-industrial complex' and a 'neo-corporatist system of negotiation' (Sachße, 1986, p. 231).

The Weimar Republic, then, brought the institutional consolidation of a 'split' welfare state (Hernes, 1986). *Sozialpolitik* proper identified a realm of contributory and work-related benefits, associated with institutions of corporative negotiation in which the beneficiaries were directly represented; at its centre stood the productive worker and head of household, normatively male. The complement to this was a system of *Wohlfahrt*, in which benefits were related to assessed need rather than contributions. It was family-focused and associated with caring or disciplinary intervention and with agencies whose function was advocacy rather than representation. At the centre of this system stood women and children. The state acted as guarantor and integrating agency for both functions. The failure of Weimar democracy, its collapse precipitated by conflicts over the financing of mass unemployment, can be seen as a consequence of the first crisis of the modern welfare state, caught between the promises it could not materially afford to fulfil and the hostility of those who saw both *Sozialpolitik* and *Wohlfahrt* as unacceptable burdens on profitability (Weisbrod, 1981; Evans and Geary, 1987).

National Socialism

In some significant ways, the period of National Socialist rule represents an interruption in the continuous development of Germany's economic and political institutions; representative government, civic equality and the federal system, all destroyed by the Nazis, were successfully restored after 1945. The operations of the capitalist economy were barely touched, and even the trade unions, one of Hitler's earliest targets, regrouped and established their status as a 'social partner' in the post-war economy. All of this applies to West Germany, of course; in East Germany the collapse of Nazism was the occasion for the creation of an entirely new set of institutions in the name of socialism. Here too, though, it is clear that the experience of National Socialism did not in itself prevent later recourse to historic models, for example in the democratic constitution of 1949 or, indeed, in the adoption of a rationalised version of pre-war social insurance legislation as the basis for a social security system that lasted the life of the GDR (Hentschel, 1983). If we consider the heritage of National Socialist policy for the Federal Republic, the impact of the Nazi experience on the development of social policy and its conditions appears to have been different in different areas. At the core of social policy, work-related social insurance, Nazi policy built on and reinforced existing values and institutions, although it interrupted the growth of democratic corporatist institutions associated with their administration. In the areas historically marginal to the core, the sphere of welfare and population policy and of policy towards outsiders, the historical function of Nazi practice is more complex. Here, National Socialism brought about a radical culmination of existing trends in policy. As a result, certain kinds of direct intervention by the state, particularly in the area of reproductive and family policy, and to some extent the whole principle of state intervention, were discredited. At the same time, Nazi policies towards foreigners, and particularly foreign labour, simply highlighted a continuity in the enforcement of discriminatory and ethnically delimited definitions of citizenship which has begun to work itself out in the pattern of ethnic conflict in Germany following unification in 1990.

Between 1933 and 1945, two imperatives defined the direction of social policy. The first was the 'nationalisation' of the working class; the second the 'rationalisation' of the genetic 'stock' of the German population to fit Nazism's redefinition of the nation as a biological unit. The aim was a *Volksgemeinschaft* – a national or racial community. Over the whole period of the regime, social welfare remained an important function of the state. It was the functions of public welfare that were redefined; the welfare agencies of the Weimar Republic were developed into a machinery for enforcing National Socialist values on the genetically healthy and racially valuable population and screening others out (Hansen, 1991; Otto and Sünker, 1989).

Eugenics, the proposition that social ills could be overcome by improving the physical 'stock' of the population, had been influential in both medical and social policy circles since before the First World War (Usborne, 1992; Weindling, 1993). Under the Weimar Republic, a eugenic consensus among professionals across the political spectrum fuelled the liberalisation of abortion law and the flowering of public initiatives in the fields of family planning, ante-natal care and maternal and infant health. But even before 1933, financial pressures on the public welfare system were encouraging the deployment of medical and genetic definitions of deviance as a basis for sorting and selecting among those who called upon public services.

After 1933, the public health aspect of the eugenic movement became entirely subordinate to genetic definitions of character. Deviants, including criminals, juvenile delinquents, prostitutes, vagrants, the chronically unemployed (as far as they were confirmed to be work-shy) and homosexuals, were presumed to be incorrigible. They were subject to measures which were essentially punitive. Social hygiene was displaced by race hygiene (*Rassenhygiene*), which was promoted by both positive and negative means. Under legislation of 1933 which linked biological and labour market policy, healthy women were encouraged to leave work and have children by a system of marriage loans. The network of health advice and care for pregnant women, mothers and infants was extended. Eligibility for these benefits was limited according to capacity to reproduce, or genetic health, and the same clinics and bureaux that confirmed the entitlement of healthy parents identified the genetically diseased. These people, including alcoholics, epileptics and the morally or intellectually 'feeble-minded', selected on the basis of tests with a strong social bias, were subject after 1934 to compulsory sterilisation. From 1939 on, incurably ill, hereditarily diseased, mentally infirm and physically disabled children and adults housed in institutions were systematically murdered as a matter of state policy (Bock, 1984; Czarnowski, 1991). Jews and Gypsies, identified *a priori* as racial outsiders, suffered systematic discrimination, exclusion, and finally mass murder (Burleigh and Wippermann, 1991).

Nazism incorporated an ideology of work as an absolute value (Lüdtke, 1993). An expression of the principles behind Nazi social policy and an important feature of the regime's public face was the diversion of resources from support for the unemployed to public works projects and programmes for labour service, both voluntary and compulsory. Nazi policy towards workers in work was designed to extirpate socialist traditions and incorporate the working class in a national community free from social conflict. The trade unions and other organisations of the labour movement were smashed in 1933, to be replaced with a single organisation of workers and employers, the *Deutsche Arbeitsfront*. The workplace was redefined as a factory community (*Betriebsgemeinschaft*), with the employer at its head. The Nazi state attempted to compensate workers for their loss of independence with an elaborate programme for the improvement of conditions at the workplace and with new forms of activity outside work. The *Kraft durch Freude* (Strength through Joy) organisation offered recreation, group travel and the opportunity to buy one's own car, the *Volkswagen*, through periodic contributions. The state thus invited workers to participate in a developing consumer culture. Official assertions about the dignity of work and the worker within the *Volksgemeinschaft* were backed up by measures to give workers access to the bonuses and paid holidays which had previously been the prerogatives of salaried staff, and to erode the favoured status of the latter within the social insurance system (which was retained and extended to the non-manual self-employed) (Recker, 1985; Prinz, 1986; Mason, 1993).

Although working conditions and living standards declined under conditions of forced rearmament and labour-market saturation in the last years before the war, Nazi policy appears to have reinforced certain processes of social levelling and integration within the German population. To some extent, national solidarity was confirmed by the presence of identifiable outsiders or enemies within the body politic. In addition to the racial enemy (the Jews) and, in wartime, the national enemy (the Allied powers), Germans had encounters with captive foreign workers during the war. Evidence suggests that the presence of these workers, constituting a kind of underclass and always working under German managers and foremen, contributed to an increase in relative status for native workers and an acquiescence, at least, in the notion of ethnic solidarity (Herbert, 1983). If we can see the privileged position of Germans in relation to foreign workers in Nazi Germany as foreshadowing the situation of *Gastarbeiter* in West Germany (see Chapter 9), it is worth noting that modern Germany has always relied on the economic contribution of foreigners, and that their treatment, in terms of both civic and work-related rights, has been a matter for public debate and policy since the nineteenth century. As early as 1908, Prussia introduced both a system of formal registration for foreign workers and officially sponsored machinery for recruiting foreign agricultural labour, confirming the existence of a secondary and discriminated labour force as a permanent feature of the economy (Herbert, 1990).

The foundations of social policy in West Germany after 1945

The basis for the present institutions of social policy in Germany was largely laid down in the years following the decision in the summer of 1948 to create a new West German state (Hockerts, 1980). After Germany's capitulation in 1945, the occupying powers collectively proposed an entirely new system of social insurance, unifying and rationalising the various types of provision which had existed formerly, but this proved unacceptable to all the interested groups. In the meantime, the old system continued to operate under Allied administration, though the dimensions of social need and galloping inflation meant it was far from adequate. As the breach opened up between the Soviet Union and the western Allies that spelt the beginning of the Cold War, the original Allied proposal for a unified insurance system was summarily adopted in the Soviet Zone, where it would form the basis for the GDR's social security system. In the West, the drafting of a new system was delegated by the British and American military governments to the German representative bodies responsible for the administration of the unified economic area (*Bizone*) created out of their respective zones of occupation. Almost simultaneously, the Parliamentary Council began to deliberate on a draft constitution for the new West German state, and plans for social security reform were shelved pending the creation of a new and legitimate governmental machinery.

As a result, it was the Christian Democrats (CDU/CSU) who dominated the making of a new social policy; in coalition with the liberal Free Democrats (FDP), they governed the first *Bundestag* with a small majority and gained ever-larger majorities in successive elections until the mid-1960s. In contrast to the creative contribution that its predecessor, the Centre Party, had made to the development of the Weimar welfare state, the CDU/CSU approach was not an expansive one. Reform was limited in the first instance to increasing the benefits within the social insurance system, or, in the terms of the legislation, adapting them to changes in wages and prices. This reflected the urgent need to raise benefits to a realistic level. The minimalist approach to reform was in keeping with the neo-liberal principles of the social market economy which formed the economic programme of the CDU/CSU in government and guided the reconstruction of West Germany's economic institutions. A contributory system constituted a form of collective self-help and an incentive to work, and guaranteed that economic growth would be reflected directly in improved social benefits. It was thus the appropriate adjunct to an economic doctrine that saw the citizenry as a collection of free economic agents and approved of state intervention only to guarantee competition as the basis for freedom of consumer choice. It also had two generations of effective operation behind it, which weighed heavily against any proposals for reform that would have created new financial burdens on the population or reduced the influence of interested groups, including employers and the voluntary sector in particular.

Under the first government of Chancellor Konrad Adenauer, the system of social insurance as it had existed before the war was substantially restored. Structural reforms were considered during his second term, but the only major change came in 1957, with the reform of the old-age pension: for the first time, the pension was treated as a substitute for earnings rather than a supplement; the amount payable, determined by formula, worked out at 60 per cent of gross income after forty years of insured work and was linked to the cost of living and average earnings. The message of this reform was ambiguous. On the one hand, it confirmed that maintaining the standard of living of individuals was one of the functions of state policy. On the other, it was variously supported by the proposition that the old-age pension was a specific reward for a lifetime of work and the idea that it represented the debt owed by each generation to the preceding one (Hentschel, 1983). In short, the claim to dignity in old age was to be regarded as an earned entitlement, rather than a human right.

The explicit commitment to direct social benefits and public assistance that had characterised the Weimar Republic was not resuscitated with the same energy after 1945. This was in spite of the fact that the social need produced by the Second World War was apparently far more serious than the conditions to which the first welfare state was a response: the German civilian population suffered critically from hunger and homelessness in the first years after the war, at the same time as the western zones were flooded with millions of refugees, displaced persons and Germans expelled from Eastern Europe. To their urgent needs were added those of disabled veterans, prisoners of war (some of whom did not return to Germany until the mid-1950s) and the survivors of the fallen. While the long-term solutions to war-induced social distress and problems of the integration of new groups into the population were left to the workings of the economic recovery, war victims were the first beneficiaries of positive welfare legislation, the Federal Law on State Benefits (*Bundesversorgungsgesetz*) of 1950. On the whole, though, the Weimar experience provided a cautionary example rather than a model. Just as the drafters of the Basic Law strove to make the political system proof against the pre-programmed self-destruction inherent in the Weimar constitution, the acknowledgement of employers and the newly consolidated trade unions as 'social partners' proceeded without the kind of prescriptive legislation that had directly embroiled the Weimar state in industrial conflicts. The comprehensive welfare commitments of post-1918 governments were perceived as having overextended the system politically and financially and fed the spiralling inflation of 1919–23, whose spectre has haunted German economic policy ever since.

A more wide-ranging commitment on the part of the new state to social welfare thus had to await the first upswing in the economy. The *Wirtschaftswunder* (economic miracle) began to make itself felt for the population at large from about 1957 on, after a period of relative austerity compounded by policies designed to prevent any return of inflation and to direct resources into investment rather than consumption (Abelshauser, 1983). In 1961, a new Social Welfare Act (*Sozialhilfegesetz*) decreed a reorganisation of the direct benefit system inherited from the Weimar Republic; it confirmed the right of all citizens to public assistance to maintain a standard of living that would allow them not only to answer their physical needs but also to participate in social and cultural life. The stated aim of *Sozialhilfe* was to enable the needy to help themselves, but from the beginning benefit rates were low and schematically applied. Eligibility was established only when an individual could demonstrate no other source of income, including relatives' contributions.

The single substantive innovation in welfare policy in the early years of the Federal Republic was the introduction of *Kindergeld*, or child benefit. The idea of *Kindergeld* had been raised in the immediate post-war years, but it was vetoed by the occupying powers as a relic of National Socialism:

a policy for paying people to have children. Indeed, in nearly all areas of policy towards the family, the reference to National Socialist policies could be and was deployed to discredit state intervention. Christian Democrat policy-makers in particular invoked the horrors of Nazism to encourage the return to a family policy directed at reinforcing the authoritative position of the male head of household (Moeller, 1993). Liberal and individualising policies like the equality of women (*Gleichstellung*), which the GDR authorities were in the process of writing into law, were equated with the Nazi policy of atomising and coordinating the population (*Gleichschaltung*). The power of legal and customary tradition is demonstrated by the paradox of the Equality Law of 1957: the guarantee of equality of men and women enshrined in the Basic Law was translated into reform of the marriage law provision of the civil code only after seven years of deliberation, and three years after the deadline laid down in the Law. Until 1976 it included the stipulation that a married woman could engage in paid employment only so far as it did not conflict with her primary duty to her family. In the case of *Kindergeld*, supporters of the patriarchal family used welfare policy as a means of privileging some families over others. The first *Kindergeld* legislation of 1954 provided for payment only from the third child on and only to the families of economically active citizens, and funded the system through contributions. By 1961, payments had been extended to the second child, and the additional costs covered out of general taxation. *Kindergeld* was made payable to all children only in 1974.

The extension of *Kindergeld* was part of a second 'new course' in social policy, precipitated by economic difficulties in the mid-1960s that brought the SPD into government, first as a member of the 'Grand Coalition' composed of Christian and Social Democrats, and then, after the elections of 1969, at the head of a cabinet in coalition with the FDP. In the late 1960s and 1970s, legislation was introduced which extended the competence of government to intervene in the economy, widened the social safety-net, and elaborated corporatist institutions, such as co-determination in industry (*Mitbestimmung*), which had stopped short in the 1950s. These measures attest to politicians' awareness that the *Wirtschaftswunder* was over; it was no longer possible to be confident that the natural expansion of the economy alone would suffice to overcome social inequality or avoid conflicts over the distribution of the social product. The reforms of the 1970s addressed these two problems by adapting the mechanisms of political participation in policy-making and augmenting the redistributive functions of the state, without fundamentally altering the character of the system. As direct expenditure on social assistance, child benefit, training and education increased, the welfare element of social policy acquired a higher profile than ever before, but 'even in 1980 the social security system was still . . . a system of social insurance with welfare elements, and not the other way around' (Hentschel, 1983, p. 209).

Guide to further reading

There is no up-to-date survey of the history of German social policy available in English, and nothing that takes into account both *Sozialpolitik* and welfare policy. Many of the standard and most recent works involve a comparative element, including Flora and Heidenheimer (1981), Mommsen and Mock (1981), Hennock (1987) and Baldwin (1990), all of which focus on the development of social insurance. New research has resulted in a number of publications on specific aspects and periods of social and welfare policy: Linton (1991) and Harvey (1993) on youth; Usborne (1992) and Weindling (1993) on eugenics and population policy; Allen (1991) on the role of the women's movement; Steinmetz (1993) on municipal welfare. A useful compendium of articles on the Weimar Republic is Evans and Geary (1987). The standard work on policies towards workers in Nazi Germany is still Mason (1993), although the new English edition is largely a translation of the German original of 1977, and subsequent research has overtaken it to some extent. Burleigh and Wippermann (1991) provide a good survey of racial policies. For the post-war period, Moeller (1993) provides an in-depth study of policy-making with a focus on the crucial area of family and gender policy. Herbert (1990) is the standard general work on foreign labour.

In German, there are now a number of authoritative general surveys of aspects of both social policy and welfare to set beside a proliferating specialist literature: Hentschel (1983) is primarily a history of the social security system and industrial relations policy since 1880. Gladen (1974) focuses on social security, but also includes material on poor relief. Tennstedt (1981) places policy since the eighteenth century in its social and economic context. Sachße and Tennstedt (1980, 1988) give a detailed account of the history of poor relief and social service since the Middle Ages. Sachße (1986) provides a historical survey of the development of social welfare in the context of a study of the growth of social work as a feminised profession; more recent studies that focus on the relationship between women and social work are Meyer-Renschhausen (1989), Baumann (1992) and Eifert (1993). Landwehr and Baron (1983) provide a general survey of the development of social work.

Chapter 2

The impact of unification

Steen Mangen

Until 1990, a radical reform of the total institutional arrangements of the welfare state had not been attempted in any Western European country since the early post-war years. Innovations since then had remained at the sectoral level, the creation of the national health service in Italy in 1978 being a prime example. Unification of Germany imposed an agenda for comprehensive welfare reform unparalleled elsewhere in the EC, for it rendered largely redundant the organisation and many of the goals of GDR social policy. Despite some initial protests from elements on the left, a policy of a more or less total and rapid assimilation of the eastern system into the federal model was adopted. This strategy has accrued serious economic, social and political costs for, in effect, it created in the 'united' Germany a two-tier welfare state in which most easterners' access to welfare compares unfavourably with that of their western counterparts. Moreover, economic and social indicators unambiguously confirm that the medium-term effects of this strategy will stretch into the next millennium.

This chapter briefly reviews the solutions adopted in the first phase of the transition, as well as discussing current policy lines concerning funding and administration in this, the second phase. It then speculates on longer-term welfare problems arising from the very modest projections of economic performance in a Germany that, with unification, slipped from second to eighth place in the EC in terms of per capita GDP. However, equally important is the fact that many of these problems are the consequence of policies adopted in the old West Germany where the welfare model was already being challenged by the mounting issues of an ageing population, long-term unemployment and the threat posed by the 'two-thirds' society. The need to generate political consensus meant that relatively short-term palliatives were voted that failed to address critical long-term structural problems. Thus, the incorporation of the GDR has seriously exacerbated but, for most substantive areas, did not create these fundamental problems which will unavoidably require further political resolution. There is an emerging agreement in the academic literature that significant changes will be needed in the operation of the present German polity necessitating the federal government to adopt a more dirigiste role than was the case prior to 1990. Such a process has perforce already been occurring and must call into question the viability of the old model of concerted federalism.

The socio-economic impact of unification

In comparison with the former West Germany (see Introduction and Chapter 1), the official perception of those aspects of welfare that constituted a legitimate public good was much more extensive in the GDR. There welfare was delivered via a unified and substantially centralised system under the hegemony of the Communist Party (*Sozialistische Deutsche Arbeiterpartei*, SED) (Dennis, 1988). Local authorities and voluntary welfare agents were under tight supervision and best understood as operating field services for East Berlin. Apart from the absence of unemployment coverage, which because of guarantees of rights to work did not exist until right at the end of the GDR era, all-risk social insurance was administered by the trade unions for employees and by the state for the relatively few self-employed and for the large number of party officials. Unlike in West Germany, social security was not principally organised on earnings-related, performance achievement lines (*Leistungsprinzip*) (Lötsch, 1992), although this did assume more importance in the 1980s (Scharf, 1987). Rather, the system was characterised by 'citizenship' welfare rights fulfilled in general by the provision of universal, albeit modest, flat-rate benefits. A critical welfare role was undertaken by employers (largely state corporations), who were major suppliers of such popularly esteemed social services as kindergarten and primary health facilities. Welfare activity extended well beyond conventional western definitions. Thus, although the level of benefits might have been low, they were supplemented by wide-scale heavy subsidies of essential items such as food, housing, certain clothing, energy and public transport, items which in total represented about one-third of average weekly household expenditure (Lampert, 1990).

Unification has begun to stimulate propensities towards a greater individualisation of life-styles in the East and an accompanying differentiation – some might argue, atomisation – of social structure (Zapf, 1991). These developments have inescapably given rise to new inequalities, particularly projected in the area of income distribution, which had been relatively uniform in the GDR era. The transition has already had serious consequences for the major national parties arising from the polarisation in the East of winners and losers, as well as from the inevitable reinforcement of the great economic division between West and East.

The demise of the old paternalistic social policy of the GDR has transferred burdens to individuals for functions previously assumed by the state. There have been qualitative and quantitative dimensions to this transition: changes not only in institutional organisation, but also in the level of service provision. Social security was the sector where the impact has been the most immediate, but, according to initial impressionistic assessments, all welfare sectors in the East were in substantial need of upgrading. With regard to services, although for different reasons, it is perhaps in education and housing where the difficulties are most acute: the former at the ideological level and the latter because of the sheer qualitative deficiencies. Education as the key mechanism for cultural reproduction was the area of social policy most tightly controlled by the SED. Housing problems remained acute during the GDR era, despite the massive building programmes that were implemented. In 1990 almost 15 per cent of all flats lacked a bath or shower and sole access to an indoor lavatory (Lötsch, 1991). Housing is clearly the major sector of social infrastructural investment; indications are that the initial requirement will be for an upgrading of one-third of a million units annually up to the end of the century. Furthermore, housing problems have scarcely been alleviated by the principle adopted by the outgoing GDR government of rights to restitution rather than compensation for former owners of property confiscated by the state on the institution of the GDR.

Among the gainers from unification have been eastern wage-earners, pensioners and certain other welfare recipients. Trade unions in the West, anxious to avoid chronic regional salary inequalities which might encourage jobs to move East, have been keen advocates of income parity and have been supported by the Ministry of Labour and Social Affairs, which sees in this strategy a means of increasing receipts from social insurance contributions (Schmidt, 1992). Concessions in this direction have been forthcoming because the employer's side in the eastern federal states has been over-represented by heavily subsidised industry which is confronted by few immediate budgetary constraints (Paqué and Soltwedel, 1993). Furthermore, western employers were not eager to see the mushrooming of low-cost competitors in the new *Länder*. However, the opinion of many economic organisations, including the OECD, is that, given prevailing productivity levels, this has been a recipe for eastern workers to price themselves out of jobs (OECD, 1992c). Ancillary costs of labour had been steadily growing in the old West Germany and by 1992 represented 84 per cent of expenditure on wages. Unit costs in the East are 60 per cent higher than in the West and the wage–productivity ratio there is still deteriorating. Nevertheless, one should not overstate the wages problem. Less than a quarter of the workforce will be covered by full wage parity agreements by 1995 and, even within these sectors, workers have been willing to moderate their demands in the light of economic realities, as the 1993 revised strategy of the powerful *IG Metall* union has demonstrated. Two years after unification, average net income was approaching three-quarters the western equivalent, although this is reduced to just over 60 per cent when overtime is taken into account.

According to one of the major economic forecasting institutions, in the first two years since unification there has been only a slight increase in income inequality in the former GDR, though this is set to increase (DIW, 1993a). Survey evidence for the same period suggests that, despite mass unemployment, over half of eastern households have improved their real incomes, although one household in seven – largely those where all adult members are unemployed – is worse off. Surprisingly, these data indicate that the situation of single-parent households has stabilised (Berger *et al.*, 1993).

More spectacular has been the change in the fortunes of the losers from unification, the principal representatives being the unemployed, since the immediate impact of the transition was severest on the labour market. In the first two years, more than half of all industrial jobs were destroyed and productivity fell by almost two-thirds. By the end of 1991, three-quarters of a million eastern workers over the age of 55 had opted for early retirement. The federal scheme permits them to receive full pay for up to five years and it has also functioned to reduce alternative claims for social assistance by the older unemployed (Chamberlayne, 1992b). Wolf (1991) has argued that the social consequences of early retirement are appreciably different in the East because of the abrupt change of life for the people concerned, the large degree to which it was an enforced decision and the different social and moral worth historically attached to work in the GDR. As for other measures, about 20 per cent of employees in the East were subsidised for short-time work, including 'zero-time' work, in a special scheme which ended in 1991. Thereafter, the number of short-time workers fell by more than half (DIW, 1993b).

In 1991, 70 per cent of expenditure on labour market measures in the East was allocated to 'passive' interventions (that is, solely allocating welfare benefits to the unemployed). Subsequently, the government has attached greater priority to active measures involving retraining and job creation, although this policy line has been compromised by budgetary deficits and, for a time, funding of new retraining programmes was suspended. Per capita costs for participants in these schemes are considerably higher than for unemployment benefit recipients: job creation places, for example, on average cost almost two-thirds more (in 1992, DM 24,000 as opposed to DM 15,000 [Parkes, 1992]). Unlike western applicants, people in the East may transfer directly from employment to short-term job creation schemes without the need to qualify through a period of unemployment and there the full wage costs are paid from federal sources, compared to 75 per cent in the West. The consequence has been that the western long-term unemployed have far less probability of participating in labour market reintegration measures than their eastern colleagues.

Individuals have also been taking their own active measures, either by migrating or commuting to the former West Germany. It is estimated, for example, that currently there are 400,000 such commuters (DIW, 1993c). Typically, they are young, blue-collar workers, many of whom have had to accept employment inferior to the level of their skills, in part due to a tendency of western employers to downgrade East German qualifications (OECD, 1992c).

Chronically high levels of unemployment must call into question present labour market policy. A strategy of 'going for growth' has had little impact on long-term unemployment, although the federal government points to the new jobs created as a result. There has also been greater emphasis on flexibility of labour market regulations – draft legislation has been approved in cabinet – and on what has become known as 'atypical' work, much of which exempts employers from making contributions to social insurance for their staff. As in Britain, a 'create your own job' through self-employment policy has also been advocated. One product of these sorts of solutions, irrespective of the dubious benefits they may confer, is the fundamental restructuring of the relationship between the state and the individual as regards indemnifying major social risks.

Despite some short-term recovery, unemployment in one guise or another will continue as the most intransigent problem facing the East. The official rate, at 15.4 per cent (August, 1993), is double that of the West, where it has also been rising after a downward drift over the previous six years. The number of people in the second labour market – on short-time or in training or job creation programmes, for example – has also declined, suggesting that hidden unemployment is being transformed into real unemployment. Women in the new *Länder* have been particularly affected: they suffer double the male unemployment rate. Furthermore, the eastern unemployment profile differs from that in the West and indicates that possession of skills is no guarantee of finding appropriate work: three-quarters of claimants are skilled compared with half in the former West Germany.

At the time of writing, active and passive unemployment measures – benefits, early retirement, subsidies for short-time workers, job creation and retraining – incorporate well over four million East Germans: 1.2 million are registered unemployed and more than three million have been siphoned out of the regular labour market by one or other of the measures mentioned above (Employment Observatory, 1993). In the short term, a further small rise in eastern unemployment is projected and in the longer term possibly as many as one-fifth may continue to be unemployed or to remain in the second labour market (Paqué and Soltwedel, 1993).

In a welfare state such as Germany's where unemployment insurance is operated by the semi-autonomous Federal Labour Office and funded through insurance contributions, the intransigence of long-term unemployment threatens the continuing feasibility of insurance-based compensation. Increases in the contribution rate from 4.3 per cent to 6.8 per cent of gross pay in 1991 have not prevented the scheme from regularly amassing a large deficit, a problem which the Federal Labour Office currently predicts will persist, calling into question the future viability of the insurance principle as the basis of funding this social risk (Blanke *et al.*, 1992). The scheme has become routinely reliant on federal subsidies to make good its deficits. Even so, as a result of budgetary capping, the Federal Labour Office announced that it could not fund new retraining programmes for 1993, despite increased revenue from the rise in the contribution levy. Moreover, expenditure on federally funded unemployment assistance, awarded to the long-term unemployed when insurance entitlements expire, has also risen sharply.

Perhaps of greater concern is the fact that in the West since the 1980s outlays on social assistance, which is primarily funded by local authorities, accelerated sharply, largely as a result of rising long-term unemployment. Gone are the days when it amounted to a relatively small budget principally directed to those elderly with inadequate pensions entitlements. In the old *Länder*, problems of funding social assistance have been progressively deteriorating, causing tensions between the federal government, the *Länder* and local authorities, particularly in those areas most affected: the declining regions of the former industrial heartland. The federal government has been attempting to reduce the fiscal burden on local authorities, primarily via prolonged rights to unemployment insurance benefit for older workers and through job creation programmes where remuneration for former social assistance recipients is set at slightly higher levels than their original benefits (Wilson, 1993; see also Chapter 3). As a result, in the early 1990s there has been some improvement in the West, so that currently slightly fewer than 30 per cent of social assistance recipients are unemployed; however, in the East just over 50 per cent of social assistance claimants receive benefits because they are out of work (*Der Spiegel*, 1993).

The reliance on social assistance in the former GDR will grow as the cohort of unemployed with insurance benefits exhausts its entitlements. This inevitable development is expected to contribute substantially to the projected need to increase local authority expenditure there by 30 per cent annually until 1995 (DIW, 1993d). Accordingly, the government has sought to intervene to reduce the liabilities of all local authorities. With an eye to the reformulation in 1996 of subsistence criteria used to calculate benefit levels, it announced that, henceforth, social assistance would not necessarily be index-linked. Indeed, a real cut in benefit was implemented in 1993 and defended on the grounds that the growing 'poverty trap' had to be resolved.

The transition and the welfare agenda

The welfare agenda was essentially determined by the speed of the transition. Under these circumstances, legislative activity had to proceed at an intense pace; emergency and *ad hoc* funding strategies were unavoidable; the administrative structure had to be radically reformed partly through reliance on the posting of western bureaucrats to key positions; and in the introduction of the plural welfare system, the East has been heavily dependent on powerful western voluntary organisations.

Social policy assumed a central significance in the management of the transformation process (Schmähl, 1992a), since it was a vehicle to legitimise the new state and also to fend off the worst economic consequences arising, at least in the short run, from the union. However, although the GDR's negotiators of the State Treaty that legislated unification did succeed in establishing parity between a 'social' and an 'economic' union (Glaessner, 1992), there was no question that this was to provide an occasion whereby positive institutional features of the systems in both parts of Germany – even partially – could be merged. Eastern negotiators were hardly in a strong bargaining position and that meant that the policy flow was to be one-way, resulting in a preference for a rapid absorption of the western model, although, subsequently, abortion legislation and the social supplement to pensions were to be deviations from the rule. Thus, the State Treaty ended any serious idea that better attributes of the old GDR welfare system would be retained in anything but the short run: the longest survivor was to be the primary care *Polyklinik* network, but, even here, a longevity of only five years was assured (see Chapter 4). Gradual transition was rejected, since most eastern participants were anxious for immediate unification; speed, too, was attractive to the Chancellor in the run-up to the 1990 general election. SPD representatives did express reservations about the adverse funding implications of rapid unification, in which, in any case, they saw no short-term electoral advantage. But the government was intent on avoiding unleashing a general debate about welfare which would resurrect issues that had been so controversial only in the very recent past, when health, social security and tax reforms had been legislated (see Chapters 3 and 4). Accordingly, the negotiations did not provide the opportunity to re-examine the institutional arrangements of the existing western welfare model or the future viability of long-held welfare principles. The outcome was that little effort was invested in devising – or funding – a comprehensive implementation strategy. All hope was placed in sanguine projections of an economic miracle in the East (*Aufschwung Ost*) and rapid adoption of the western welfare structure.

In 1990, preparatory to unification, the GDR established for the first time a social assistance scheme, as well as legislating new job creation programmes consonant with those in the West. Immediately on unification the Federal

Labour Office took financial responsibility for unemployment insurance. The multiple sickness insurance schemes of the West were introduced in 1991, although there was to be no financial union with their western counterparts and, therefore, no possibility of cross-subsidisation. In the same year the further and higher educational promotional scheme (BAFöG), the childrearing allowance scheme and federal child benefits were introduced. The pensions system was integrated in a financial union in 1992. Owing to the low level of unemployment and pensions benefits in the East, a federally funded 'social supplement' was created to top up entitlements. Local authorities assumed immediate responsibilities for housing, hospitals, many welfare facilities previously provided by state enterprises, the subsidies for essential items and for administration of the social assistance scheme. (Further details are provided by Mangen, 1992.)

The funding agenda

The agenda in the first phase of the transition was determined by the need to infuse emergency funding into the East, principally to alleviate the most urgent social situations there, but also to establish the organisational structures of the western plural social security and welfare systems. The source of funding was largely federal and was intended to be short term and a 'seedbed' stimulating self-perpetuating projects. In the second phase, politicians have expended energy on the search for longer-term budgetary stability, mainly through formulating a new inter-state fiscal equalisation scheme to be established in the sixteen *Länder* in 1995, thereby attempting to force the western states into a more central role in funding unification than is presently the case. The official 'fiscal mood' between the two phases has been radically modified: from initial expectations of growth-led solutions to a current emphasis on the need to impose fiscal restraint.

Eager to improve its appeal in the first all-German election in 1990, the government stressed that unification would stimulate a self-generating impulse for growth which would mirror – and improve on – the mini-boom that the Federal Republic had enjoyed in the late 1980s. Federal pump-priming programmes were therefore deliberately time-limited. From the beginning, there was a serious failure on the part of the government to estimate the real funding requirements of the new *Länder* (Glaessner, 1992). This lack of a strategic economic programme to revitalise the East squares ill with the traditional anticipatory style of policy-making in the old West Germany. And, subsequently, it has led to an uncharacteristic reliance on *ad hoc* and emergency funding measures to supplement the main funds, the German Unity Fund (*Deutsche Einheit*) and the joint programme to stimulate an economic upswing (*Gemeinschaftswerk Aufschwung Ost*), as well as the panoply of other short-term federal subsidies and credit programmes. All these measures meant that additional fiscal sources were urgently needed to honour commitments. Part of the means have been raised by sharply increasing the borrowing requirement, which has seriously exacerbated the public sector deficit. Politically embarrassing as it was for the Chancellor, a one-year income tax increase, meretriciously called a solidarity levy, was instigated in 1991, reneging on electoral promises made only a few months previously. But it has been western social security contributors who have been the favoured target to supply additional revenue through regular increases in insurance levies.

For a brief period there was, indeed, an economic upturn stimulated by the union, but it occurred in the West and to some extent in other EC countries. The collapse of the GDR economy was startling both for its immediacy and its depth and surpassed the worst prior predictions. Within the first year, GDP in the East declined by almost one-third. To make matters worse, West Germany sunk into recession: even its own optimistic short-term projections indicated more or less zero growth; and, whilst eastern GDP may increase by as much as 7 per cent, this is from a very low base as a result of economic collapse there immediately on unification.

Public sector transfers from West to East in 1991 amounted to over 5 per cent of West German GDP (Ganssmann, 1993). Embarrassingly for the government, the rapid increase in public expenditure since unification – twice that originally forecast – profoundly reversed trends in the 1980s in the West and wiped out the budgetary reductions and tax gains of the *Wendepolitik* (the policy of rolling back the frontiers of the state and espousing self-reliance). Over half of this expenditure in the East has been financed through borrowing, and without a change of course, by 1995, over one-fifth of federal tax revenues will have to be allocated to debt servicing. With the deficit set to increase to 7 per cent in 1993, the government was determined to steer a new course of strict fiscal constraint on itself, on the *Länder* and on the local authorities.

To add to the government's difficulties, some economic forecasts in the second phase of the transition suggest that the new *Länder* will continue to require over DM 150 billion a year (in 1990 prices) to the end of the century in order to approach the living standards of the West. Accordingly, in 1992, Chancellor Kohl launched negotiations on a 'Solidarity Pact' which was to determine the level and distribution of future funding from 1995 onwards, when the *Deutsche Einheit* programme was due to expire and the government was to take over the combined debt of the old GDR state and *Treuhand*, the state holding enterprise.

The Pact, which was concluded in 1993, was a conscious attempt to restore an accommodation between the main parties and the social partners through seeking an agreement ostensibly espousing the principles of solidarity and social justice. This tactic of the government was designed to counter criticisms of the lack of equity of the means initially exploited to fund unification.

Apart from borrowing, the cabinet had pushed a large proportion of the burden on to social security contributors, so as to avoid long-term tax increases. Bearing in mind that insurance levies operate with an upper income ceiling, this strategy has a necessarily regressive redistributive impact. Similarly regressive was the across-the-board increase in VAT. There was general popular resentment that certain privileged occupational groups were, thereby, substantially exempt from shouldering their share of the burden: principally, civil servants (a status that embraces many more workers than in Britain), who benefit from non-contributory welfare benefits, and the self-employed (Ganssmann, 1993). Employers and the *Bundesbank* complained about overburdening employer–employee-funded social insurance which was contradictory to the government's goal of improving Germany's international competitiveness by reducing non-wage labour costs.

At the heart of the discussions about the Pact were two inter-related issues: how to finance the budgetary transfers eastwards, which could amount to about DM 150 billion annually: and, critically, how to integrate the new states into a revised inter-*Länder* fiscal equalisation scheme to guarantee the survival of cooperative federalism. Unification had rendered the old scheme redundant. The new states simply had too weak a tax base for it to have continued: they contained 20 per cent of the population but generated only 6 per cent of total public sector tax revenue. Local authorities in the East were in even direr straits, two-thirds of funds being derived from federal transfers and credits, double the ratio of their western counterparts (DIW, 1993d). And, since they had been allocated an enormous role in rebuilding the welfare state, their fiscal futures scarcely improved. To make matters worse, many could not count on an increase in the proportion of transfers the *Länder*, in turn, allocated to them. To gain some indication of their plight, Schneider (1993) argues that many communal social services in the East would have collapsed, had it not been for extensive reliance on federal job creation programmes to supply staff.

The old federal states were concerned to limit their liabilities with regard to equalisation transfers. Regional disparities in united Germany, however, are enormous and, *ceteris paribus*, they would have called forth enormous transfers, even from some of the poorer western states. This would have necessitated these *Länder* losing a large slice of previous budgetary awards. Two things were clear: extra taxation funding would have to be generated and the role of the federal government in the process would, perforce, be more salient than previously. The old *Länder* were successful in getting a lot of their own way on fiscal issues. But, critically, by agreeing to a strategy which allocated to the federal level the principal responsibility for funding the new states, they assisted in changing the balance of power within the federal polity.

The urgency of concluding the Solidarity Pact was underlined by the fact that, by 1992, it was clear that the projected budgetary deficit for 1995

would rise to over DM 100 billion. The Chancellor did not want to resort to immediate tax increases which were being urged upon him by the SPD, since he did not wish to increase his unpopularity by reneging twice on electoral commitments. The poor showing of both major parties in the state elections held at this time in Hesse – their share of the vote declined to the advantage of the right-wing Republican Party on the uncharacteristic basis of a low turn-out – concentrated minds wonderfully and concessions were forthcoming whereby the SPD agreed to a delay in an income tax increase until 1995 in return for a guarantee by Chancellor Kohl that there would be no substantial cuts in welfare.

Originally, the government was seeking savings of some DM 18 billion, but in the negotiations this was whittled down by about half. In terms of proposals with direct implications for the welfare sector, four principal means were agreed: another temporary 7.5 per cent 'solidarity' surcharge on income tax; increases in wealth and property taxes; a rise in petrol tax; and expenditure cuts of some DM 9 billion, to be effected in part by stricter policing of abuse of the welfare system. Significantly, a working party of *Länder* finance ministers was set up to explore means of attaining further cuts of DM 9 billion up to 1995. All in all, the fiscal measures amounted to some 3.5 per cent of GDP and could hardly fail but lead to a real decline in German living standards.

The Pact's total fiscal package amounted to a transfer from West to East of about DM 110 billion for the base-line year, 1995. Its proponents argued that the arrangement, at least, offered the new *Länder* the opportunity to engage in a more viable medium-term planning. Yet, the most significant achievement of the Pact is at the political level, for it marked a partial reinstatement of the primacy of the consensus politics that has been the hallmark of the federal model, and, moreover, it heralded a new sense of realism about the liabilities of German unification.

But there were detractors. Even before the Pact was signed, fears were expressed – by the *Bundesbank* among others – that the measures would not be sufficient to reduce the mounting public sector deficit. The agreed tax reforms were specifically identified as totally inadequate. The agreement seemed to have veered away from addressing many serious fiscal issues and did not sufficiently specify the means of achieving the savings. A fundamental flaw was the underlying over-optimistic assumption of economic recovery. Elements on the left maintained that, in reality, there was not much solidarity in the Pact since the weakest in society were being hit the most; for them the agenda was wage restraint and belt-tightening, appeals to solidarity being a device to attempt to conceal a far-reaching savings programme. Some pointed to the dangers of raised expectations if the Pact, after all the insistence on its fundamental importance for the future of Germany, did not deliver.

Whatever their position, its critics were agreed that the Pact was largely a short-term measure achieved by deferring too much to an outdated model of concerted federalism. Indeed, the attempt to implement it soon encountered resistance among the various interested parties, including within the federal ministries that failed to manifest the propensities for restraint they demanded of others. As regards the regional states, the 3 per cent guideline in growth of expenditure agreed in the Pact seems to have been largely ignored, especially by SPD-controlled western *Länder*.

But spiralling economic problems could not be repressed for long, particularly as forecasts of growth were constantly being revised downwards in contrast to those in respect of the budgetary deficit. Seizing on the recommendations of the *Länder* finance ministers' working party, the government only a few months later set aside its declared intention in the Pact to maintain the real value of welfare benefits. It announced plans for a 3 per cent cut in social and unemployment assistance, child allowances and benefits for participants in retraining programmes, despite inevitable protests from the SPD. Estimated savings derived from these cuts were incorporated in a medium-term retrenchment plan approved by the cabinet shortly afterwards. The objective was to reduce the federal deficit by over 40 per cent by limiting annual federal budgetary growth to 4 per cent to 1997, largely in an attempt to avoid bringing forward tax increases in 1994, an election year. Unlike the Solidarity Pact, this plan primarily relied on expenditure cuts rather than tax increases, but it broke the promise to reduce the unemployment insurance levy. It was stressed that, if the *Länder* complied with the strategy, reductions in the deficit could be significantly more. However, at the time of writing, the proposals face considerable opposition, especially in the *Bundesrat*, where the SPD command a majority, although much of the plan circumvents the need for approval of the upper house. Nevertheless, the government is anxious to perpetuate the broad consensus that the Pact secured. It is attempting to reach a compromise with the SPD, which seems prepared to approve the social assistance and child benefit cuts in return for waiving the proposed cuts in benefits for those on training programmes.

The administrative agenda

From the instigation of the union, the eastern states have had to build an administrative competence practically *ab initio*. More than one-quarter of a million former GDR officials were suspended from their duties in administration and university teaching on suspicions of political unacceptability (Roesler, 1991). The immediate imposition of West Germany's federal structures was to prove beyond the capabilities of those left in post and an emergency transfer of 20,000 western administrators was instigated, many of whom were shocked by the working conditions they encountered: initially even telephone contact with the West proved difficult. Attracting sufficient numbers of suitably qualified officials from the West has remained a problem.

In the meantime, the professionalisation of eastern administrative staff has progressed more slowly than the government had hoped (von Beyme, 1992). Particularly problematic has been the situation of local authorities. As already stated, many social service responsibilities – particularly in the field of occupational welfare – were transferred to them. However, the existing staff at senior levels were typically political appointees who lacked the necessary professional competence to cope with their new duties, especially with regard to negotiating the plural system of social services which affords a prominent role to the non-governmental sector. Rather, they had been more accustomed to executing the decisions of the central government. Part of the blame for the current problems must be laid at the door of the government, since the State Treaties scarcely made prescriptions for eastern local authorities and crucially failed to make provisions to ensure an operational administration there.

The question of personnel capacity in the new states is complex. There is an urgent need for expert administrators coexisting with a serious overstaffing in other areas, particularly in the social sector: relevant expenditure is almost 40 per cent in excess of the relevant per capita ratio in the West. Although local authorities in the first three years since unification shed about a quarter of their staff, current stipulations make further dismissals difficult and the costly staffing ratios in certain services are making them unattractive for take-over by potential bidders in the voluntary and private sectors (DIW, 1993d).

The lack of sufficiently qualified administrators was exacerbated by the equally serious deficiency of local authority and *Länder* politicians skilled in negotiating the complexities of the social market economy with its reliance on a heavily legalistic procedure. Paradoxically, then, the introduction of the decentralised pluralistic western model necessitated a large degree of dirigism from the centre (Backhaus-Maul and Olk, 1992).

Additional problems are caused by the complexity of federal regulations – in building, for example – which has resulted in lengthy administrative processing times. Moreover, the new *Länder* inherited a welfare system that was deficient in research and intelligence; the serious lack of data has frustrated the creation of an effective monitoring system and renders forward planning particularly hazardous.

The GDR style of local administration, accustomed to passivity on the part of the electorate, was unreceptive to local citizen initiatives; neither was it strong on community consultation with relevant interest groups. To add to difficulties, the propensities of the GDR population to engage in voluntarism and, with it, to negotiate effectively the pathways of interest mediation have remained critically below those in the old Federal Republic, notwithstanding the burgeoning of multifarious but short-lived citizen groups in the dying throes of the GDR. So-called 'voluntary organisations' in the former GDR had been effectively incorporated in the SED hegemony and were largely state-initiated and -financed. As such, they lacked the social and ethical justification of their western counterparts, although in terms of responding to the transition those organisations that had existed under the old regime – the Red Cross, *Caritas* and *Diakonie* – had obvious organisational advantages over the newcomers (Backhaus-Maul and Olk, 1992). The relative political naïveté of eastern voluntary welfare agencies with regard to the western pluralist system has caused some analysts to question whether the German voluntary sector will suffer from a declining influence within the polity (Bialas and Ettl, 1993). In any case, in instigating the federal model of social services it was inevitable that eastern agencies would be subject to colonisation by western counterparts (see Chapter 7).

Testing the limits of the German social state

The former GDR has undergone the most radical metamorphosis of any country in Europe in terms of its speed, depth and extensiveness (Bialas and Ettl, 1993). As such, it does not conform to the experiences of transition in other states because, in essence, the process was not one of gradual adoption but of total assimilation of another country's model in all but minor detail. Such a profound change in social, economic and political structures on such a grand scale could scarcely but unleash great insecurities, contrasting sharply with the securities of the 'niche' society that had endured under the former regime. Herder-Dorneich (1991) notes that the essential features of the transition – its speed, the accompanying mass emigration and the dominance of materialism over preferences for any specific democratic ideology – inculcated a deep sense of popular apathy. Among certain sections of the population the reaction to those insecurities has tragically culminated in a rapid rise in crime and delinquency and the outbreak of organised racist attacks.

But it is not only in the East that unification has taken its toll. For, undoubtedly, it has seriously threatened the viability of long-held western welfare principles that have traditionally formed the core of the federal model: subsidiarity, concerted federalism, solidarity and, in social insurance, the equivalence principle. The old tried and tested political means are proving insufficient to the task of finding long-term solutions to growing social problems. In fact, there has been a perceptible drift in German politics since the union and some of the more negative features of the system, particularly its immobilism, have exercised a dominant influence. The result is that the traditional anticipatory style of economic and social policy-making has been sacrificed in favour of *ad hoc* reliance on short-term solutions (Schmähl, 1992a). Meanwhile, the electorate is responding with historically atypical volatility, the major parties having lost considerable ground, none more so than the CDU in the East.

Schmidt (1992) has analysed the effects of the transition on governance. Although he sees the principal features of the federation continuing, a more prominent and dirigiste role of the centre and, with it, a changing power base within the parties are discernible. There has also been an intensification of conflicts between economic and social policy, and relations between the social partners are more tense. These developments prompt Schmidt to question how much of the 'middle way', with its emphasis on consensus, continuity and social stability, will be compromised. Ganssmann is more pessimistic: quite simply 'the institutions of the old West German welfare state are not sufficient to manage the transformation of East Germany' (Ganssmann 1993, p. 88).

The Solidarity Pact did, at least, stimulate substantial inter-party agreement about the scale of unification costs and the need to adopt a more long-term strategy. With the election of Rudolf Scharping, the new leader of the SPD, who, like Chancellor Kohl, is a consensus politician, one can expect this to continue, despite arguments about welfare cuts proposed almost before the ink on the Pact was dry; certainly, the resolution of policy differences on immigration point that way. Significantly, there is no serious talk of an eclipse of the social state, but clearly on the agenda is a renegotiation of the distribution of liabilities which will further the aims of the original *Wendepolitik* by prioritising a greater degree of self-reliance and private provisions, whilst also guaranteeing a statutory basic coverage.

Recently, the government released a discussion document on the social and economic future of Germany, the *Standort Deutschland*, that advocated radical measures to improve international competitiveness through a reduction in the period spent in further and higher education, more flexibility on the part of trade unions in negotiating wages and ancillary costs, a gradual move to a longer working week and an extended working life. It argued that the 'Standort-Killer' has been high labour costs, large borrowing requirements, rising budgetary deficits requiring high interest rates, and rising inflation, which, in turn, produced social and labour market unrest. The *Standort* policy is not without dangers. Policy horizons have been pushed even further into the future, delaying in the East the achievement of the constitutional guarantees of the German social state. Thus, in a united state, a two-tier welfare system East and West will be perpetuated; moreover, it is being grafted on to pre-existing social inequalities of the West German 'two-thirds' society. Large sectors of the population have felt understandably aggrieved that they are paying more than their fair share of unification costs: the social insurance contributor and the unemployed – East and West – most justifiably so. The serious political and social risks arising from a prolonged transition cannot be discounted in a country where the maintenance of social stability through consensus political management has been such a dominant preoccupation.

Guide to further reading

The majority of sources on unification which have a direct relevance to social policy are in German. For English-language reviews of developments in the former West Germany prior to 1989, see, for example, Mangen (1991a). East German social policy is treated in McCauley (1983), Krisch (1985), Dennis (1988) and Adams (1990). Landua (1993) reviews the social dimension of the transition. A valuable chronology of relevant events is provided by the German Embassy newsletter (*Labour and Social Affairs Report*).

Otherwise the principal literature is in German. Particularly useful in a period of rapid change are the weekly reports (*Wochenberichte*) published by the *Deutsches Institut für Wirtschaftsforschung*. Von Dohnanyi (1991) provides an easily understandable and speculative account of the economic and social task implied by unification. More scholarly are the two edited volumes by Kleinhenz (1991, 1992) and an article by Müller (1991). Bäcker (1991) offers a concise and more digestible account of the same topic. The problem of unemployment has been the subject of regular review in *Der Spiegel* and a useful orientation is provided by Heier (1991). Finally, *Internationes* publishes a regular *Sozialreport* which is available free of charge.

Part II

Social provision and social policy

Chapter 3

Social security – the core of the German employment-centred social state

Jochen Clasen

In the context of British social policy, the term social security has come to refer to the entirety of cash transfers to individuals or households which are administered, or at least controlled, by a single government department. In Germany, the picture is more complex. In official publications, the term social security (*Soziale Sicherung* or *Soziale Sicherheit*) is used but not always unambiguously applied. It is often narrowly defined as social insurance (see BMAS, 1990), but at times it even includes labour regulations such as workers' rights to co-determination in companies (BMAS, 1991, 1993). To some extent, this terminological ambiguity corresponds to the fragmentary character of social security in Germany. The loss of earnings due to risks such as unemployment, injury, old-age and ill-health is dealt with by a multitude of public and semi-public organisations. Separate schemes cover different social and occupational groups. Social insurance benefits are centrally funded while assistance benefits are financed by local authorities and municipalities. Some benefits are administered by insurance agencies independent of government, others by public authorities at the federal, regional state (*Land*) or communal level. The purpose of this chapter is to make this picture clearer. The first section provides a brief reflection on the historical origins and development of German social security. This is followed by a description of the characteristics, structures and institutions of the current system as well as, for illustrative purposes, the way these affect the living conditions of a typical family. Although fairly successful by international standards, gaps in the system, prevalent for some time, have become more acute in the last two decades. The chapter discusses their causes and consequences, as well as the position of political parties and other organisations involved in policy debates about social security.

A brief history of social security

Leaving early municipal support for the poor and forms of workers' self-help aside, the origins of the form of social security provision which is still dominant in Germany today go back to the 1880s. With the intention of securing loyalty to the constitutional monarchy, Chancellor Bismarck initiated the implementation of the world's first public health insurance (1883), accident insurance (1884) and invalidity and old-age pension insurance (1889). The provision of an albeit minimal public pension in particular would, it was hoped, integrate workers into the social and political order and make them less susceptible to the influence of the Social Democratic Party (SPD) and socialist trade unions (see Chapter 1).

Bismarck's original plans for old-age and invalidity schemes bore similarities to the social insurance schemes later introduced in Great Britain. In the first draft of the German Social Insurance Bill of 1887, he proposed low, flat-rate contributions and benefits which were not differentiated according to former earnings levels (Hennock, 1987). He also envisaged a major involvement of the state in the financing and administration of the schemes, but the lack of sufficient support for a new tax as its funding base, as well as opposition from both employers and parliament (with the conservative Centre Party as the major influence), resulted in a compromise. Contributions by employers and employees became the main source of finance for the schemes. The fact that they were compulsory was counterbalanced by arrangements for their self-administration by employer organisations and trade unions. The SPD, largely excluded from political power until the 1920s, continued to envisage a more egalitarian system but was anxious not to antagonise better-paid workers who insisted on a system of differential benefit levels determined by prior earnings (Ritter, 1986). Gradually the schemes expanded so that, at the turn of the century, more than half of all wage-earners were members of social insurance schemes. White-collar employees, too, were integrated by means of a separate scheme. This institutional separation according to occupational status (blue collar, white collar and civil servants) remains a characteristic feature of German social security.

Despite adverse economic circumstances for long periods in the 1920s, the number of contributors rose further during the Weimar Republic. The SPD's previously hostile position towards statutory social provision gradually changed when it became clear that its particular features (self-administration, separate institutions, graduated contributions and benefits) – contrary to

Bismarck's intention – strengthened rather than weakened the links between workers and their political organisations (Ritter, 1986; Hennock, 1987). In fact, the SPD became a driving force for further expansion of the system and for the introduction of an unemployment insurance scheme which, based on by then conventional funding and benefit structures, was eventually implemented in 1927 (Clasen, 1994, ch. 2).

The principles and institutions of social insurance proved to be remarkably resilient to change. For the most part, they remained in place even under the Nazi regime, although self-administration was practically abolished (Hentschel, 1983; Schmidt, 1988). After the Second World War, inspired by the Beveridge proposals being discussed in Britain, the Allied Control Commission set out to implement a more comprehensive social insurance system in Western Germany (Baldwin, 1990). German resistance was widespread, however, ranging from private insurance companies, occupational groups and the traditional insurance funds to sections within the trade union movement who feared that a universal scheme would mean low benefit rates. This opposition has to be interpreted in the light of plans for a unified and centrally controlled social security system which had been devised (but not introduced) by the Nazis. Perceived as having been abused by the fascist regime, the traditional fragmented social insurance system was one of the few institutions which was regarded with pride in post-war West Germany (Hockerts, 1980).

The onset of the Cold War altered the scenario. For the United States it became more important to come to an agreement with prevailing West German views than to reach an accord with the Soviet Union. The task of introducing a new social security scheme was transferred to the new West German coalition government which was elected in 1949. It was led by the conservative Christian Democratic Union (CDU) as the strongest party, which, having 'nailed the defence of the traditional social insurance system to its mast' (Hockerts, 1981, p. 320), reintroduced the fragmentary system and implemented a limited child benefit and housing benefit scheme during the 1950s (Schmidt, 1988, p. 69). Based on high economic growth rates, social security spending increased considerably during this 'take-off' phase (Alber, 1988a, p. 100). The introduction of a major reform of retirement pensions in 1957, which involved a steep rise in pension levels and a link to developments of gross wages, is widely believed to explain the CDU's convincing victory in the general election of the same year (Michalsky, 1985). It contributed to a process of reorientation within the SPD, which gradually abandoned its post-war ideal of a more comprehensive and universal social insurance model in favour of endorsing traditional structures and principles.

Relatively lower economic growth rates slowed down the expansion of social security in the 1960s. A new Federal Social Welfare Act (1961), providing the legal basis for a last safety net against poverty, and a major reform of unemployment insurance and labour market policy (1969) were the two most important reforms of the decade. In 1969, the CDU lost political power for the first time since the Second World War and the SPD formed a coalition government with the liberal FDP. Although differences between these two parties with respect to social policy were greater than in other policy fields, a new phase of rapid expansion began, marked by the inclusion of new groups (such as farmers and professionals), the coverage of new risks and needs (such as family allowances) and increases in benefit levels (Alber, 1989). This phase came to an end in the aftermath of the economic crisis of the mid-1970s. Rising unemployment resulted in decreased revenues from contributions and increases in social security spending to which the government responded with cutbacks. After the second oil price crisis in the early 1980s, government coalitions led by the SPD (up to 1982) and then by the CDU pursued austerity policies. However, unlike in Great Britain, there was no major welfare backlash or full-blown attack on traditional institutions or principles by either party. Instead, the pattern was one of the consolidation of social security spending and the adaptation to a changed economic and labour market context by way of a succession of small selective changes. These affected mainly 'peripheral' groups without lengthy and stable records of insured employment, rather than long-standing contributors to social insurance funds, who continued to enjoy barely diminished benefit rights and levels of security (Offe, 1991). Before examining the reasons for this pattern of policy-making, a little more detail is needed of what German social security is about.

Structures, institutions and principles

Perhaps the best starting-point for a description of the structure and organisation of social security in Germany is the 'social budget', which is the total sum of all types of social expenditure (in cash and kind), excluding education and capital spending on housing. In 1990, the 'social budget' amounted to DM 703 billion (approximately 30 per cent of GNP), two-thirds of which was spent on monetary transfers (BMAS, 1990, p. 128). About two-thirds of the revenue was raised via contributions from employers (37 per cent) and employees (28 per cent), the remainder stemming from general taxation. It is therefore no surprise that by far the largest section of the 'social budget' (about 62 per cent) accrues to expenditure on the so-called 'general system of social security', that is, to social insurance and (to a much lesser extent) child benefits. The remaining items are transfers to specific groups, for example to tenured public sector employees (9 per cent), expenditure on social assistance and services, which also includes student grants and housing benefit (9 per cent), and benefits paid by employers such as sickness payments and occupational pensions (9 per cent), as well as indirect transfers such as tax allowances (BMAS, 1990, p. 149).

This indicates that the predominant orientation of the German welfare state is directed not simply at delivering monetary transfers but also at a particular form of benefits, that is, contributory benefits. Traditionally there have been four separate areas of social insurance (pensions, sickness, accident and unemployment insurance), with a fifth branch, covering need for long-term care, to be phased in during 1994 (see below). Common characteristics of these insurance schemes are as follows:

- Membership is compulsory for all economically active people who are employed for more than eighteen hours per week (fifteen hours in pension insurance), with the exception of tenured public sector employees (*Beamte*) and self-employed people. This makes social insurance coverage almost universal (about 95 per cent of all Germans are insured against sickness and accidents and 85 per cent are members of statutory pension schemes).
- Insurance funds are financed by employers and employees, each paying half of a fixed proportion of employees' monthly earnings (up to a certain ceiling) as earmarked contributions to separate insurance funds (accident insurance is funded by employers alone).
- Insurance funds are jointly administered by employers and unions in semi-autonomous agencies (the so-called *para fisci*). Representatives of public authorities participate in the administration of unemployment insurance and the government also retains the right to fix contribution and benefit rates.
- Benefits are based on a firm legal entitlement with rates differing according to former earnings and length of contribution records (the 'equivalence' principle). The main objective is to compensate for lost earnings and to provide some form of status-maintenance rather than to redistribute income or to alleviate poverty by providing a minimum income.

Despite more than a hundred years of reform, social insurance has remained the 'core institutional principle of the German welfare state' (Alber, 1988a, p. 100). It represents a 'third way' (Schmidt, 1988, p. 97) of providing social security between the liberal, market-oriented and residual type of income maintenance prevalent in some countries (such as the United States) and the egalitarian, universal and redistributive, citizenship-oriented systems of others (such as Sweden) (see Esping-Andersen, 1990; Leibfried, 1992). The main principle is that provision of benefits is determined by previous earnings. Consequently, as will be shown below, it is full-time and continuous participation in employment which guarantees access to adequate and sufficient income security in Germany. Non-employed persons (such as dependent family members) either rely on benefits derived from the insured (mainly male) breadwinner or, together with those in precarious forms of employment, are referred to social assistance.

Since the organisation of health insurance funds is discussed elsewhere in this book (see Chapter 4), the remainder of this section is confined to a few remarks about the pension, unemployment and accident insurance systems. Germany is a big spender on public pensions: relative to national economic resources, expenditure is almost twice as high as in the United Kingdom (see OECD, 1988, p. 140). It comes as no surprise, therefore, that statutory pensions are the most important source of income for the majority of retired employees in Germany. Occupational pensions are nevertheless drawn as supplementary income by 27 per cent of male and 12 per cent of female statutory pensioners (BMAS, 1990, p. 47). There are different statutory insurance schemes for blue- and white-collar workers, while the scheme for tenured civil servants is entirely financed by general taxation. Levels of retirement (and invalidity) pensions are determined by the number of years spent in insured employment and the amount of lifetime earnings. Weakening the work nexus somewhat, certain activities are treated as equivalent to, or as substituting, insured employment (such as military service, university education and so-called 'baby years', i.e. years credited for raising children) and are therefore taken into account for the calculation of individual pension levels. Widows and widowers of former contributors receive a 'survivor' pension, representing 60 per cent of their spouse's entitlement.

How adequate are pensions? A hypothetical model pension of someone with forty-five years of insurance on average earnings amounted to about 72 per cent of his or her previous net income in 1989 (BMAS, 1990, p. 217). In absolute terms, a 'standard pension' (forty-five years' contributions) in 1993 was worth DM 1,868 or £750 per month in the old and £540 in the new *Länder* (assuming a rate of DM 2.50 to £1). However, in 1988 just over half of all male and less than a fifth of female pensioners fulfilled the assumptions made even for a pension after forty years of employment, so that actual pensions were on average closer to 40 per cent (for blue-collar workers) and 60 per cent (for white-collar workers) of former earnings (Bäcker *et al.*, 1989, p. 254). Reflecting the orientation towards status-maintenance, pension levels differ significantly: average white-collar pensions are higher than average blue-collar pensions, invalidity pensions lower than retirement pensions, and pension levels for men on average far above pensions for women. Differences between men's and women's pensions are smaller in the East since women there have generally worked for longer periods (see Chapter 8). While the degree of vertical redistribution within German pension arrangements is limited and there is no actual minimum pension (apart from a temporary arrangement for pensions in the new *Länder*, see below), claimants with at least twenty-five insured years (employment and substitute periods) who received less than 75 per cent of average earnings are entitled to a pension calculated at that level.

Unemployment insurance is administered by a single body, the Federal Labour Office (*Bundesanstalt für Arbeit*) in Nuremberg, which is controlled by a tripartite board comprising representatives from unions, employer organisations and public authorities. Benefits as well as so-called 'active' labour market programmes (e.g. vocational training, retraining and job creation schemes) are financed by earmarked contributions, but the federal government is obliged to subsidise them if deficits occur in the annual budget. Against fierce criticism from the opposition and from trade unions, cuts in benefit levels (of up to 3 per cent) were implemented in January 1994. Since then, provided contributions have been paid for a sufficient period, unemployed people receive unemployment benefit (*Arbeitslosengeld*) which represents 67 per cent of previous net income for a maximum standard duration of one year. The figure for claimants without children is 60 per cent, and entitlement periods are extended for older workers with longer contribution records (see Clasen, 1994). Unemployment assistance (*Arbeitslosenhilfe*) is received by claimants who have exhausted *Arbeitslosengeld* and by those who have been in insured employment for at least six months prior to becoming unemployed. *Arbeitslosenhilfe* is subject to a means-test and, although administered by the *Bundesanstalt*, is paid for out of general taxation. However, benefit levels are also based on former net income (since 1994 57 per cent for claimants with children, 53 per cent for others). A further restriction introduced in January 1994 was the limitation of the receipt of *Arbeitslosenhilfe* for claimants without prior receipt of *Arbeitslosengeld* to a maximum duration of one year.

Finally, there is a multitude of statutory accident insurance funds, mainly organised along occupational lines. As in the event of absence from work due to illness, employers are obliged to continue paying full wages for the first six weeks to employees who suffer a work-related accident. After that, an allowance of 70 per cent (80 per cent for employees with dependent children) of previous gross wages is paid during periods of rehabilitation. If the accident is so serious that the capacity for full participation in paid work is reduced, a full or partial invalidity pension is granted, the amount of which is once again determined by previous earnings.

Apart from the insurance principle, two other principles are relevant for what are, in expenditure terms, less important benefits. First, there is the 'principle of provision' (*Versorgungsprinzip*) according to which certain groups have a legal entitlement to tax-financed statutory benefits, for example as victims of war or in recognition of 'services rendered to the state' by civil servants and other tenured public employees who enjoy a privileged income security (see below). Second, there is the principle of 'welfare' or 'charity' (*Fürsorgeprinzip*), which is the basis for social assistance (*Sozialhilfe*). *Sozialhilfe* operates in a similar way to the British Income Support scheme, but unlike in the United Kingdom it can top up low wages and, more importantly, is financed and administered on a local level by municipalities and local authorities. There are two basic forms. First, there is 'assistance in particular circumstances' for specific groups in need such as people with disabilities, the blind, homeless people and pregnant women (see Brühl, 1989, p. 8). The second form is called 'assistance with the cost of living', which is supposed to provide a subsistence level of income. Only when other sources of income such as earnings from work, other social security benefits and savings have been exhausted can a full or supplementary payment of *Sozialhilfe* be made as a last resort. There is also an obligation on the part of partners, parents and adult offspring to pay income maintenance if their income exceeds certain levels (according to the principle of subsidiarity). Usually, benefit levels are uprated in line with the rise in prices but, while there were some deviations in the early 1980s, the upratings for 1994, 1995 and 1996 have been limited by the federal government.

Differences between these three benefit principles are not only institutional and administrative but are also of an ideological nature. Both insurance and 'provision' benefits are based on a strong legal codification and are perceived as legitimate 'wage replacement' benefits. Since 1980, entitlements to statutory pensions have even been treated as property rights (Schmidt, 1988, p. 99). By contrast, *Sozialhilfe* recipients are officially referred to as 'applicants' (*Antragsteller*) for whom, although they have a right to benefit, the type and amount of the transfer is determined by individual circumstances. In effect, this represents a 'split' in the German welfare state between insurance systems (labour policy), on the one hand, and the provision of social assistance (welfare policy), on the other (see Leibfried and Tennstedt, 1985). With Offe (1991), one could go further by distinguishing five 'welfare classes' in Germany (see also Lepsius, 1979; Krätke, 1985). First, there are tenured public sector employees who receive special child benefit allowances and other subsidies and can look forward to more generous pensions than either blue- or white-collar employees (without their incomes being reduced by compulsory contributions to either pension or unemployment insurance funds). The second group are employees in relatively secure full-time work who are covered by mandatory insurance systems. In the third category are those who were previously in the second but now rely on insurance benefits. Less organised and financially in a less secure position, they are nevertheless able to fend off the most serious attacks on benefit levels due to widespread suppport for the 'wage replacement' insurance schemes, especially on the part of trade unions (see below). The fourth category is a heterogeneous group of both the long-term and the young unemployed, single parents, elderly people with low pensions (especially women) and those who were previously in low-paid employment. Their common characteristic is that they are without any or sufficient entitlement to insurance benefits and therefore have to rely on local social assistance. Finally, there is a group who do not 'unequivocally enjoy basic privileges that are tied to national citizenship' (Offe, 1991, p. 145), which includes refugees and asylum seekers who, as a form of humanitarian help rather than legal entitlement, receive social assistance, albeit often at less than the usual rate (see Chapter 9).

Before closing this section, it should be noted that there is other tax expenditure and there are also other, mainly tax-financed, social security transfers such as child benefits which form part of what is officially referred to as *Soziale Sicherung* (BMAS, 1993). While social security transfers will be further discussed below, a few remarks about tax allowances seem appropriate. Functioning as an equivalent to social security by increasing households' disposable income, they are an important type of income-maintenance in Germany. As in other countries, a number of these allowances favour families on low wages and those with children. The financially most important form of tax expenditure, however, is the so-called 'married couples' tax-splitting'. Its total volume, amounting to £9 billion in 1990 (again assuming DM 2.50 to £1), is almost as much as all other forms of tax allowance (for children and savings, and for the cost of housing, social care and so on) put together (BMAS, 1990, p. 182). It has been criticised since it has little justification with respect to social policy criteria. For tax purposes, married couples' combined income is treated as if each partner earned exactly half of it. Due to the progressive income tax system in Germany, this reduces the overall annual tax burden especially for single-earner couples (and for couples with large earning differentials) by up to £10,000 (Pfaff and Roloff, 1990). Because of this preferential treatment of single (mainly male) earner couples at the expense of two-earner couples and the implicit discouragement of working wives, demands for reform and abolition have been made frequently.

The Schmitz family – an illustration

The way the social security system works in practice can be illustrated with reference to a hypothetical family. Of course, certain assumptions about the family have to be made and it should be noted that a change in those assumptions, especially with respect to family type, total family income (and its structure) and the occupational status of the parents, would alter the following picture considerably. The regional location is important, too, since earnings in the new *Länder* are on average lower than those in the West, and this has implications for the level of social security transfers. However, for illustrative purposes, let us imagine a family headed by Frank and Doro Schmitz. Frank is a manual worker employed by a large car company in West Germany. He earns about the average gross wage for industrial workers, which was about £1,450 per month in 1991 (Statistisches Bundesamt, 1992, p. 585). Doro is a part-time secretary and earns about

£550. Their three children are Christoph (aged 25), who is a student living away from home, Andrea (18), who is an apprentice, and Ludwig (16), who goes to school. In which ways is this family affected by the tax and social security system?

Apart from other types of less important direct and indirect taxes (the rate of VAT is currently set at 15 per cent), both parents pay income tax after deduction of certain allowances. The most important of these allowances are the personal tax allowance (£2,250 each in 1993), the child tax allowance (£1,640 per child) and educational tax allowances for all three children. The remainder is taxed on a progressive scale with a starting rate of 19 per cent and a ceiling of 53 per cent. The average tax burden is about 18 per cent. Additionally, both Frank and Doro (since she works twenty hours per week) pay contributions to their respective pension funds (8.75 per cent in 1993), the unemployment insurance fund (3.25 per cent) and into one of a multitude of sickness insurance funds (rates vary with an average employee contribution of 6.7 per cent). Thus, in addition to direct taxation, a total of 18.7 per cent of each of their gross wages is transferred to social insurance schemes. Mainly due to the cost of German unification, which to a large extent has been financed by transfers from social insurance funds (Ganssmann, 1993), contributions to pension insurance will be increased in 1994. Employees will also contribute to the new care insurance fund. This means that the total sum of social insurance contributions will rise above 20 per cent of gross earnings for the majority of employees in 1994.

What is the Schmitzes' entitlement to social security benefits? Currently the family receives universal child benefit for each of the three children (even for Christoph since he is in education and younger than 28). Amounts above certain guaranteed levels vary with a maximum of about £28 per month for the first child, £52 for the second and £88 for the third. The actual rates for Andrea and Ludwig are lower than the maximum, since the combined income of their parents is too high to qualify for the receipt of the top rates (see BMAS, 1993). Depending on the level of his parents' earnings, Christoph might be entitled to a student grant up to a maximum of £380 per month, 50 per cent of which constitutes an interest-free loan which has to be paid back after the completion of his studies. About a third of all students in West Germany were in receipt of such a grant in 1991 (with an average payment of £240). Considering usual rent levels this amount is hardly enough to live on, which explains why part-time work has become very common among West German students. In 1991, 80 per cent were in some form of gainful employment (*Times Higher Education Supplement*, 23 July 1993).

Women are entitled to maternity benefit (*Mutterschaftsgeld*) for six weeks before and eight weeks after the birth of a child. The amount depends on the level of previous earnings, with a maximum of £10 a day. In Doro's case, since her income is higher than that, her employer would be obliged to top the statutory benefit up to her full previous net wage. If she or her husband do not work for more than nineteen hours per week, one of them can also receive a childrearing benefit (*Erziehungsgeld*) of £240 per month for two years. According to the level of a claimant's additional earnings, however, this amount could be reduced from the seventh month onwards. Finally, one parent can take up to three years' unpaid child-rearing leave (*Erziehungsurlaub*) with the guarantee of a job to return to, as long as the other spouse continues working.

If Doro or Frank fall ill, they receive full pay from their employer for six weeks. After that, they are entitled to sickness benefit from their health insurance fund for not more than seventy-eight weeks in three years. Benefit levels represent 80 per cent of regular gross earnings, but not more than net earnings. If the illness lasts longer than the specified period covered by insurance, they might have to turn to means-tested local social assistance (see below). Work accidents are similarly covered by employers for six weeks. After that, accident insurance benefits would be paid and eventually an invalidity pension if the person's full capacity for employment is not restored.

As outlined earlier, Frank would receive unemployment benefit (*Arbeit-slosengeld*) if he lost his job. Currently (1994) he would receive 67 per cent of his previous net income. However, since the latter does not include any bonus payments, overtime pay or the widely paid thirteenth monthly wage, the actual replacement value of unemployment benefit is normally lower. If Frank remains unemployed for more than one year, he will receive the lower unemployment assistance (*Arbeitslosenhilfe*) of 57 per cent of former net earnings. Depending on Doro's earnings and both partners' savings, the actual amount of benefit might be lower. If Doro were also made redundant, the total amount of unemployment benefit received would be unlikely to be sufficient for the whole family to live on. The last resort would then be social assistance (*Sozialhilfe*).

Let us assume that following recurrent periods of unemployment both Frank and Doro are without insurance benefits and Frank decides to apply for *Sozialhilfe*. How much would the family be entitled to? Rates differ slightly between *Länder* (and especially between East and West), with an average West German standard level (*Regelsatz*) of £203 per month in 1993. Supplements are paid for each family member (80 per cent of the *Regelsatz* for spouses and between 50 per cent and 90 per cent for each child, according to age), while the costs of rent and heating (unless the accommodation is considered 'inappropriate') are normally covered in full. There are also supplements for clothing and household items. However, according to the overriding principle of subsidiarity, mentioned earlier, which stipulates that *Sozialhilfe* is paid only when all other forms of income have been exhausted, Frank's entitlement might be reduced in proportion to other income. This includes savings, as well as other benefits, and his own earnings or those of his wife, his children and his parents, even if they are not part of the same household (see Schulte and Trenk-Hinterberger, 1988). *Sozialhilfe* would certainly be reduced (or even withdrawn) once Frank receives his retirement pension. The statutory retirement age is 65 but there are a number of ways of taking retirement earlier, for example after unemployment. In fact, for male blue-collar workers invalidity pensions became all but the most common form of entering retirement in the late 1980s when the average age at retirement was about 59 for men and 62 for women (Bäcker *et al.*, 1989, p. 221). The way pensions are calculated has already been discussed. It should be noted, though, that Frank would have to pay sickness insurance contributions out of his pension.

This description of the way in which social security affects a typical family could easily be extended, addressing more details, covering more contingencies and illustrating the effect of benefits which are perhaps less important to the Schmitz family but more so to others (e.g. single parents, or families on low wages). The aim here was simply to give a picture of the 'work-oriented' nature of social security in Germany. Average insurance benefit levels are certainly generous by international (and especially UK) standards, but it is important to recognise that the generosity of the system is targeted towards compensating wage-earners, so that the degree of income security individuals enjoy depends on the level of their earnings and the extent of their participation in full-time employment. For those temporarily out of work, benefits become less adequate the longer the absence from paid work lasts. In an appropriate analogy, Wagner (1984) has likened this social security model to a safety net turned upside down. For those in the middle of the tightrope of employment, a fall into the net is brief and relatively well cushioned. However, the longer one remains in the net the harder it is to avoid a gradual slide towards its edges, that is, towards ever more precarious forms of income security. This is an in-built or structural problem in the German income maintenance system. The next section examines its consequences as well as some of its advantages in more detail.

Achievements and gaps in the system

Data produced by the Luxembourg Income Study (LIS) show that, as a result of its tax and social security system, disposable income was more equally distributed in Germany than in a number of other countries, including the United Kingdom (Mitchell, 1992, p. 76). In the 1980s, about 10 per cent of the German population lived at or below the poverty line, defined as 50 per cent of average equivalent expenditure, compared to over 15 per cent in the United Kingdom (Room, 1992, p. 57). One in twelve elderly people (over 60 years of age) in Germany lived in poverty in 1980, against one in six in the United Kingdom (Kohl, 1992, p. 135). These figures conceal differences in the incidence of poverty, however. For example, while 8.8 per cent of

German nationals lived on less than half average incomes at the end of the 1980s, the rate was close to 25 per cent for foreigners (Hofemann, 1992, p. 294).

Standard *Sozialhilfe* rates are slightly more generous than income support levels in the United Kingdom. However, these values vary considerably according to family type. For example, a couple with two children received about 70 per cent of per capita income in West Germany in 1988, but single people without dependants only 20 per cent (Room, 1992, p. 53). Take-up rates of *Sozialhilfe*, estimated to be less than 50 per cent (Hofemann, 1992, p. 293), appear to be considerably lower than those of social assistance benefits in Great Britain (see Hartmann, 1985; Room, 1992, p. 50). This suggests that an application for the former is perceived as even more degrading than for the latter. This is probably because of the institutional, administrative and ideological divisions which exist in Germany between insurance and assistance benefits. However, although means-tested benefits have traditionally been a more common source of state support for a much larger proportion of social security claimants in the United Kingdom than in Germany, over the past two decades there has been a considerable increase of *Sozialhilfe* recipients in Germany, rising to 3.7 million in 1990 (Statistisches Bundesamt, 1992, p. 505). In relative terms, just 2.5 per cent of the population in former West Germany lived on *Sozialhilfe* in 1970, 3.5 per cent in 1980 and 5.9 per cent in 1990 (Hofemann, 1992). Owing to the payment of temporary supplements to insurance benefits in the new eastern *Länder* (see below), the rate there was considerably lower.

How can this rise in the number of social assistance claimants be explained? Until the 1970s, social insurance coverage had been extended to an ever-increasing share of the population who could rely on relatively generous benefits granted on a firm legal basis (see Alber, 1989). The traditional 'wage-labour-centred' (Vobruba, 1990) social security system had proved adequate and effective for a wage-earner society, and for those on better and even medium pay levels, insurance benefits continue to guarantee relatively efficient and adequate protection against lost earnings. Yet latent problems and gaps in the insurance-based system have become obvious, caused partly by social and cultural changes with respect to family structures, the life-cycle and so on, but, perhaps more importantly, by changes and problems to do with the labour market. Throughout the 1980s, at any one point in time around two million workers in West Germany (about 9 per cent of the workforce) were jobless and about a third of them had been out of work for more than a year. A large proportion of the unemployed either exhausted their entitlement to unemployment benefits or never fulfilled the necessary conditions for the receipt of insurance transfers (see Clasen, 1992, 1994). The loss of a job succeeded insufficient pensions as the most important single reason for the application for *Sozialhilfe* (see Table 3.1).

Table 3.1 *Sozialhilfe* recipients and unemployment as reason for claim, West Germany, 1979–1991

Year	Recipients (millions)[1]	Loss of employment as main reason for claim (%)[2]	Also in receipt of unemployment benefit (%)[3]
1979	1.31	—	6.6
1981	1.29	12.3	9.9
1983	1.73	19.3	14.3
1985	2.06	25.0	17.8
1987	2.33	32.7	19.7
1989	2.78	32.6	12.6
1991	2.78	28.7	8.9

Sources: (1) *Wirtschaft und Statistik*, various years; individual recipients who claimed *Sozialhilfe* (*Hilfe zum Lebensunterhalt* only) at least once during the year (multiple claims included); (2) Welzmüller (1989, p. 373); for 1981: Büchtemann (1985, p. 455) (household basis); *Wirtschaft und Statistik*, various years; no earlier data available; (3) Welzmüller (1989, p. 373); for 1979: Alber (1989, p. 181; household basis); for 1981: Büchtemann (1985, p. 455; household basis); *Wirtschaft und Statistik*, various years; since 1988 figures based on a new definition (see *Wirtschaft und Statistik*, 1990, p. 424).

Moreover, the number of those in precarious forms of employment (insecure self-employment, part-time work, fixed-term contracts, low-paid work) has increased. By 1990, more than 10 per cent of the total workforce was employed on a temporary basis; the share of part-time employment (overwhelmingly occupied by women) was 15 per cent (Blackwell, 1992, pp. 133, 135). While these types of employment might or might not be voluntarily chosen, the implications are that for those outside a 'standard employment relationship' (Hinrichs, 1991) access to efficient and adequate forms of social security (i.e. social insurance) becomes harder or even impossible.

In short, while for a long time the traditional system of social security in Germany was in 'ideal correspondence with an industrial society characterized by the features of full employment, strong families, large and homogeneous corporate collective actors, and a balanced demographic structure', these characteristics have become increasingly obsolete while the social security system itself remains structurally unchanged, thus becoming at the same time 'less social', in that it provides support for a smaller proportion of the population, and 'less secure' (Offe, 1991, p. 124). More specifically, a number of problems in the German social security system have become more evident over the past decade or so. These would include the following:

- The inadequacy of the financial support for people in need of long-term care (this is about to be addressed with the introduction of a care insurance system as a fifth pillar of German social insurance, see below).

- The wide income differentials, particularly within the retirement and invalidity pensions and especially at the expense of women. As a result, a significant proportion of women in West Germany receive pensions below social assistance levels (Bäcker *et al.*, 1989, p. 254).
- The lack of social security coverage for women, and other people caring for relatives, independent of an employed breadwinner (see Leibfried and Ostner, 1991).
- The absence of a minimum level of insurance benefit which would avoid people having to apply to locally financed social assistance (for a transitional period such a 'floor' has been introduced in East Germany in order to avoid overburdening the new *Länder*, see below).
- The lack of transparency and the high degree of institutional fragmentation within the system of social insurance. For example, depending on the cause of invalidity, an invalidity pension can be paid either from accident insurance or from pension insurance, the former usually being higher than the latter. This reflects yet another traditional principle (the so-called *Kausalprinzip*) in German social security – it is the cause of a risk, rather than the degree of need (the so-called *Finalprinzip*), which determines the level and type of state support.
- The inadequate financial basis of insurance agencies. For example, the *Bundesanstalt für Arbeit* is the main source of funds not only for transfers to unemployed contributors but also for labour market policies which benefit other social groups as well as society as a whole. Yet tenured public sector employees and self-employed people are exempt from any contribution to the agency.

Although some of these problems have been identified for some time, policy changes have been piecemeal and the preservation of traditional social security structures and institutions paramount, irrespective of the party in power. In fact, the German income-maintenance system developed in a rather depoliticised way up to the 1970s and even into the 1980s. Since then, however, controversies and demands for reform have become more frequent. The next section comments on the position of the major parties and other actors with respect to recent social security debates.

The politics of social security

For a long time the development of social security in Germany has been a remarkably consensual one, without any intensive conflict between labour-force participants, on the one hand, and welfare clients, on the other. It has been suggested that this is the result of the 'middle mass of the economically active population' being firmly integrated into the major statutory programmes (Alber, 1988a, p. 118). Particular features of the system, such as contributory rather than tax-financed benefits, separate and corporatist funds and the principle of status-maintenance according to a logic of restitution rather than of redistribution have allowed a broad compromise between parties. Conservatives support existing arrangements because they keep social security issues out of class conflict by giving both workers and employers a stake in the system; socialists accept social insurance as a form of 'institutionalized class solidarity', while liberals appreciate its actuarial principles and limited options for state interference (Offe, 1991, pp. 127–8).

This picture began to change in the early 1980s, when the regaining of power by the conservative CDU/CSU amid economic difficulties in 1982 was accompanied by rhetorical calls for severe cut-backs in social security programmes. However, in practice the aggressive policy of retrenchment which took place at the same time in the United Kingdom was not echoed in Germany. This was partly due to working-class representation in the German CDU being stronger than in the British Conservative Party, and to the different ideological background of the CDU (see Padgett, 1989). The CDU's position with regard to social policy has always been ambivalent (Michalsky, 1985; Mangen, 1989). In the 1950s, ideological tensions between Catholic social theory, on the one hand, and belief in market liberalism, on the other, led to the 'verbal compromise' of a 'social market economy' (Michalsky, 1985, p. 59). Even today, divisions within the party frequently become evident during discussions about social security reforms. Backed up by the liberal FDP and employer organisations, the 'economic wing' of the CDU, normally in charge of the Ministry of Finance, tends to emphasise the need to cut back on the cost of labour for reasons of international competitiveness. Its 'social policy wing', on the other hand, often relying on the support of trade unions and also of the SPD at times, sees itself as the main defender of traditional social security structures and benefit rights.

The SPD, for its part, is certainly another ardent defender of current social security structures and institutions and has been ever since post-war plans in favour of a more universal and comprehensive scheme were dismissed (see Baldwin, 1990). By opening up social insurance to a greater number of occupational groups and introducing more redistributive elements (such as those within pension insurance), the party actively contributed to social insurance becoming a virtually universal system by the 1970s. In recognition of problems which have become more evident since then, reform proposals have been put forward which, if implemented, would not abolish the employment-centred and earnings-related character of social security but would complement it by the introduction of a minimum benefit floor. This would prevent unemployed and other claimants being excluded from the system and having to apply for social assistance (see SPD, 1988).

Supported principally by groups which do not contribute to the statutory social insurance schemes, such as the self-employed, professionals and tenured public sector employees, the FDP is the party most interested in more substantial reform. Demands for a greater range of private forms of social security are made frequently, as well as for cutbacks in benefit (especially in respect of unemployment insurance) and a system which would limit the amount of risk-sharing by differentiating benefit entitlements more strictly according to individual contribution records (see Clasen, 1994). Holding between 5 per cent and 10 per cent of the vote, the Liberals have managed to exert a considerable influence in government coalitions with either the SPD or the CDU ever since the 1950s. However, their impact in the field of social policy has been limited and even the FDP has never seriously rocked the boat. Proposals for change have been directed at benefit levels and entitlements without seeking radical alterations to the structure of the system.

German trade unions, and their association the DGB, play a larger role in social security affairs than do their counterparts in Great Britain, not only because of their participatory role in the administration of social insurance but also because of the perception of insurance benefits as 'deferred' wages to which workers have a contractual right. As a consequence, any reductions in benefit levels or restrictions of benefit rights for current wage-earners are seen by the unions as a direct attack on 'earned' acquisitions. The adherence to traditional social security structures and the defence of the 'equivalence' principle (i.e. the link between contributions and benefits) in particular has therefore been of paramount importance to unions in Germany (Nissen, 1988). It is fair to say that employer organisations, too, are committed to the traditional structure of social insurance (Nissen, 1988). In times of economic difficulty, however, they stress the need to lower contribution rates and reduce levels of benefit, especially for unemployed claimants.

Social security debates in Germany cannot be properly understood without taking account of the *Länder*. It is the *Länder* and local communities who have to pick up the bill if gaps in the fragmented funding and administrative systems of social insurance widen. For example, the combination of mass unemployment and diminishing tax revenues in the early 1980s led governments to restrict access to insurance benefits by targeting social security on 'better contributors'. Local authorities found themselves in financial difficulties as a result, since *Sozialhilfe* payments to unemployed claimants soared. Some local governments responded by employing *Sozialhilfe* recipients for a period of time just long enough for them to regain eligibility for unemployment insurance benefits. On being made redundant again, unemployed persons would requalify for insurance benefits from the *Bundesanstalt* rather than having to claim assistance benefits from local government. While this illustrates a perverse effect of the fragmented structure of social security in Germany, it is noteworthy that this structure can also induce the building of political coalitions able to exert significant pressure for, or conversely to block, the implementation of particular policies. For example, the combined protest by opposition parties, unions, *Länder* (including CDU-governed ones) and municipalities was a major cause of the halt brought to the erosion of insurance protection for unemployed claimants in the mid-1980s. By comparison, it can be argued that the unprecedented decline of unemployment insurance coverage in Great Britain during the 1980s was facilitated by the absence of a financially and institutionally independent local social security system (Clasen, 1994).

There is evidence that the picture of social security as a field of 'depoliticized rigidity' (Offe, 1991) is changing. Debates about the shape of social security have become more frequent and controversial in recent times. Nevertheless, no major structural reform has yet been suggested by any political party except the Greens, who advocate a total break with wage-labour-oriented principles of income-maintenance in favour of the introduction of a minimum guaranteed income for all and the appreciation and remuneration of areas of work outside insured employment (see Die Grünen, 1986; Opielka and Ostner, 1987). Meanwhile, changes to the existing system have recently been implemented in response to demographic shifts, the impact of unification and economic recession.

Paying for care and the cost of unification

In 1992, a major reform in pension insurance was implemented in anticipation of increasing expenditure as a result of growing numbers of elderly people, both in absolute terms and as a proportion of the population. Some measures of the Pension Reform Act were aimed at reducing future expenditure (such as the lowering of the pension adjustment basis to average net rather than gross earnings, the increase in the retirement age and changes in eligibility criteria), other changes were to increase revenue (e.g. higher contribution rates). The background to and details of the reform are described elsewhere (Schmähl, 1993). The discussion which follows here will therefore concentrate on two other debates and developments which will impinge on the future shape of social security in Germany.

First, the funding of long-term care, especially for elderly people, has been a problem for some time. The inadequacy of many personal pensions means that about 70 per cent of all people who live in homes providing care have to rely on *Sozialhilfe*. Although it has been known for some time that, for demographic reasons, this situation would become even more acute in the future (see Glendinning and McLaughlin, 1993, p. 86), it took until 1993 for the CDU/FDP government to agree on a reform.

Supported by employer organisations, the FDP initially favoured compulsory membership in a private scheme rather than a new statutory insurance system which would cover the cost of institutional and domiciliary care. Contributions for the latter would raise high labour costs even further, it was argued, and thus weaken an already struggling economy. In contrast, the CDU, and especially its 'social policy wing', emphasised the need for a fifth branch of mandatory insurance modelled on traditional structures and principles. This idea was eventually accepted by the Liberals after concessions were made regarding increased costs for employers. Thus, after lengthy discussions between the ruling coalition parties and also between government and opposition (the reform depended on the agreement of at least some SPD-led *Länder* in the *Bundesrat*), it was recently (March 1994) decided that employers and employees will share mandatory contributions of 1 per cent of gross wages to be paid to the new statutory care insurance scheme from 1995 onwards. This levy will rise to 1.7 per cent in July 1996. As a compensation for increased costs to employers, one public holiday will be cut.

Whatever its final form, the new care insurance will apply to both West and East Germany, as do all other social security regulations already. After unification, West German structures and institutions of social security were simply extended to the new *Länder*. However, contrary to traditional equivalence principles, a 'social supplement' for low insurance benefits just above *Sozialhilfe* rates was introduced, on a temporary basis, as a 'floor' below which no East German should fall. In unemployment insurance this floor was about £200 per month for claims made before the end of 1992. Until 1996, a third of all pensions are to be topped up with a supplement which guaranteed a minimum benefit of £240 (£380 for married couples) in 1992. The abolition of these supplements will hit women especially, and in ways similar to those in which elderly women have been disadvantaged in West Germany.

How far everybody else in the East will be affected depends on the speed of the equalisation of average wages. At the end of 1991, blue-collar workers in the East earned 73 per cent of their counterparts in the West; the figure for white-collar workers was 68 per cent (Huster, 1993, p. 25). Though hindered by the slowness of increases in productivity, a rapid equalisation of wages and the expansion of employment remain very much a necessity, given that adequate social security continues to depend on principles of reciprocity and equivalence between earnings and benefits. Due to the breakdown of the economy in the East, and with it the labour market, living conditions in the new *Länder* are widely determined by social security benefits, with up to two-thirds of all households depending completely or mainly on them (Bäcker, 1993, p. 189). The reason for this is simple. Only about half of the 9.8 million people employed in the former GDR continue to receive full earnings. Over four million are either unemployed or receive early retirement pensions or short-term working allowances, or participate in job creation schemes, or commute to work in the West (Employment Observatory, 1993). Thus, in the new *Länder*, tax revenues and social insurance contributions remain low. As a consequence, transfers from West to East (especially in the form of income maintenance payments) amounted to £60 billion in 1991 and £72 billion in 1992. This latter figure represented more than three-quarters of East German and about 6 per cent of West German GDP (Bäcker, 1993, p. 195).

Both the opposition and the trade unions have attacked the government's method of raising revenue for these transfers. Instead of increasing income tax rates, which would have shared the costs more equitably, a large part of the burden of unification was put selectively on low- and middle-income groups by means of increased contributions to social insurance funds. As described earlier, the self-employed and tenured civil servants are exempt from these. The controversy over whether it is 'legitimate to use funds raised by the contributions of the members of a particular social insurance programme to address problems which are seen as problems of society as a whole' (Ganssmann, 1993, p. 86) became even more fierce in mid-1993, when the government decided that social security claimants themselves should pay for part of the transfers to the East. Against the background of the recent economic crisis and rising unemployment in East and West, the burden of massive public debt and the unwillingness to increase taxation more substantially, cuts in social security programmes were regarded as inevitable. Current plans envisage savings which amount to over £8 billion for 1994, to be achieved by severe reductions of benefit rates and limitations of entitlement which will affect *Sozialhilfe* recipients and the unemployed especially (see Kühl, 1993).

Conclusion

The basic principles and institutions of social security in Germany, which go back to the end of the last century, have proved remarkably resistant to change despite major historical breaks, such as the reform plans after the Second World War and, more recently, German unification. Compulsory social insurance remains the core of the system, with semi-autonomous legal entities providing benefits on the basis of insured employment and thus preserving status and earnings differentials which are only mildly softened by elements of vertical redistribution. As described in this chapter, it is precisely these features which have contributed to the stability and relatively uncontroversial development of social security. As Germany developed into a society based on high levels of employment of (mainly male) wage-earners, the traditional features of its social security provision became increasingly effective for an ever-growing proportion of the population.

However, economic, social and demographic changes over the past two decades have started to erode the previously 'ideal correspondence' between the 'wage-labour-centred' social security model (Vobruba, 1990) and its social environment. Also, as in other countries, the recent economic recession has added pressure to the search for options which would relieve the state of responsibility to devote an ever larger share of public spending to social security. So far, only limited reforms have been implemented which accommodate social security to a changed economic and social context without challenging traditional structures and institutions. Whether a more radical overhaul can be avoided depends on two factors. First, provided there is no change in the way funds are raised for covering the cost of German unification, calls for a more streamlined social security system are likely to become more forceful the longer a significant economic recovery in the new *Länder* fails to materialise. Second, because of the particular funding and institutional principles of social insurance in Germany, it is the shape of the labour market which will determine both the 'size and nature of the problems which the social security system will have to absorb, as well as the financial means that the system has at its disposal' (Offe, 1991, p. 131). In turn, since unemployment is more likely to increase further than decline significantly before the end of this century (Kühl, 1993), new rounds of cutbacks seem as inevitable as continued debates about more substantial reform.

Guide to further reading

For readers of German, current income maintenance programmes and principles are discussed in Bäcker *et al.* (1989), Lampert (1991) and also Schmidt (1988). Structural problems with respect to social insurance and social security are dealt with in Bieback (1986) and in Vobruba (1990). Leibfried and Tennstedt (1985) concentrate on manifestations of the 'split' in the German social state in 'worker' and 'poverty' policy. Official publications on policy issues are covered in irregular publications of the *Sozialbericht* and other information from the Ministry of Labour and Social Affairs (e.g. *Arbeit und Sozialpolitik*, *Bundesarbeitsblatt*) and also other government departments and social insurance agencies. Publications by the *Statistisches Bundesamt* (e.g. *Fachserie* 13 on social security benefits, *Wirtschaft und Statistik*) provide information about expenditure, benefit levels, claimant groups, etc. A number of journals such as *Zeitschrift für Sozialreform*, *Sozialer Fortschritt*, *Soziale Sicherheit*, *WSI Mitteilungen* and *Blätter der Wohlfahrtspflege* include reports on social security issues on an irregular basis.

For readers of English, access to information regarding social security developments in Germany has improved somewhat due to EC publications on changes in the structure, organisation and legislation of national social security programmes within member-states (e.g. MISSOC, 1993). See also the 'European Observatories' on family policies (Dumon, 1992), policies to combat social exclusion (Room, 1992) and social and economic policies towards older people in Europe (Walker *et al.*, 1993). The impact of social, political and economic influences on the shape of income maintenance programmes in Germany and their particular 'regime' character in comparison with systems in other nations has been the subject, or is part of, a number of studies (see Esping-Andersen, 1990; Heidenheimer *et al.* 1990; Ginsburg, 1992; Leibfried, 1992; Wilson, 1993).

Ritter (1986) provides an excellent comparison of historical origins of social security principles in Germany and Great Britain before 1914 (see also Hennock, 1987, and Baldwin, 1990). The period between the end of the Second World War and the mid-1980s is discussed by Alber (1986, 1988a; see also Schmidt, 1988). Offe (1991) explains the remarkable historical rigidity of social security in Germany and Michalsky (1985) remains a useful source about the position of political parties towards social security (see also Alber, 1988a). Particular aspects or fields of social security are discussed by Clasen (1994) (unemployment benefit policies in Great Britain and Germany); Jacobs *et al.* (1991) and Schmähl (1993) (retirement pensions); Bradshaw *et al.* (1993) (support of families in EC countries); and McLaughlin and Glendinning (1993) (who include a useful chapter on the lack of adequate funding for care in Germany). The male-biased character of German social security is discussed by Leibfried and Ostner (1991) and the dependence of sufficient and effective social protection on participation in standard, full-time and lengthy forms of employment by Hinrichs (1991). Apart from the usual social policy and social science journals, the *Journal of European Social Policy* in particular has recently been a valuable source for articles on specific aspects of German social security policy.

Chapter 4

Health care policy

Michael Moran

The importance of health care policy

Health care policy is of great importance to the welfare states of advanced capitalist nations, and Germany is no exception. It is impossible to understand German social policy without a grasp of the country's health care system. For the student of public policy generally, however, health care in Germany has a wider importance, because the German system has three features which give it a broad comparative interest.

The first feature is the way health care is financed. The funding of modern health care systems has evolved along three distinct routes. The largest system in the world, the American, relies heavily on the market: citizens are expected to buy care themselves, either by paying directly at the moment of treatment, or by purchasing health insurance in the marketplace. An alternative is provided by the British system, which guarantees everybody health care free at the point of treatment, and funds care largely from taxes collected by central government. Germany's significance lies in the fact that it was the pioneer of a third major funding principle, usually called 'compulsory insurance'. Workers and employers are obliged to make contributions to designated health funds which in turn pay the treatment costs of their members. (The historical origin of this principle, which underlies much of the German welfare state, is described in Chapter 1.) The German system has been immensely influential abroad. Many nations on the mainland of Europe, and some important non-European states like Japan, have adopted variants of compulsory insurance. In examining Germany we are therefore looking at a model of health care organisation which has proved important internationally.

The analytical importance of the German system is reinforced by its size. Even before reunification, the German system was the biggest in Western Europe, measured by citizens covered, personnel employed or money spent. The addition of the 16 million citizens of the former German Democratic Republic has created a superstate in the heart of Europe – and a health care system of corresponding magnitude. Table 4.1 provides a comparison of some of the most important aspects of the German system before unification with those of other major capitalist nations, and also compares Germany against averages for all countries in the Organisation for Economic Cooperation and Development, the organisation which covers all the most economically advanced capitalist nations.

Pioneering principles and sheer size make the German system important to any student of the welfare state, but a third feature gives health policy a special interest to anyone concerned with the government of modern industrial societies like Germany. The Federal Republic is a state where policy is made by bargaining and compromise – indeed it is probably the best example of such a style of policy-making among the leading capitalist nations. In his study of the policy process in the former West Germany, Katzenstein (1987) identified this cooperative federalism as a key governing principle. The principle dictates that policy-making should be guided by the search for a consensus between the major interests in the policy process, especially the major territorial interests. Since Germany is a federal state, the federal government should not – and in practice probably cannot – impose major policy innovations from the centre on the member-states of the federation, the *Länder*.

The principle of cooperative federalism faces policy-makers with great dilemmas. On the one hand, following its dictates provides a way of creating a consensus over policy, thus increasing the likelihood that decisions can be implemented effectively. On the other hand, the need to secure agreement among a wide range of interests can make the search for reforms a long, frustrating and ineffective business. For almost twenty years debates about health policy in Germany have been dominated by the search for reforms, principally with the objective of containing costs. There have been successive piecemeal attempts at reform – the latest as recently as 1992 – and each of these has involved the painstaking attempt to conciliate the different interests in the system. There is a remarkable contrast here with the United Kingdom, where central government has since 1989 imposed radical reforms on powerful interests. In health care, both the United Kingdom and Germany have faced the same acute policy dilemma in trying to introduce reforms: whether to maximise consensus and sacrifice radical decisiveness, or whether to impose radical reforms and run the risk that the continuing resistance of unconciliated interests will destroy the reforms at implementation. The value of the German experience to British readers is that Germany has opted for the former, while we have

Table 4.1 Germany and the health care systems of other advanced industrial countries: selected comparisons

	% total GDP on health 1991	Beds per 1,000 population 1990	Physicians per 1,000 population 1990	Male life expectancy at birth (years) 1990	Female life expectancy at birth (years) 1990	Infant mortality (deaths per 1,000 live births) 1990	Per capita health spending in US dollars 1991
Germany	8.5	10.4	3.1	72.6*	79.0*	7.1	1,659
Canada	10.0	6.6*	2.2	73.8	80.4	6.8	1,915
France	9.1	9.7	2.7	72.7	80.9	7.2	1,650
Italy	8.3	7.2*	1.3*	73.5*	80.0	8.2	1,408
Japan	6.8	15.8	1.6	75.9	81.9	4.6	1,307
UK	6.6	6.4	1.4	73.0	78.5	7.9	1,043
USA	13.2	4.7	2.3	72.0	78.8	9.1	2,868
OECD average	7.9	9.0	2.4	72.6	78.8	9.7	1,305

Note: *indicates a 1989 figure.
Source: Schieber *et al.* (1993).

opted for the latter; we can thus observe in Germany a way of solving policy problems very different from ours, both in its successes and in its failings.

The remainder of this chapter is shaped by the threefold importance of the German system. The next section looks in more detail at the fundamental principles by which the system is organised. Then the chapter turns from principles to practice – to the working features of health care organisation. Following this, it sketches some of the main policy problems which exist in the Federal Republic, and looks at the attempts to produce solutions to those problems.

Principles

Three important principles underlie the German health care system. They may be summarised as compulsory insurance, federal organisation and the segregation of ambulatory and institutional health care.

Most health care in Germany is free at the point of treatment. The bills for care are met by health insurance funds, and it is these institutions which are central to the compulsory insurance system. Almost all German workers are obliged to join a health insurance fund (exceptions are some highly paid employees who can take out insurance with private firms). Funds levy a contribution equally on employers and employed, expressed as a percentage of workers' income. The contribution rate is determined annually. Out of this income, the funds contract with providers, for instance the Associations representing doctors in local practice, for the provision of care for their members. The historical evolution of the system means that there are large numbers of funds (presently in excess of 1,100). In practice, three kinds are particularly significant: district funds, which are organised territorially; factory or workplace funds, which cater for the workers in a particular enterprise; and 'substitute' funds, a rather unsatisfactory literal translation of the name (*Ersatzkassen*) of a group of funds organised nationwide and designed to cater in the main for white-collar workers like civil servants.

Although the organisational structure of the funding system is thus quite complex, the basic principles are straightforward. While it is conventionally said that Germans pay for health insurance, in reality the insurance premium is a payroll tax, with the tax 'hypothecated' (allocated) to health care. Membership of a fund covers not only a worker but also dependants, while those not catered for by the occupationally based scheme, such as the retired, are covered by other means. As a consequence, virtually every German shares an entitlement to free, or nearly free, health care. To receive treatment from a doctor in local practice, for instance, it is necessary only to produce the *Krankenschein* (sickness certificate) issued by the health insurance fund as proof of eligibility; the doctor provides the appropriate treatment and then submits the bill.

If 'compulsory insurance' defines a key principle by which the health care system is funded, 'federalism' defines the dominant principle of organisation. The influence of federalism can be seen at three levels. First, the fact that the wider system of government is organised along federal lines deeply influences the allocation of authority in health care policy-making and implementation. A simple example of this is provided by the way federal principles constrain the ability of the government in Bonn to reform the health care system. Any reform legislation has to pass both houses of the German parliament, and the upper house – the *Bundesrat* – is designed to represent the interests of the *Länder*, the delegates being sent and instructed by the *Länder* governments.

The principles of 'national' federalism spill over, not surprisingly, into 'health care federalism' – in other words, the most important institutions within the health care system tend to be those organised along federal lines. The executive responsibilities of the Health Ministry in Bonn are few, the responsibility within the governmental structure being largely the domain of the governments of the *Länder*. On the side of payers, the most important institutions in negotiating with the providers of care are Associations of Insurance Funds organised at *Land* level (though national-level institutions also play some role). On the side of providers also it is the *Land*, rather than the national level, which provides the most significant institutions. For doctors, the important regulatory bodies are the *Ärztekammern* (doctors' chambers) organised separately in each of the *Länder*: they license practitioners, control medical ethics and professional discipline and are responsible for continuing education. For doctors in local practice the key institution to which they need to belong in order to be paid for treating members of the insurance funds is the Association of Insurance Doctors organised for the *Land* in which they live and practise. These doctors' Associations both negotiate with the insurance funds over rates of payment and administer the system for reimbursing doctors.

The final important aspect of German federalism which shapes the health care system concerns not so much the allocation of authority between different institutions as the way allocation is codified. Germany's is not only a federal system, it is a federal system with a written constitution (the Basic Law). Disputes about the meaning of that constitution are adjudicated by an independent Constitutional Court. The result is that many of the most important policy issues in health care are debated in the language of constitutional law, and the Court itself is a significant actor in the policy process. In considering measures to reform the health care system, for instance, policy-makers have to take into account not only factors familiar to policy-makers in the United Kingdom – are measures effective, do they have public support, are they capable of commanding a majority in the legislature?

It is also necessary to ensure that measures are consistent with the higher law of the constitution itself. This is by no means a formality. In the United Kingdom, for instance, numbers entering the medical profession are tightly controlled from the centre of government. In the Federal Republic, attempts to exercise much weaker controls over those entering medical schools, and those entering local practice, have not been implemented because they violated constitutional guarantees of the right to practise a profession.

The principles of compulsory insurance and of federalism deeply influence, on the one hand, the funding and, on the other, the institutional structure of health care in Germany. A third principle, more particular to the health care system itself, shapes the way care is actually delivered. This is the sharp separation, embodied in law, between ambulatory care and institutional care. (Ambulatory care refers to care where patients can literally walk in for treatment, and walk out afterwards, of the kind that in the United Kingdom is delivered in the surgeries of general practitioners and in the outpatient departments of hospitals.) In the Federal Republic before unification the law more or less prohibited hospitals from providing the kind of care delivered to day patients by outpatient departments in Britain.

The operation of this principle has in turn had important consequences for both the delivery of care and the structure of the single most important organised group in the health care system, the medical profession. Whereas local practice – or general practice as it is usually called in the United Kingdom – has often been one of the less prestigious branches of medicine in this country, doctors in local practice in Germany have long been among the leaders of the profession in both prestige and in pay. Their monopoly of ambulatory care means that a far wider range of medical procedures are performed by German local practitioners than are performed in the GP's surgery in this country. One important visible index of the difference that immediately strikes even the most casual visitor from the United Kingdom is the contrast between the technological sophistication of the offices occupied by German doctors and the simple, low-tech surgery at the disposal of the traditional British GP. This in turn is reflected in the range of specialisms available. In Britain 'general practitioner' is virtually a synonym for the doctor operating in the community out of a surgery. Specialists in Britain are usually only accessible to patients by reference from their GP. In Germany, by contrast, general practice in the British sense is comparatively rare, and a wide range of medical specialists can be consulted by patients simply walking off the street into their offices. The widespread presence of specialists in local practice is of course one more reason why the prestige of local practice is so high in the German medical profession.

Compulsory insurance, federalism and the separation between ambulatory and institutional care are important shaping principles in the health care system. How those principles work out in practice is the concern of the next section.

The system in practice

Looking beyond bare principles to see how policy is made, three features are immediately obvious: institutional fragmentation, corporatism and medical domination. Institutional fragmentation grows out of the federal principle, but is not solely a product of federalism. It also reflects the complex history of the German system and the diversity of interests produced by that history. The most obvious kind of fragmentation is, however, territorial. The most important executive responsibilities are lodged with the governments of the individual *Länder*. It is the *Länder* which have prime responsibility for education, including medical education; they control a large part of the hospital system; and *Länder* governments oversee the self-regulatory bodies like the chambers that govern the medical profession. The federal government in Bonn has little say over the actual delivery of health care. But the split between a federal centre and its constituent parts is only part of the story. The federal government itself is fragmented. Leading politicians – like the Health Minister – usually have power bases in their home *Land*. The government is invariably a multi-party coalition, and individual ministers tend to operate with considerable independence; the concept of collective responsibility which generally obliges British cabinet ministers to defend common policies in public is much weaker in Germany. In the circumstances it is very difficult to establish common lines, on health care or on other thorny issues. A tiny sign of this fragmentation at the centre was provided until 1991 by the way executive responsibility for health policy in Bonn was organised. Until then, the health portfolio did not exist separately, but was part of a package of responsibilities spanning Youth, Women, Family and Health.

In short, the structure of government in Germany is designed to fragment decision-making, and it is successful in that aim. But for health care this is only the start of the story of fragmentation. The institutions with the most important executive responsibilities are not even within the state structure at all. The cost of treatment, we have seen, is met by over 1,100 separate self-governing insurance funds. This structure is partly a product of historical development. When compulsory health insurance was first introduced in the 1880s, existing voluntarily created funds were given responsibilities under the new system. The compulsory system inherited over 18,000 separate funds. In the intervening century, two developments occurred: insurance cover rose from 10 per cent of the population (principally in the working class) to nearly 100 per cent; and the number of funds was greatly reduced by amalgamations. Even after a century-long process of consolidation, however, the country is still left with the present large number of separate funds. On the side of providers, fragmentation, though not as marked, is still considerable. The institutional separation of ambulatory and hospital care means that payers have to negotiate separately with hospitals and with the doctors who provide ambulatory care. Among the most prestigious group of doctors – those practising in the local community – these forces for fragmentation are reinforced by a powerful anti-collectivist ideology. Local doctors picture themselves as independent professionals and are suspicious of anything which might move them in the direction of a salaried service. They are even hostile to the formation of group practices: whereas solo practitioners are a dying breed among GPs in Britain, they remain the norm in local practice in Germany.

One reason for the fragmentation of the German system is the historical route through which its institutions have evolved. But a second cause of fragmentation is the corporatist nature of the system. Corporatism has endowed a wide range of separate organisations outside the state structure with responsibilities for making and implementing health care policy.

Corporatism exists where important functions of regulation are delegated by the state to privately organised interests, and where in return for carrying out those functions the organisations are given legal powers of compulsion over their members. The most distinctive feature of the German health care system – compulsory insurance – is corporatist. The insurance funds, by collecting contributions from employers and employees, carry out tax-raising functions which would otherwise have to be undertaken by government. In return, the legal obligation on workers to join guarantees members for the funds, while the state recognises them as central actors in the policy-making process. A corporatist bargain also defines the state's relationship with doctors. Membership of their *Land* chamber is obligatory for physicians, and in return the chambers 'govern' the profession, in matters like the regulation of professional ethics. (In this sense, the chambers occupy a position in regulation that in some important respects resembles the position of the General Medical Council in the United Kingdom.)

Even in cases where legal compulsion is not formally present, corporatist features are marked. For instance, while doctors in local practice are not statutorily obliged to join an Association of Insurance Doctors, in practice they must do so as a condition of economic survival. This is because the Associations play a key part in reimbursing doctors for treatment given to insurance fund members. As we have already seen, virtually all Germans have the cost of their health care covered by contributions to one insurance fund or another. The funds will only reimburse doctors who are members of an Association of Insurance Doctors. Hence, in practice, working as a doctor demands membership. But it goes beyond eligibility. In characteristic corporatist fashion the Associations administer important parts of the health care system. They negotiate the rates of reimbursement with the insurance funds, and then receive annually a single sum from the funds. Doctors in local practice apply for reimbursement, not to the funds but to their Association, which pays out of this single global sum. Because they are paymasters the Associations have also acquired other functions. It is up to them to check that claims are not fraudulent and, increasingly, that they do not breach economic guidelines designed to contain costs. But if the Associations are the immediate paymasters, it is the insurance funds and their members who must ultimately fund the bill through the insurance premiums. The rising cost of health care in Germany, and with it the increased level of health insurance contributions, has given the insurance funds an increasing interest in the way health care is delivered. In short, the single most important aspect of health care policy – the cost of care – is largely determined in Germany by negotiations between funders and providers outside the state structure.

The functioning of the health care system represents a particularly well-developed case of the deep-rooted German system of self-administration or -regulation (*Selbstverwaltung*). In health care, its effect is to strip an already fragmented state structure of a wide range of functions. This contrasts with Britain, where there is tight central control and where state institutions dominate the way health care is costed and delivered.

Corporatism and medical domination are in turn connected to each other. Most modern health care systems give the medical profession a large say in health care policy-making. The German system is no exception, though it is true that not all doctors are powerful. The profession is itself internally divided. There are growing numbers of poorly paid and relatively powerless doctors working in hospitals, and there are reckoned to be about 15,000 unemployed qualified physicians in the country. Nevertheless, parts of the profession enjoy great power, high prestige and generous rewards. When the pay of doctors in Germany relative to the rest of the population is compared with the relative pay of doctors in other countries, the German medical profession emerges as one of the best paid in the world (Alber, 1988b). Doctors in local practice are particularly privileged. Not only do their own Associations negotiate pay rates, they actually administer the payment system. The method of calculating reimbursement reinforces the independence of the doctor as an autonomous professional. Payment is based on 'fee for service' in which the doctor makes an independent clinical judgement about the treatment required by the patient and bills the payer accordingly. Although pressure to contain costs has put this system under pressure in recent years, its endurance is both a symbolic and a substantive sign of the power and status of the local practitioner.

Institutional fragmentation is not a peculiarity of health care; the dispersal of power is central to both the principle and the practice of German government. It is a conscious response to the country's political history, especially its history of tyranny in the Nazi years. But the legacy for health care is problematic. The country is committed to delivering free, or nearly free, high-quality care to its citizens. It has to meet all the policy problems which that commitment creates with an institutional structure which places great limitations on the authority and administrative resources of the state, which scatters executive responsibility among numerous extra-state institutions, and which buttresses the privileged position of one group of deliverers, the medical profession. The kinds of problems these circumstances create, and the sorts of solutions attempted, are examined in the next section.

Achievements and problems

The German health care system is highly successful. It has managed to avoid many of the faults apparently endemic in the alternative systems of health care organisation sketched at the start of this chapter. Unlike the market-based system of funding in the United States, the German system ensures that the whole population has adequate health insurance cover. (About 35 million Americans have no health insurance cover at all, and a much larger number are inadequately covered [OECD, 1992a]). Virtually every German has access to what is, even by the standards of the richest countries in the world, an exceptionally high quality of medical care.

The German achievement in providing the whole population with care free at the point of treatment is matched by the centrally controlled, tax-financed system of the United Kingdom. Germany has, however, been able to provide a higher standard of care than has Britain (measured, for instance, by the greater availability of single-room accommodation for patients in hospitals and readier access to the most advanced medical technology). Germany has also been much more successful than has the United Kingdom in avoiding long waiting lists for treatment, and offers more patient choice than has been available under the National Health Service. The most obvious indicator of greater choice is in the field of ambulatory care, where patients not only have direct access to a wide range of specialists (in the United Kingdom they must await referral from a GP) but also have more freedom in choosing which local doctors to use as their family physician (though the range of choice is widening in Britain.)

Universal coverage and freedom of choice have also been achieved comparatively economically. Like every modern health care system, Germany has been attempting for two decades to contain costs. Nevertheless, when the proportion of national income spent on health care is compared with like figures for similar countries, the German system emerges as no more than averagely expensive. As Table 4.1 (above) shows, it spends considerably more than does the United Kingdom; but it spends much less than does the United States (which commits over 13 per cent of its total domestic expenditure to health care). In short, for anyone unfortunate enough to be sick, Germany before reunification was probably the best country in the world in which to be treated for ill health, regardless of whether a patient was rich or poor. This outstanding record is worth bearing in mind while considering the undoubted problems of the health care system.

For purposes of discussion, these problems can be examined under four headings: impact, control, equity and the special problems created by reunification. The first of these itself springs from a wider question in the study of health policy: what is the purpose of a health care system, and, in particular, how far is the effectiveness of health care policy to be judged by its impact on the health of the population? It may seem odd to raise such a question when health care consumes so many resources. If health care does not lead to better health, what is the point of all the costly activity? But while only a few argue that modern medicine is useless or even positively harmful, there is widespread uncertainty in all modern health care systems about the actual connection between medicine and health. This is because it is demonstrable that the actual health of a population is determined by a wide range of factors – the quality of the physical environment, the extent of poverty, diet and life-style. Where the quality and amount of health care fit into this causal chain is unclear (for a discussion, see McKeown, 1976).

Uncertainty about the impact of health care poses a problem in all advanced industrial nations because all invest heavily in modern medicine, but it is a particularly serious problem in Germany because the scale of the resources committed is so great. Measured by standard indicators of health care, like life expectancy, the former West Germany scores less well than many other leading industrial nations (Alber, 1988b.) Table 4.1 (above) shows that on some important indicators Germany before unification performed better than did the United Kingdom, but whether the marginal differences in performance justify the very large differences in resources committed is debatable. Japan, the advanced capitalist nation with which Germany is so often compared, seems to achieve better health outcomes with fewer resources. The cost and technical sophistication of German medicine has not, apparently, produced corresponding results in the health of the population. Other countries achieve more by spending less.

The suspicion that, at the very least, the country has not been getting value for its money is strengthened by the way the providers of health care are paid. There is a heavy reliance on 'fee for service' in paying the medical profession and in paying for hospital care. (Under fee for service, providers bill for each item of treatment.) This system provides powerful economic incentives to providers to increase the level of care and, at the extreme, simply to offer quite unnecessary medical procedures. The fee for service system has not evolved as a natural response to the health needs of the population. Its use reflects the historically dominant position of the medical profession over other groups, notably the health insurance funds. It originated in political struggles between doctors and the health insurance funds, in which doctors emerged victorious. For the most prestigious group of German doctors – those in local practice – fee for service payment is a guarantee of their status as free professionals superior to occupations that are paid by salary. In short, this method of payment has not developed as a response to the health care needs of the population but as the result of the interests of the most powerful group of providers in the system (see Tennstedt, 1977; Stone, 1980).

The problematic impact of health care policy, and the way this is linked to the organisation of the system, is particularly well illustrated by the fate of policies designed to prevent ill health in the Federal Republic. Recognition of the fact that curative medicine has a limited, perhaps a highly limited, impact on health lies behind contemporary interest in preventive policy. But the history of prevention in Germany is unimpressive. In an already fragmented policy-making and implementation system, the institutions of preventive medicine – notably in public health – are themselves fragmented and institutionally marginal. At the federal level, preventive policies have been employed by different governments to represent their different ideologies. As Freeman (1994, p. 12) puts it: 'prevention has been used at the federal level by the Left to seek to extend government authority over the health sector (1968–1970), and by the Right to legitimate a strategy of cost containment (1987–1989).' The powerful medical profession, while sceptical on ideological grounds of measures which imply state intervention, has opportunistically used some preventive measures – such as screening – to boost its income under the fee for service system. For the insurance funds, prevention has been seen as a possible mechanism for long-term cost containment. In short, prevention policy is pulled hither and thither by the many institutions involved in health care. It serves a wide range of functions: to legitimise competing health care ideologies; to boost the income of some interests; to advance cost containment. Against these more or less latent functions, the manifest function of actually improving the health of the population seems to be unimportant (for a comprehensive discussion, see Freeman, 1994).

As these remarks suggest, power relations in the German health care system are also at the root of the second problem identified above: the problem of control. At the most fundamental level there are huge accountability gaps in the system; at the more immediate operational level these manifest themselves as problems of cost control and control over the distribution of human resources.

The historical development of the German system originally endowed it with institutions in which there were powerful traditions of democratic control and participation. This was especially noteworthy of the health insurance funds controlled by their own members which developed in the nineteenth century. The subsequent evolution of the system has all but destroyed that tradition of popular control. The introduction of compulsory insurance in the 1880s, and the transformation of previously voluntary funds into agents of state compulsion, began that process. Bitter struggles between the funds and the doctors' associations in the early decades of this century effectively wrested control of health care delivery from the funds and gave doctors the lion's share. The Nazis purged the funds of their social democratic activists, and since their reconstruction after the Second World War they have been democratic in little more than name. Participation in internal fund elections is very low, and control is exercised by oligarchies of officials. On the doctors' side, despite the efforts of radical left-wing groups of mostly young doctors, the profession is dominated likewise by oligarchies. In short, despite all the institutional fragmentation – the profusion of organisations, the federal system, the delegation of important functions to organisations outside the state structure – the whole health care system is strikingly hierarchical. The most obviously democratic parts of the system are the institutions of the state, whose political leaders at least have to win the support of citizens in competitive elections. Yet the organisation of the system strips the state of most important executive responsibilities in health care. The ability of elected governments to reform the system is constrained by the power of the interests in health care. The reforms introduced in Britain and in Germany after the late 1980s are a clear illustration. In Britain after 1989, central government imposed a wide range of reforms against the vocal opposition of the medical profession. In the same year, the federal government in Bonn implemented a Health Care Reform Act which, Webber (1989) has shown, had been fundamentally reshaped by powerful sectional interests in the medical profession and in the pharmaceutical industry. There are, in short, large control deficits in the German system, and these deficits are caused by the basic principles of health care organisation.

These control deficits are revealed at the operational level in problems of ensuring cost control and efficiency. The 'cost control problem' might in the German case be more accurately labelled a 'burden allocation' problem. It is not so much that health care costs in Germany are high by international standards; it is more that compulsory insurance makes costs highly visible and distributes them in a particularly onerous way. In Britain, the fact that the health service is paid for out of taxation means that taxpayers never see in their pay packets a deduction specifically allocated to health care. That is exactly what German workers and employers see in the contribution premium due to the health insurance fund. That premium has risen over the long term: in 1950 the national average was under 6 per cent, by the early 1990s over 12 per cent. The rise in contribution rates forced the federal government into a major reform of the health care system at the end of the 1980s, but that cost containment measure has been a failure. In 1991 total costs rose by 10 per cent, and at the end of 1992 the federal government was obliged to introduce another round of measures (see below).

The control deficit is not confined to costs. It extends to the planning and utilisation of capital resources. Like many other health care systems of advanced capitalist nations, Germany suffers from a 'bed mountain' – an overprovision of hospital beds relative to need. But the most serious control problems have occurred in the provision of human resources for health care. The country has simultaneously managed to achieve a shortage of nurses and a gross oversupply of doctors.

The crux of the problem in controlling doctor numbers is political – especially the problems of authoritative decision-making created by the federal constitution. Since control of education is a responsibility of the *Länder*, it is exceptionally difficult for the national authorities to create and enforce a policy limiting the numbers entering to study medicine at university. And even if a highly restrictive national policy could be articulated, it is doubtful that it could be constitutionally enforced. Previous efforts to restrict entry to parts of the medical profession have been struck down by the Constitutional Court on the grounds that they contravene constitutional guarantees to citizens of their rights to practise a profession. Despite an agreement among the governments of the *Länder* to raise entry standards and cut numbers entering courses, the universities accept 10,000 new first-year medical students every year. In 1991–2 there were 97,500 medical students in the reunited Germany (Federal Government, 1993). The problems faced by policy-makers in controlling numbers entering medicine show just how different Germany is from the centralised British system. In this country, a central department, the Department of Health, lays down and successfully enforces exact targets for recruitment to medical schools, following advice from a Medical Manpower Standing Advisory Committee, itself appointed by the Department. Likewise the numbers entering general practice are tightly regulated, under guidance from central government, in the interests of controlling both the total supply of GPs and their geographical distribution.

The control deficits in the German system are one source of the third major problem identified earlier: the lack of equity, especially in the distribution of the costs of health care. The decentralisation of health insurance, and the lack of a strong central authority capable of allocating costs between unequal groups, combine to produce large variations in the costs borne by different groups. These variations penalise the poorest. The nub of the problem lies in the main principle on which the health care system is founded – compulsory insurance organised by a large number of autonomous funds. Each fund is a self-governing entity with an obligation to balance its books (an obligation which many now find impossible to meet). The obligation leads to large differences in contribution rates between funds. Around the national average for health insurance contributions of just over 12 per cent lies a range between 8 per cent and 16 per cent. Part of this difference may lie in efficiency variations between funds, but the most important reasons lie elsewhere: in the different health demands of members, and in their unequal incomes. The two most important kinds of fund are those organised territorially in districts and those based on the workplace. Funds which organise in the poorest parts of the Federal Republic, even before unification introduced the poverty-stricken East, were forced to charge well above average rates, both because they contained disproportionate numbers of the poor and unhealthy, and because members with low incomes provided a less lucrative tax base than was available to funds organising in prosperous districts. This structural inequality has been reinforced by the actions of individuals intent on banding together in funds which exclude low-income and high-risk members: thus, in recent years, 'factory funds' have been formed to allow workers to 'exit' from high-premium district funds (see Moran, 1990, for details).

The problems of equity and control sketched here existed in the Federal Republic before reunification with the former German Democratic Republic in 1990, but reunification has both intensified existing problems and added new ones. It has led to an institutional revolution in the five new *Länder* created out of the old German Democratic Republic. Most of the main features of communist health care are being swept away. A centrally controlled system of health insurance and medical education has been dismantled. The health insurance funds already established in the West have extended eastwards, and new district funds have been created. Under communism, doctors were mostly (badly paid) salaried employees; now as many as 80 per cent in local practice are independent contractors on the former West German model (Freudenstein, 1992). The single most distinctive feature of health care delivery in the old German Democratic Republic was the *Poliklinik*. This was a health centre employing the full range of medical professionals and providing a full range of ambulatory care, often attached to a hospital. The first intention on reunification was to phase out financial support for the *Polikliniken* by 1995, though in the health care reforms introduced for the whole of Germany at the start of 1993 they have been given a reprieve (see below). Nevertheless, their long-term future looks bleak. *Polikliniken* violate one of the key principles of the old West German system, the strict separation of ambulatory from institutional care. Since that principle works to the economic advantage of the powerful section of the medical profession which is in local practice, the *Polikliniken* have formidable enemies in the new Germany. Similar pressures are also destroying the old communist system of salaried dentists in favour of the establishment of independent contractors as in West Germany (Nippert, 1992).

Part of the problem created by reunification is therefore novel: how to bring about revolutionary changes in health care in a democratic society? There is widespread argument about the appropriateness of trying to replicate the former West German system in the new *Länder*, but that a revolution was needed is without doubt. The old GDR left a lamentable legacy: badly paid and demoralised health care professionals; inefficiently organised and poorly equipped hospitals; scandalous connections between parts of the medical profession – especially psychiatry – and the old communist tyranny; and a population whose health status is markedly worse than that achieved in the former West Germany, or indeed in the poorest countries of Western Europe (Rowland, 1991).

Many of these failings only intensify the problems of cost containment and of equity which existed in the former West German system. Raising the five *Länder* to the level of the rest of Germany will be hugely expensive, especially in spending on hospitals (Kurbjuweit, 1991). The extension of the West German funding system to the East further magnifies the difficulties. Reunification has been an economic catastrophe for the former GDR, leading to mass unemployment, the collapse of large parts of productive industry and the exposure of huge gaps in wage levels between East and West. The new *Länder* just do not have the resources to run a health insurance system based on the principle that funds should balance their books. This was recognised at the foundation of the new system in 1990 by the provision of financial support from the federal government to meet the deficits of the funds in the East (Deutsche Bundesbank, 1991).

The political significance of this financial support is that it creates a precedent for federal government intervention in the funding system across the whole nation, and gives the system a sharp push in the direction of greater centralisation – a direction in which the health care system has been edging for two decades, under pressure to solve problems of cost containment and equity. As long ago as 1977, the Federal Republic established a system of 'Concerted Action' in health care. This created a national forum where all the main parties are brought together in the attempt to produce agreement on common targets for important objectives like cost containment. In 1989, the federal government passed a major Health Care Reform Act which further intervened in the bargaining relations between the doctors and the funds. These reforms failed in their most important objective, which was to curb the rising level of health insurance premiums. That failure, coupled with the added problems brought by reunification, has produced renewed institutional change and policy innovation. In 1991, a new, separate Health Ministry was created for the first time. The change signified the rising salience of health care as a political issue, and signified also the government's determination to get a grip on the costs of the health insurance system. The new Minister, Gerda Hasselfeld, had a mandate to produce a reform package designed to curb costs. She failed to produce an agreement, and in May 1992 resigned. The political sensitivity of the cost of care has nevertheless driven the federal government further towards intervention, and her successor has introduced another reform package, effective from the start of 1993. When finally implemented, fundamental changes will take place in the structure of the compulsory insurance system. From 1997, contributors will be free to choose their own health insurance fund, thus increasing the pressure on funds to compete with each other by offering economical rates. Imbalances between funds will be removed by transfer payments between funds in deficit and those in surplus. There are to be financial incentives to increase the level of treatment offered outside hospitals, thus cutting into the large bill for institutional care. There will be fixed drug budgets for the health insurance funds, and excess drug costs will be met by a levy imposed on the pharmaceutical industry. Associated reforms in the recruitment of doctors are intended to cut numbers, reduce medical unemployment and cut the costs doctors impose on the health care system. From 1999, doctors will be obliged to retire at the age of 68, and immediate restrictions are to be imposed on entry into ambulatory practice in the areas where numbers of doctors are already high. These latter proposals, though modest, already face the prospect of being challenged in the Constitutional Court as an infringement of citizens' rights to practise their chosen profession (Oldiges, 1991; Karcher, 1992; Tufts, 1992).

Conclusion

The state which was created in West Germany after 1949 was highly decentralised both territorially and functionally: the governments of the individual *Länder* had a great deal of authority; and organisations representing the main interests in the economy played a large part in making and implementing policy. Decentralisation was designed to ensure that the Federal Republic would, unlike some German regimes in the past, be democratic and limited in its power over citizens. That design was outstandingly successful, but it risked creating a system of government so concerned with compromise and bargaining that strategic decision-making would be impossible. In economic management this danger was partly avoided because the big banks and their allies in the large industrial concerns were a powerful force for cohesion. It has proved exceptionally difficult to create any similarly effective strategic institutions in health care. The 'Concerted Action' introduced in 1977, though undoubtedly useful in pushing the interested parties to think in terms of the needs of the whole nation, offers nothing like the sort of direction which has existed in economic management. There is compelling evidence from the way other advanced capitalist nations have responded to the challenge of cost containment that increased central control over policy is a functional response to the needs of modern health care systems (Moran, 1994). There are indeed signs that German health care, too, is being pushed towards greater centralisation. But in German politics and society the fears of centralisation in the light of German political history, the powerful territorial interests in the *Länder* and the powerful functional interests in the medical profession and in the insurance funds are all a great obstacle to the creation of more effective central steering mechanisms.

Guide to further reading

Readers of German will want to start with a historical understanding of the evolution of the system. Tennstedt (1977), though specifically about the history of the insurance funds, illuminates very well the political struggles which have shaped the system. Two major works by Alber (1987, 1989) set the German system in context: the first traces the historical development of welfare states in Western Europe; the second examines the welfare state in Germany itself. Alber (1988b) uses OECD data to construct a comparative statistical portrait of the modern health care systems against which the German system can be measured. Two landmark articles by Webber (1988, 1989) trace the history of reforms to the system, emphasising the historical power of doctors and the modern problems of securing decisive reform in the decentralised Germany of today. The argument of these papers also recurs in English in Webber (1991).

As a result of reunification, the German system is undergoing rapid change. Fortunately for the reader of German there is an excellent trade press and the 'quality' German newspapers cover health care policy extensively: of the former, the journal of the district insurance funds, *Die Ortskrankenkasse*, is particularly accessible; of the latter, *Handelsblatt* and *Frankfurter Allgemeine Zeitung* provide particularly good coverage. Basic statistical data about the German system are to be obtained from three sources: *Daten des Gesundheitswesens* (Stuttgart: Kohlhammer, bi-annual); *Statistisches Jahrbuch* (Wiesbaden: Statistisches Bundesamt, annual); and OECD (1993, both in text format and on diskette).

For readers of English, coverage of the system is patchy, and is rather biased towards recent events. Stone (1980) is a standard historical introduction which stresses the central role of the medical profession. Light and Schuller (1986) is a comparison of the two German systems which has been made somewhat redundant by recent events, but several of the pieces – notably Rosenberg's – contain valuable material on the historical development of the system. Heidenheimer (1980) provides an informative account of the historical development of the medical profession, with the added bonus of a comparison with Scandinavia. Alber (1991) has provided an overview which is good both at comparing the German system with others and at examining the political context of health care reform. Moran and Wood (1993) compare the regulation of the medical profession in Germany, the United Kingdom and the United States. OECD (1992b, ch. 5) examines the reform of the system and includes useful passages on the impact of reunification. The other chapters in the same volume give some comparative perspective on German changes. Deutsche Bundesbank (1991, available in English or German) is excellent on the funding of the system. Henke (1991) examines the fiscal problems of reunification. Döhler (1991) compares health policy networks in the Federal Republic, the United States and the United Kingdom.

Acknowledgements

The paper on which this chapter is based was originally given to a study day on 'Social Policy in Germany' organised by the Social Policy Association in February 1992. I am grateful for the many helpful comments received on that day. I am also grateful to Jochen Clasen and Richard Freeman for their comments and criticisms on earlier drafts of this chapter.

Chapter 5

Housing policy and the housing system

Mark Kleinman

In all countries, housing lies at the intersection of social policy with a number of other policy areas, such as economic policy, land-use planning and urban and regional policies. The form that housing policy takes – its scope and rationale – can therefore act as an indicator of the balance between economic and social goals, or between the relative weights given to free markets and to state intervention in that country.

In Germany, housing policy since 1945 has to be seen within the context of the commitment to a social market economy. While housing policies in all countries reflect a mixture of state intervention and market forces, the particular form taken in Germany reflects this wider vision. Specifically, this means the consistent emphasis on market provision within a framework of laws, and the reliance on market forces, supplemented by regulation and limited state support. Housing is not provided as a social service, but government retains important responsibilities both for ensuring the housing standards of the mass of the population, and for meeting the needs of the most disadvantaged.

Any study of German housing policy in a comparative context will bring out similarities and differences with policies in Britain, for example, or in other European Union (EU) countries more generally. Many of the main trends in German housing policy in recent years, such as the switch from 'bricks-and-mortar' production subsidies to means-tested personal housing subsidies, or the reduction in new social house-building, or the encouragement of owner-occupation, are common to most if not all EU countries (see, for example, Hills *et al.*, 1990; Ghekiere 1991, 1992; Boelhouwer and van der Heijden, 1992; Kleinman, 1992, 1993). But the exact form of these policy developments reflects the specific German context.

In a comparative context, a number of aspects of the German housing system immediately stand out. First, there is the importance given to market conditions. Policy is sensitive to the current stage in the economic cycle, and policy-makers try to work with the cycle rather than cut across it. What would in other countries be described as changes in policy are sometimes defended in Germany as changes in emphasis, because of different economic conditions, rather than shifts in direction. This was certainly the case following the reintroduction, in a limited way, of federal housing subsidies in the late 1980s.

Second, in comparison with Britain, there is no large local authority sector, indeed there is no local authority sector at all. However, as described below, local authorities do have nomination rights into the social housing stock and do in some cases hold controlling interests in local housing companies. The term 'social housing' therefore describes a method of *financing* housing together with a set of *regulations* and *responsibilities* about allocation of tenancies, rent levels and standards, rather than a physically identifiable stock of dwellings. Flats which were at one time let as social housing can, once the subsidised loans with which they were built have been paid off, be let as non-social private rented housing. One result of this is that there is in general less segregation of social and private housing. Social housing is more evenly spread throughout the stock:

> Compared to Britain, the spatial distribution of the different segments
> of the housing stock throughout the cities of West Germany is relatively
> homogeneous. Old, and therefore cheap, social housing can be found in central
> locations with high accessibility and in attractive environmental settings with
> tall trees, having been built during reconstruction on the site of buildings
> demolished during the war. (Kreibich, 1991, p. 78)

However, while this is the general pattern, there are also large estates of social housing built on the peripheries of the major cities during the 1960s and early 1970s. According to Power (1993, p. 129), fourteen 'giant' estates, each with over 5,000 dwellings in blocks of thirteen storeys or more, were built in this period.

Third, while in Britain the private rented sector has declined continuously over the last fifty years and now plays only a very minor role in the housing system, in Germany, private renting remains a large, diverse sector, housing more than two out of five households. Its diversity means that it plays a major role in providing accommodation for all income levels. Investors in the sector include individuals as well as companies.

Fourth, and as a corollary to the last point, fewer German households are owner-occupiers, by comparison not only with Britain, but also with other

EU countries (Table 5.1). Although policy has supported the encouragement of owner-occupation, and the level of home-ownership has risen in recent years, it remains the lowest in the EU. The reasons for this are complex. The greater size and diversity of private renting means that there is an alternative to owner-occupation for middle- and higher-income households. House prices are much higher in Germany, even taking into account relative incomes. High house prices and the way that housing finance is organised mean that owner-occupation is not an option for lower-income households as it is in Britain, and that first-time buyers need to spend a number of years saving for a deposit and to qualify for a low-interest loan from a savings bank (*Bausparkasse*, see below). Entry to owner-occupation hence occurs in the middle of the life-cycle, and there is relatively little trading up and down within the stock. The average first-time buyer in Germany is aged 36 and stays in the property for 28 years. This contrasts strongly with the British pattern of early entry to owner-occupation and frequent movement, often of a wholly or partly speculative nature, within the sector.

Fifth, although means-tested housing benefit (*Wohngeld* – which can be claimed by owner-occupiers as well as both private and social tenants) has been available in West Germany since 1965, a much smaller proportion of tenants is dependent on benefit to pay their rent. In 1992, only 10 per cent of tenant households and 1.2 per cent of owner-occupier households in the western part of Germany were in receipt of benefit. The numbers of recipients in the former GDR were much higher: 31 per cent of tenant households and 20 per cent of owner-occupier households. But this is still far below British levels, with more than 60 per cent of social tenants in receipt of housing benefit. (The comparison with the former GDR does of course

Table 5.1 Housing tenure in the EU (percentage)

	Owner-occupier	Private renting	Social renting	Year
Spain	88.3	10.6	1.2	1989
Ireland	74.4	10.1	12.4	1981
Greece	70.0	26.5	–	1981
UK	67.0	7.0	26.0	1989
Italy	64.0	23.5	5.3	1990
Belgium	62.0	30.0	6.0	1986
Luxembourg	59.2	35.1	–	1981
Portugal	55.9	35.5	4.4	1981
Denmark	55.5	22.1	21.2	1988
France	54.2	19.7	17.2	1988
Netherlands	43.7	13.0	42.9	1988
West Germany	40.0	43.0	17.0	1989

Source: Ghekiere (1991).

in part reflect the fact that rents there remain below levels in either western Germany or in Britain.)

Finally, the development of housing policy and the housing system in Germany has been crucially affected by its economic situation. For most of the post-war period, until very recently, West Germany has been characterised by low inflation, low and stable interest rates and, compared with other EU countries, low unemployment. This has had profound effects on the housing market. Low inflation and low unemployment have contributed to a 'savings culture'. Fixed interest rates on housing loans (to both owner-occupiers and investors) have until recently been the norm. Germany has not had the Anglo-Saxon experience of high inflation, negative real interest rates, house price booms and windfall gains for mortgagers. Home-ownership in Germany is both expensive and a long-term commitment, and it is perceived to be so by the mass of housing consumers. Conversely, the environment for investment in rented housing has been more attractive than in other countries not only because of the specific legislative and taxation arrangements, but also because of the relatively stable economic conditions underpinning loan repayments, rent levels and costs.

Since unification in 1990, much of the economic and social stability which has underpinned, and in part explains, the nature of the post-war West German housing system has come under threat. Inflation is rising, as is unemployment, and in the early 1990s, real take-home income began to stagnate. In addition, the relatively balanced urban and regional system which obtained in the old Federal Republic, and which contrasted greatly with both Britain and France, each of which is dominated by its capital city region, came to an end. In its place came a very unbalanced distribution between West and East together with the possibility of a much more skewed urban hierarchy developing as Berlin sought to become a 'global city' to rival London and Paris (Dangschat, 1993). Alongside this, in the wake of the great changes of 1989 and subsequently, came the large migrations of ethnic Germans from Eastern Europe and non-German refugees which put additional pressures on the housing system. German housing policy is therefore a story of a relatively stable system in the forty years or so after 1950, based around the core West German idea of the social market economy, which in the last few years has been faced with a very different economic and social situation (see also Chapter 9).

This chapter is arranged as follows. The next two sections examine the development of housing policy in the post-war period and the structure and operation of the current German housing system, looking at each tenure in turn. The subsequent section describes the outcomes of the system in terms of the overall match between supply and demand, the dwelling stock, housing costs for households, urban renewal and gentrification, and the extent of unmet housing need. Following a general assessment of housing policy in West Germany, the chapter concludes with a section on housing issues in the new *Länder* and a discussion of key issues for the 1990s.

Housing policy in the post-war period

The federal nature of the political system in Germany makes for a relatively complex policy-making and implementing environment, with roles for the federal government, the *Länder* and the local authorities. The federal government determines its own overall level of support to housing, while the *Länder* have considerable power to determine their own housing policy within these constraints. In particular, the *Länder* decide on the form of support to social housing, and its allocation between home-ownership and rental programmes. The *Länder* are required at least to match federal funds, and in practice they contribute more (Boelhouwer and van der Heijden, 1992). The allocation of federal resources between states is formula-based, mainly reflecting population size. Local municipal authorities can and do contribute their own resources to housing programmes. These local authorities have both direct control over local social housing companies that they own, and indirect control via a system of nomination rights (see below).

There is therefore considerable scope for differences in housing policy at the level of both states and cities. Moreover, as outlined below, national housing policy has gone through different phases, reflecting both economic developments and changes in political power at the federal level. However, as a general comparative point, the formulation and implementation of housing policy in Germany rests on a greater degree of consensus-building and agreement than is the case in Britain between different levels of government, and between government at all levels and other agencies. This is of course not specific to the housing sphere, but reflects institutional aspects of the Federal Republic in the post-war period, such as coalition politics and the broad commitment to the social market economy. However, it is important to emphasise that this does not mean that housing policy has somehow been 'de-politicised', but rather that the form that the politics of housing takes differs in Germany from that in Britain. The constitutionally defined relationships between the different levels of government in Germany protect state and local governments from the centralisation of power at the national level which has been the dominant characteristic in Britain over the last fifteen years. But there are nevertheless conflicts between federal and other levels of government in Germany over questions of housing policy.

Very broadly, we can divide housing policy in the post-war period into five decade-long categories (Tomann, 1990; Boelhouwer and van der Heijden, 1992). The immediate post-war period was characterised by an acute crude shortage of dwellings, caused by a combination of war damage and an influx of refugees. In 1950, the shortage was estimated at between 5.5 and 6 million dwellings. The first phase, the 1950s, was hence a period of reconstruction. The First Housing Act in 1950 introduced rent controls and subsidies to new housing. Loans covering between 40 and 50 per cent of the costs of construction were provided by the state interest-free to both private investors and non-profit associations. In exchange, landlords had to accept government controls over allocation of the dwellings, protection for tenants and minimum standards with regard to size and quality. These conditions were to apply during the period the loan was in force only; at the end of this period, unless the landlord were a municipally controlled association, the dwelling would cease to be part of the social sector and become part of the private sector. This principle has continued in German housing policy with important consequences in the 1980s and 1990s as much of the stock built with subsidies comes out of the social sector, as we shall see below.

The 1950 Act was followed by the Second Housing Act in 1956, which, subsequently modified and extended, remains in large part the framework for social housing. In Germany, instead of direct government loans, investors obtain loans on the private capital market. The government, however, provides interest subsidies for a certain period of time to enable the dwelling to be let at a below-market rent. This social rent is determined by the government, and the size and quality of the dwelling are also regulated. Apartments built under these provisions can only be let to households whose income is below a certain level. A second category of social housing, which has received public funds since 1967, can be let to middle-income tenants whose incomes are up to 40 per cent above the ceiling for the first category of social housing (Duvigneau and Schonefeldt, 1989).

In the 1960s, the second phase, full employment and the effect of additional supply in creating a more balanced housing market led to a reduction in the role of the state. Rent controls were gradually phased out, so that by 1968 they remained only in Hamburg, Munich and Berlin. Housing benefit was introduced in 1965, and supply subsidies were extended to owner-occupation as well as social rented housing (Tomann, 1990).

The third phase of policy in the 1970s saw a return to greater government involvement under SPD–FDP coalition governments. Chancellor Brandt declared that the government's aims were to increase owner-occupation among broad strata of the population, develop a long-term programme of social housing construction and improve housing benefit (Boelhouwer and van der Heijden, 1992). This led to a housing boom, with output peaking at 714,000 in 1973, before falling rapidly to under 400,000 in 1976. After 1976, under Chancellor Schmidt, there was a change in policy towards improvement rather than new building, and a greater emphasis on owner-occupation rather than renting. This change in policy was justified in part by the overall balance between the numbers of households and dwellings. Urban renewal was encouraged by the 1971 Urban Renewal Act and subsequent legislation, which provided for the costs of renewal to be shared between the three levels of government. Under the last SPD–FDP coalition government of 1980–2, there were sharp rises in interest rates and a reduction in the resources available to government. A more market-oriented policy was gradually introduced, a move which continued and accelerated under the CDU–FDP coalition which took power after 1982. In 1982, the government introduced the 'additional rent tax' (*Fehlbelegungsabgabe*). This allowed (but did not compel) the states to levy an additional charge on social tenants whose incomes exceeded by 20 per cent or more the income ceiling for social housing, the money raised being required to be used to provide more social housing by local authorities (Boelhouwer and van der Heijden, 1992). This was an attempt to correct for poor targeting of subsidies which meant that some tenants in subsidised dwellings were on average or above-average incomes.

The fourth period of housing policy, between 1983 and 1989, is marked by the greater influence of neo-liberal economic ideas and consequent policies of deregulation and liberalisation. While in Tomann's (1990) view it would be wrong to speak of a fundamental change of policy, there has certainly been a shift from supply subsidies to housing allowances and to deregulating social housing. The new government's policy aimed to relax rent controls further, provide more assistance to owner-occupation, remove tax exemptions for social housing companies and further cut the level of subsidies.

In 1986, the government abolished federal subsidies for social rented housing. Even more radically, in June 1988, it decided to abolish the special tax status of non-profit housing companies, effectively turning them into private landlords. Changes were made to the rent legislation to permit rises above the rate of inflation, and the tax framework for owner-occupation was reformed in 1987. Owner-occupation was treated as a consumption rather than an investment good and hence both mortgage interest tax relief and tax on the imputed rental value of the property were abolished (Boelhouwer and van der Heijden, 1992, p. 129). New tax allowances for owner-occupiers related to family size were introduced and subsequently increased. However, by the end of the 1980s, pressure in the housing market led to a partial reversal of policy and the reintroduction of subsidies to social rented housing.

The fifth and current period of housing policy is one characterised by extreme pressures in the housing market, and policy responses by government to this increasing pressure. By the end of the 1980s, 'balanced' housing markets had clearly given way to excess demand and acute shortages of accommodation, particularly but not exclusively in the big cities. From an assumed surplus of dwellings of 100,000, the 1987 census showed a shortage of 1 million units. One poll in a major urban area in the early 1990s found that 46 per cent of people saw housing need as the most important problem, ahead of environmental pollution (44 per cent), traffic (34 per cent) and crime (17 per cent) (Wilderer, 1993). The causes of this are complex. The numbers of households continued to increase, as household size fell; in addition, real disposable income rose throughout the 1980s. Living space per person rose considerably, from 24 square metres per person in 1968 to 35.5 square metres per person in 1987. Urban renewal and redevelopment and conversion of inner-city apartments to larger units or to commercial uses had reduced the supply of poorer quality, cheaper accommodation. At the same time, the increase in demand was coming from young people, students, small households and immigrants, who required precisely this type of accommodation. Hence the new shortage or new crisis in the West German housing system arose initially for essentially domestic reasons. But these pressures were compounded by the flow of migrants. For example, the Institute for Economic Research estimated that 2 million *Aussiedler* will emigrate to the area of the former Federal Republic by the year 2000 (Boelhouwer and van der Heijden, 1992, p. 132).

Government responded to these pressures with a variety of policy measures. Private investment was encouraged through improvement in the tax treatment of housing investment. Federal subsidies to social housing were reintroduced, albeit mainly under a new 'third subsidy system', which was less generous than previous federal subsidies and operated for a shorter period. This new subsidy system was more flexible, and involved greater negotiation and agreement with states and local authorities. Altogether, around DM 40 billion was allocated for social housing for the four years 1990–3, representing around 500,000 new social units (Boelhouwer and van der Heijden, 1992). By relaxing certain building regulations, the government aimed to promote additional supply through the conversion of other property such as commercial premises and attics.

Overall, the federal Housing Minister set a target in 1989 of 1 million new dwellings over the following three years – a target that was in fact very nearly achieved (see below). Housing policy in the 1990s shows the degree of sensitivity of the federal government to the new housing shortage. At the same time, the policy response maintains the underlying philosophy of looking to the market to meet most housing needs, and using state activity to support and supplement, not to replace, the market. One of the major issues for housing policy in the 1990s is, of course, the condition and ownership of the former state-owned stock in the new eastern *Länder*. This is discussed later in this chapter.

Structure and operation of the housing system

Owner-occupation

Despite a long-term policy orientation towards increasing the level of owner-occupation, home-ownership among Germans remains low by Western

European standards. Nevertheless, it has increased over the last twenty years from 36 per cent in 1970 to 42 per cent today (Haffner, 1991). House prices are high in Germany, with a ratio of 6 to 7 of house prices to average earnings. This is about twice as high as the ratio in Britain, for example.

There are no direct equivalents to building societies in Germany. Mortgage loans are provided by savings banks, mortgage banks and commercial banks. These first mortgages are restricted by law to a maximum of 60 per cent of the purchase price of the property. Home-owners must therefore top up their first mortgage with second and third loans and/or a cash deposit. Second loans are often obtained from *Bausparkassen* – specialist housing contract-savings institutions whose operations are described below.

Traditionally, the German mortgage market has been dominated by *Sparkassen* (savings banks) and *Hypothekenbanken* (mortgage banks), who still provide half of all lending (Tomann, 1993). In the 1980s, there were numerous takeovers of mortgage banks and *Bausparkassen* by commercial banks, creating financial conglomerates providing a range of financial services. Loans have traditionally been at fixed interest rates, but in recent years greater volatility in inflation and interest rates has led to greater use of variable rate mortgages and renewable interest rate loans (where the rate is fixed for five to ten years at a time).

Mortgage banks are legally restricted to providing mortgages to residential properties and loans to public corporations. They can grant second mortgages up to 15 per cent of their total outstanding loans. During the 1980s, their market share declined from a quarter to about a fifth (Tomann, 1993). Savings banks are almost all owned by local or regional government. By law they can only operate in the respective local or regional area. They provide a range of retail banking services. Savings banks have the biggest share of the mortgage market – about 30 per cent (Tomann, 1993). Like British building societies, they fund mortgages via short-term deposits. This makes them vulnerable to movements in inflation and hence short-term interest rates. Again, like British building societies, they cope with this by offering variable rate mortgages and by a relative rigidity of interest rates to depositors (i.e. savers' rates do not change as frequently as money market rates) (Tomann, 1993).

Bausparkassen are specialist housing-savings institutions. There is no direct equivalent in Britain, but they are, for example, similar to the *plans d'épargne-logement* (housing-savings plans) used in France. They work as follows. The saver contracts for a given amount and agrees to deposit a certain sum per annum, usually 5 per cent of the total amount of the contract. The saver can then choose to receive interest on this sum at a rate of either 2.5 per cent or 4.5 per cent p.a. In addition, the saver receives a bonus of 10 per cent p.a. of the sum saved, plus an additional 2 per cent for every child under 18, up to a maximum of DM 800. The bonus is tax-free, but there is a qualifying income ceiling. The scheme used to be even more generous: until 1975 the bonus was 25 per cent, and 14 per cent up till 1988. (The construction premium for savings contracts [*Bausparverträge*] entered into after 1991 is now to be paid only after the loan has been allocated, or after a minimum of seven years, instead of yearly [Borkenstein, 1993]).

When the amount saved reaches 40 per cent or 50 per cent of the contracted sum (depending on which version of the scheme is selected), the saver receives the total contracted sum, depending on the availability of funds. The remaining portion is given as a loan, at an interest rate of either 4.5 per cent or 5.75 per cent, usually over a twelve-year period. The *Bausparkasse* system is hence a separate financial circuit. Imbalances between the supply of and demand for funds are met by changes in the length of waiting time for the loan rather than by changes in interest rates. The system expanded until the late 1970s, promoted by the special tax treatment and premia. This preferential treatment was reduced during the 1980s, reducing the attractiveness of the system, a development which was compounded by the consequent longer waiting times. Recently, the system has received a boost from unification, with a boom in contract saving in the new *Länder* (Tomann, 1993).

Hence the typical home-buyer makes use of a package of loans. This might include a first mortgage from a mortgage or savings bank, a *Bausparkasse* loan and a third loan from a commercial bank. In practice, this is much less complicated than it sounds. As many mortgage banks and *Bausparkassen* are owned by commercial banks, the borrower will often be making a single monthly payment to cover all three loans, and indeed may not even be aware of the details of how the payment is made up. However, the complexity of loans and local operation of many financial institutions may be a significant factor in the low mobility found in the owner-occupied sector.

Owner-occupiers are not taxed on the imputed rental value of their home, nor do they (in almost all cases) have to pay capital gains tax. On the other hand, they do not receive tax relief for mortgage interest payments. Losses during the construction period and depreciation (for eight years) are tax-deductible. Moreover home-owners (but not tenants) receive a tax credit for each child in the family (*Baukindergeld*). This was introduced in 1987 at DM 600 but was subsequently raised, first to DM 750 in January 1990 and then to DM 1000.

Social housing

Social housing is provided both by private landlords and by non-profit housing enterprises (*Gemeinnütziges Wohnungsunternehmen*). There are more than 1,800 non-profit housing enterprises who belong to the General Association of Non-profit Housing Enterprises (*Gesamtverband Gemeinnütziger Wohnungsunternehmen*, GGW) based in Cologne. The total is made up of more than 1,200 co-operatives, who together own around 1 million units; 540

private limited-dividend companies; and 60 public limited companies. These 600 limited-dividend companies own an average stock of 5,000 units each. The fifty largest companies have an average of 20,000 units, and together own one-third of all social housing (Power, 1993). The largest social housing company, *Neue Heimat*, at its peak owned a gargantuan 400,000 rental units. *Neue Heimat* crashed spectacularly in the 1980s in a major financial corruption scandal. Much of its stock has now been dispersed to other social housing enterprises.

In 1987 there were 3.3 million socially rented units, about two-thirds of which were owned by the non-profit sector (Hills *et al.*, 1990). Social housing enterprises are sponsored by employers, trade unions, churches and by local authorities. Social landlords claim to compete with each other in terms of the quality of service they offer and value for money, especially on large estates where several enterprises are involved (Emms, 1990). In practice they will also be competing for some tenants with the private rented sector.

The federal government provides subsidies to social housing, but the form of those subsidies is controlled by the states. Both states and local authorities can add their own subsidies. The basic structure of support is that part of the building cost is covered by loans at below-market rates. Subsidy is calculated as investor's costs minus a predetermined social rent, below market rent. So the investor (social housing enterprise or private landlord) will break even, provided actual costs remain at or below calculated costs, and provided the levels of arrears and voids are controlled. The subsidies are degressive: the interest rate tapers up over time to the market level, and hence the social rents will also rise over time. In addition to these 'built-in' increases, rents can rise if the level of interest rates generally rises, or if there are increases in operating costs such as management and maintenance expenditure (Hubert, 1992).

Typically a market rent for a new unit might be around DM 20 monthly per square metre while a social rent might be around DM 8–9. Rents are set on a scheme-by-scheme basis – there is no rent pooling across the stock, as in Britain. Consequently, rents of social units can differ markedly depending on their time of construction. It can often be the case that older, centrally located and therefore more attractive flats have lower rents than newer flats much further away from the centre of town. The additional rent tax (see above) is one attempt to deal with this problem, as is the use of degressive subsidies. While the subsidised loan remains in force, the dwelling must be let as social housing. When the loan expires, the local authority no longer has nomination rights to the dwelling.

Applicants for social housing (both tenants and owners) must have incomes below a certain ceiling. This income ceiling, however, has been relatively generous. The local housing office (*Wohnungsamt*) checks a household's income, and, if it is satisfied that the household income is below the ceiling, issues a certificate of entitlement (*Wohnberechtigungsschein*). The applicant can then present this certificate to any of the private or non-profit landlords providing social housing in the area.

Local authorities have nomination rights to local non-profit social landlords whom they sponsor, meaning that they can allocate tenants to vacancies that arise. Other landlords providing social housing are free to choose from among applicants in possession of an entitlement certificate. Hence, in some cases, the local authority-sponsored housing associations can become a 'reception pool' for special needs and so-called problem groups (Heinz, 1991, p. 92). Large cities where access problems are particularly severe can be declared 'areas with increased housing need' under section 5a of the Housing Assignment Act (*Wohnungsbindungsgesetz*). In these cities, local authorities also have nomination rights into the stock of other social landlords operating in the area. These organisations can choose from a list of three applicants supplied by the city (Heinz, 1991).

In common with Britain, France and other countries, there has been a change in the type of households gaining access to social housing over the last two decades. Social housing in Germany, as elsewhere, was not originally intended for the poorest groups in society but rather for skilled and white-collar workers. Recently this has changed, with a more diverse pattern of households found in the sector. The reasons for this are complex. The expansion of owner-occupation has led to the exit of some better-off households from the sector. Social housing subsidies are now more targeted, as production subsidies have been reduced, while greater reliance is placed on means-tested housing allowances (Hills *et al.*, 1990). This has the dual effect of making newer and more expensive social housing affordable to poorer households, while also making it less attractive for better-off groups. This latter effect is in principle compounded in those areas where an additional rent tax is levied on households whose incomes rise above the income ceiling, although the rent tax does not appear in practice to have any effect on tenants' mobility. At the same time, the more balanced housing market of the 1970s led to vacancies in the social housing stock, and less pressure generally, encouraging a more flexible approach to allocations. Finally, although the private rented sector in Germany remains large, much of the poor quality, cheap segment of the sector, particularly in central city areas, has been lost through urban renewal, improvement and enlargement, and conversion to business use (Kreibich, 1991).

As a result, the types of household who rely on the social sector for their housing are relatively poor and fairly diverse. As Kreibich puts it:

> The typical client is no longer the worker's family with several children, but the old couple or the widow living on a pension and, as new tenants, the young couple with only one child and one, or even one-and-a-half, regular and average incomes, or the single parent household. (1991, p. 66)

As an example of this, Table 5.2 gives details of applicants and allocations for social housing in Cologne.

Table 5.2 Social housing: applicants and allocations, Cologne, 1987

Groups	New applicants	%	Allocations	%
Young families	3,144	21.5	1,579	24.3
Elderly	2,309	15.8	1,402	21.6
Students, etc.	3,789	25.9	893	13.7
Single parents (1/2 children)	1,938	13.3	1,200	18.4
Single parents (3+ children)	212	1.5	173	2.7
Families (3+ children)	1,227	8.4	398	6.1
Handicapped	1,986	13.6	860	13.2
Total	14,605	100.0	6,505	100.0

Source: Amt für Wohnungswesen der Stadt Köln (quoted in Kreibich, 1991).

From the 1970s on, there was increasing concern about both social and physical problems on large outer-city social housing estates. Although the scale of these problems and the degree of social segregation by housing tenure and location are considerably less than in Britain and France (Emms, 1990), nevertheless there were increasing concentrations of households on social security, the poor, the old, the unemployed and foreigners (Power, 1993). From 1983 onwards, federal government money under the Urban Programme (*Städtebauförderung*) began to become available both for research on experimental projects and for physical renewal schemes in social housing (Emms, 1990; Power, 1993). These funds were supplemented by state and local authority expenditures, as well as contributions from the social housing enterprises themselves. Renewal schemes combined physical renewal measures with changes in management style and a greater role for tenant participation. In some cases, efforts were made to change the social mix – in Hamburg and Bremen, for example, the rent tax was abolished to encourage better-off households to stay in the sector (Power, 1993).

The change to the taxation status of non-profit housing enterprises, coupled with other changes in the 1980s which made the early repayment of subsidised loans more attractive, means that the size of the social housing sector is rapidly shrinking, despite the recent increase in output under the 'third subsidy system' (see below). Kreibich (1991) calculates that in Cologne half of the social housing stock in 1987 will have changed status by 1997, and another estimate suggests that half the stock of 4 million dwellings nationally will have left the sector by 1995 (van Vliet, 1990). This development will increase trends towards polarisation in the German housing system. In the past, polarisation (or residualisation of the social sector) has not been as severe as in Britain because of the nature of the social sector and the existence of a large diverse private rented sector. But with the upgrading of much of the private rented stock, and the disappearance of a large proportion of the social sector, the poorest and most disadvantaged will more and more have to rely on the part of the social sector which remains under the control of the city authorities. These households 'will be increasingly concentrated in problem estates with unfavourable design (e.g. high-rise, high-density), peripheral location and rising rents' (Kreibich, 1991, p. 77).

Private rented housing

Investment in housing has been relatively favoured in the German taxation system (Tomann, 1990) and there is a particularly favourable tax treatment for new investment in private rented housing (Hubert, 1993). As a result, Germany continues to have a large private rented sector, the largest in the EU, in which higher income private individuals as well as large commercial companies are investors (Oxley and Smith, 1993). Until 1990, investors were not required to pay the (relatively low) annual land tax for the first ten years after construction (this advantage has now been abolished as part of a more general tax reform). As with other investments, relevant costs – interest, depreciation, management and maintenance – can be deducted from revenue for income tax purposes. Losses from rented housing can be offset against income from other sources. The depreciation allowances are an important source of subsidies to private rented housing (Hubert, 1993).

About half of the sector was built before the Second World War. Although there have been, and continue to be, high levels of new construction for private renting in Germany (unlike in Britain, where there has been virtually no new private rental construction for more than fifty years), the level of output has fallen recently: it has been estimated that only around 30,000 new units for private letting were completed in 1989, 14 per cent of total output (Oxley and Smith 1993).

Rent levels for new tenancies are unregulated, and hence set at market levels. Tenants have security of tenure, with landlords only able to secure possession on certain specified grounds. For existing tenants, the key concept is that of *Vergleichsmiete* (rent of a comparable dwelling). Landlords can increase the rent by reference to the rent of other contracts that have been agreed locally during the last three years, subject to an upper limit that existing rents cannot be increased by more than 30 per cent within a three-year period (currently reduced 'temporarily' to 20 per cent within three years). The aim is to prevent rents for existing tenants lagging too far behind those of new contracts. Recent evidence, however, suggests that rents on new lettings are in fact considerably higher than rents of longer-standing tenancies, reflecting both current shortages and the effects of the rent review legislation (Hubert, 1993).

Private renting in Germany, unlike in Britain, is a large, diverse tenure providing for a wide range of mainstream needs. In a number of important ways it is still seen as the 'normal' tenure. It provides a realistic alternative to either owner-occupation or social renting for millions of households. The majority of households who become owner-occupiers will spend many years as private tenants first. The operation of the sector provides a good exemplar of the philosophy of a social market economy: a reasonably strong regulatory framework which emphasises quality within which entrepreneurial activity provides for needs. The price to consumers is moderated by a combination of state controls and competitive market pressures. However, in the last few years, housing shortages have led to a breakdown in the broad political consensus on housing policy. In particular, the government appears divided between those who favour further legislation to limit rent increases for sitting tenants, and those who fear this will mean the reimposition of rent controls and hence disincentives to investment (Hubert, 1993).

Housing outcomes

Supply of housing

Table 5.3 gives details of the supply of new housing in the former West Germany since 1970. From an annual total of nearly 500,000 in 1970 (and over 700,000 in 1973) output fell sharply to only just over 200,000 p.a. in the late 1980s. From then on, as the private sector responded to higher rents and unmet demand, and government responded to housing need and public pressure, completions have steadily increased, almost doubling by 1992. The

Table 5.3 Housing supply in West Germany (thousands), 1970–1992

Year	1–2 family buildings	Multi-family buildings	Total*
1970	196	249	478
1975	195	210	437
1980	249	114	389
1985	152	133	312
1986	141	86	252
1987	125	71	217
1988	123	63	209
1989	141	74	239
1990	127	97	256
1991	134	135	315
1992	137	185	375

Note: * includes units in existing buildings.
Sources: Duvigneau and Schonefeldt (1989); Hamm (1993a).

target set by the Housing Minister of 1 million new homes in the period 1990–2 was almost achieved – Hamm (1993a) argues that it was only the delay in the execution of some contracts that prevented the target being reached. Output in 1993 was expected to exceed 400,000 (Hamm, 1993a). Further detail on the supply of social housing is given in Table 5.4. Output of social housing fell from over 100,000 at the beginning of the decade to under 40,000 at the trough in 1988. It then expanded rapidly to around 100,000 in each of the years 1990–2. In 1992, there were in addition another 18,000 social units completed in the new *Länder*. In 1993, it was expected that 150,000 new social units would be built in East and West Germany together (Hamm, 1993b). Looking at the allocation of the programme between rental and owner-occupied housing, we find that the proportions have changed markedly at different times. In 1986 and 1987, two-thirds of the programme was for owner-occupation, while in the last few years almost two-thirds has been for rental. In recent years, a growing proportion of social output has been financed through the more flexible, but less generous and less permanent 'third subsidy system'. Introduced in 1989 (although not accepted by all *Länder*), this now accounts for about one-third of total social output (Hamm, 1993b, Table 1).

Demand for housing

The demand for housing is a function of demographic, social and economic trends. In terms of demography, the numbers of households in Germany has continued to grow, accompanied by a decline in average household size.

Table 5.4 Social housing output in West Germany (thousands), 1980–1992

Year	Rented	Owner-occupied	Total
1980	40	57	97
1981	46	47	93
1982	59	40	100
1983	59	45	104
1984	40	40	80
1985	30	39	69
1986	17	35	52
1987	13	28	41
1988	13	26	39
1989	39	26	65
1990	62	29	91
1991	64	32	96
1992	64	35	100

Source: Hamm (1993b).

These trends are broadly in line with experience in other European countries (Table 5.5). In terms of economic factors, GDP per head at constant prices and constant purchasing power parities has risen by about 50 per cent between 1970 and 1989, about the same as in France, Britain and the EU as a whole. Earnings however have not risen as fast in Germany over this period as elsewhere (Kleinman, 1992, p. 6). Unemployment until recently has been relatively low in Germany, with a standardised unemployment rate of 4.3 per cent in 1991, compared with 8.7 per cent in the United Kingdom and 9.5 per cent in France (Britton, 1993). However, considerably higher unemployment rates exist in some urban areas.

Dwelling stock

With the exception of Denmark, West Germany has the highest proportion of dwellings per 1,000 inhabitants in the EU (Ghekiere, 1991, p. 41). Between 1978 and 1987, the stock of dwellings grew by almost four million – over 16 per cent of the 1978 stock (Table 5.6). There were 2.5 million more owner-occupied homes at the latter date, while the social rented sector had fallen by some 700,000. In terms of amenities, West Germany does better than France, Belgium and to some extent Britain, but not so well as the Netherlands and the Scandinavian countries (Table 5.7).

Housing costs

Comparisons of housing costs across countries are fraught with all sorts of measurement and definitional problems. Table 5.8 presents some indicative evidence on housing costs as a proportion of household expenditure. The data in the table are not, however, strictly comparable. This evidence suggests

Table 5.5 Households and average household size, 1970–1987

| | Households (millions) | | | Average household size | |
	1970	1987	% change	1970	1987
Netherlands	3.9	5.8	48.7	3.2	2.5
West Germany	22.0	27.0	22.7	2.7	2.4
France	16.2	20.9	29.0	3.1	2.7
Belgium	3.2	3.7	15.6	3.0	2.7
UK	18.6	22.8	22.6	2.9	2.5
Denmark	1.8	2.2	22.2	2.7	2.3
Sweden	3.3	3.7	12.1	2.5	2.3

Source: Boelhouwer and van der Heijden (1992, Tables 2.1 and 2.2).

Table 5.6 Change in housing stock (millions, percentage), West Germany, 1978–1987

	1978	%	1982	%	1987	%
Owner-occupiers	8.5	37.5	9.3	40.1	11.0	42.0
Rented	14.1	62.5	13.9	59.9	15.3	58.0
private	10.1	44.8	10.4	45.0	11.9	45.4
social	4.0	17.7	3.5	14.9	3.3	12.6
Total	22.6	100	23.2	100	26.3	100

Source: Ghekiere (1991, p. 284).

Table 5.7 Amenities (percentage), various dates, 1980–1988

	Central heating	**Bath or shower**
Netherlands	73	98
West Germany	70	92
France	68	85
Belgium	51	76
UK	66	97
Denmark	88	95
Sweden	99	99

Source: Boelhouwer and van der Heijden (1992, p. 39).

Table 5.8 Housing costs as a percentage of total household expenditure based on current prices, 1975–1987

	1975	**1980**	**1985**	**1986**	**1987**
Netherlands	13.9	15.9	19.4	19.0	18.0
West Germany	17.4	18.8	21.9	21.1	20.6
France	15.8	17.5	19.1	18.8	18.9
Belgium	15.4	16.4	18.7	17.5	17.1
UK	18.3	18.8	20.7	20.4	–
Denmark	22.8	27.0	25.4	25.2	26.6
Sweden	21.7	25.0	26.4	25.6	25.2

Source: Boelhouwer and van der Heijden (1992, p. 31).

that housing costs have risen as a proportion of the household budget in Germany over the period 1975–87, and that the current proportion is higher in Germany than in the Netherlands, France and Belgium, about the same as in Britain, but lower than in Denmark and Sweden.

House prices in Germany are relatively high in relation to incomes. Calculations show that the price of an average value house in West Germany in 1984 was equivalent to about 20,000 hours of work by the average worker, compared with about 9,000 hours in Britain and about 10,000 in France (Nationwide Building Society, quoted in Whitehead *et al.*, 1992). Putting it another way, the ratio of average house price to GDP per head in 1988 was 8.6 for West Germany, 6.3 for the United Kingdom and 5.1 in the Netherlands (Holmans, quoted in Whitehead *et al.*, 1992). Once again these international comparisons cannot be exact – for example there will be differences between countries in the quality of the 'average' house – but the tables can give a broad idea. Rents in Germany have risen faster than inflation for most of the last decade, and in 1992 rose faster than incomes too. This trend has continued: in May 1993 the annual rent rise was calculated to be 5.7 per cent with a particularly strong rise of 7.7 per cent noted in the social rented sector (Hamm, 1993a).

Urban renewal and gentrification

Urban renewal policies in the last twenty years have been relatively successful in renewing the physical fabric of central city areas, and improving urban environments. The very success of such policies has, however, worsened the position of the economically weaker groups in society. This has come about both through the physical displacement of poorer households as an area gentrifies, and through the loss of cheaper inner-city private rental housing through modernisation and conversion.

Conflict between local residents and public authorities in Berlin over urban renewal is fairly well known (see Hass-Klau, 1986, for example). But gentrification and social change associated with housing and urban renewal affect other cities also. Dangschat (1990) points out that the economic revitalisation of Hamburg was accompanied by a rise in the numbers on social assistance from 151,000 in 1987 to 167,000 the following year, and an increase in homelessness from 8,000 to 26,000 between 1988 and 1989.

Housing shortage and homelessness

From the mid-1980s on, the 'balanced housing markets' of earlier in the decade gave way to a new housing shortage. While this new shortage was most severe in the big cities, it was by no means confined to them. The crisis of the 1980s hence differed from the so-called 'new housing shortage' of the 1970s, which was more geographically specific. The origins of the shortage were internal: increased household formation and rising expectations combining with reduced construction and the loss of cheaper rented property through improvement activity. But the shortage was swiftly compounded by large-scale migration from Eastern Europe and elsewhere.

The number of *Aussiedler* migrating to the Federal Republic increased from 80,000 in 1987 to 200,000 in 1988, 40 per cent of whom went to North Rhine-Westphalia (Kreibich, 1991, p. 75).

The results of this renewed housing pressure were rapidly rising rents, longer queues for social housing and increased homelessness. Increased housing demand has not translated into increases in owner-occupation. Most of the new households – students, young people, foreigners – do not have the economic ability to become home-owners. Pressure is therefore put on the social sector at the same time as the size of the sector is diminishing. From 1988 the problem reached crisis proportions, with many cities resorting to bed and breakfast accommodation, and the use of gymnasia and other non-residential space for emergency accommodation. Cologne's Director of Housing said in 1988: 'We are fully booked up. There is absolutely no available flat in social housing' (quoted in Kreibich, 1991, p. 75).

Despite the success of the house-building programme announced by the federal government in response to the crisis, the problems continue. The gap between demand and supply remains and the *Deutsches Institut für Wirtschaftsforschung* (DIW) estimates that at least 500,000 flats need to be built each year to fight homelessness effectively by the year 2000 (Wilderer, 1993). The shortage, according to Wilderer (1993), affects middle-class as well as less well-off households. But the brunt of the problem is, of course, borne by the poorest. Estimating the number of homeless in Germany is difficult because there is no legal definition which adequately covers all groups (Osenberg, 1993). However, the numbers of homeless people who were directed into casual wards by law in North Rhine-Westphalia rose from 43,000 in 1989 to nearly 60,000 in 1992. In 1990, a federal working group on homelessness estimated 130,000 single homeless, 300,000 persons in casual wards, 100,000 persons in hotel rooms, 100,000 persons in asylums and psychiatric hospitals, and 200,000 immigrants in transitory lodgings (Osenberg, 1993).

Assessing housing policy in West Germany

Over the last twenty years the stock of housing has both expanded and been considerably improved. Most households are able to obtain adequate accommodation, and have seen their standards of housing consumption rise considerably. The German housing system is characterised generally by high quality and space standards. But a growing minority live in inadequate accommodation, unable to gain access to the mainstream stock. As in other areas of social policy, there is clear evidence of the emergence of a 'two-thirds society'. At the same time, the degree of polarisation within the housing system and social segregation by housing tenure is less than in Britain. A much smaller proportion of households depends on housing benefit to secure adequate accommodation. Despite the existence of many large social housing estates with a familiar catalogue of physical and social problems, in general social housing is distributed more evenly through the stock.

Home-ownership remains a goal of German housing policy, but not a goal that is pursued in such a relentless way as has been the case in Britain recently. Certainly, one does not have the impression of owner-occupation being regarded almost as a right. In Germany, owning one's own home is seen as a major commitment, to be entered into only when one is already firmly established within both the labour and housing markets. Lending policies are more cautious, the system is more regulated, and speculative trading within the owner-occupied sector much less common.

Equal opportunities issues are much less visible in Germany than in Britain. As discussed in Chapter 9, Germany has not to date seen itself as a country of immigration, still less a multi-ethnic society. Minority households are in a relatively weak position legally and politically, and indeed continue to be referred to as 'foreigners' despite many years of residence or, in some cases, despite having been born in Germany. As a consequence of these important legal, political and cultural differences, issues of race and housing are articulated in a very different way in Germany compared with Britain (Blanc, 1991).

Minorities in Germany often live in the very worst housing conditions. For example, 60 per cent of Turkish families in Berlin lack a bathroom and 25 per cent lack an inside toilet. Turkish households on average pay higher rents for the same size and type of accommodation compared with German households (Gude, 1991). Ethnic minorities have difficulty in gaining access to social housing and stay longer on waiting lists (Blanc, 1991). Social housing organisations often discriminate against them or adopt informal quotas to limit the number of families in a particular block. In general, the approach of public authorities to problems of discrimination and exclusion, in Germany as in France, has been to advocate a 'colour-blind' approach rather than to pursue policies of ethnic monitoring and equal opportunities as in Britain.

The development of housing policy in Germany in recent years shares several similarities with policies adopted in Britain and elsewhere (Ghekiere, 1991; Kleinman, 1992). There has been a greater emphasis on targeting state aid, by moving from production-based subsidies to personal housing allowances. Owner-occupation has been expanded, although at a slower pace than elsewhere in Europe. Greater choice and quality for the majority have co-existed with unmet needs and worsening conditions – particularly with regard to access – for a minority. Central government support to housing has been reduced as a result both of a political commitment to shift provision from the state to the market, and because of pressures on public expenditure. A greater proportion of housing costs has been shifted on to consumers.

At the same time, there are important differences between housing policy in Germany and housing policy in Britain. The housing crisis of the mid-1980s in Germany led to a strong policy response by the federal government, which clearly saw it as its responsibility to take measures to bring the housing market into balance. This contrasts strongly with British policy under the Conservatives which has been characterised by a piecemeal approach, and in particular a rejection of quantitative targets for housing output. Second, housing policy is shared between the different levels of government in Germany. The continuing importance of, and, within defined limits, independent action by, regional and local authorities in Germany contrasts strongly with the centralisation of power in Britain which has left local authorities with little autonomy, particularly in financial matters. Third, despite the rhetoric about markets in Britain, there is a greater practical importance given to markets in Germany in terms of accomplishing housing policy goals. Policy measures are very much governed by the state of the housing market, and the current point in the economic cycle. Finally, there is less adulation of home-ownership as a total solution. Renting is seen as a normal choice for millions of households, and policy initiatives deal at least equally with the private rented as well as the owner-occupied sector.

Housing issues in the new *Länder*

The housing issues and policy choices faced by the federal government and public authorities in the new *Länder* are similar to those faced by reform governments elsewhere in Central and Eastern Europe (see Turner *et al.*, 1992, for example). The difference in the former East Germany is of course the timescale involved, as the housing system of the former GDR undergoes not so much a gradual process of transformation as a sudden incorporation into a western market system.

In the GDR, housing was supplied not as a commodity for which consumers paid a (subsidised) price, but as part of an alternative, non-market reward system. Rents were extremely low, and did not cover the costs of even basic management and maintenance, let alone the construction debts. A large part of the real costs of housing were thus carried by the state. Average living space in the GDR was about one-third below West German levels. From the 1960s on, housing construction in the GDR was dominated by large-scale system-building using pre-fabricated materials. By such methods, giant estates such as Marzahn in Berlin were built. The proportion of state-owned stock rose to more than two in five dwellings by 1989 (Table 5.9). In addition, there was little if any incentive to maintain and repair the housing stock adequately. New building proceeded on the basis that once built the dwellings would need little or no further work, while the extremely low controlled rents in the private sector discouraged any spending on the stock. The lack of expenditure on repair and maintenance, and the increasingly poor quality of new construction, has bequeathed a major problem of stock

Table 5.9 Housing stock in the GDR (thousands, percentage), 1971–1989

	1971	**%**	**1981**	**%**	**1989**	**%**
State-owned	1,698	28	2,447	37	2,889	41
Co-operative	596	10	974	15	1,230	18
Private	3,763	62	3,141	48	2,883	41
Total	6,057	100	6,562	100	7,003	100

Source: Kohli (1993).

quality. Over half the flats in the new *Länder* require some work, and more than one-quarter are classified as being in severe disrepair (Kohli, 1993).

The policy response by the federal government to the problems it has inherited involves privatisation, modernisation and improvement of the stock, increases in rents, the introduction of housing allowances and the goal of creating viable credit-worthy landlords and increasing investment in the sector. Under the unification contract, state-owned properties were transferred to local authorities, which are supposed to privatise the stock step by step, first creating communal housing companies, and then selling on to investors, and, in particular, to tenants (Kohli, 1993). Outstanding debts were transferred to the local authorities along with the stock. The 1 million or so co-operatively owned units remained with the co-ops. However, while the co-ops own the dwellings, many did not own the land on which they stand, and had to negotiate with the local authority to purchase the land. As there was no price recommendation in the unification contract, these negotiations have proved protracted (Kohli, 1993). In addition, there are estimated to be over a million ownership claims from those in the West claiming to be former owners (or their successors) of houses and flats in the new *Länder*.

The continuing debt on the stock is a major problem. The 2.7 million units which passed into the ownership of the local authorities have an associated debt of at least DM 22 billion. Not surprisingly, there was considerable dispute between the *Länder* and the federal government about who should shoulder the burden of this debt (Kohli, 1993). Eventually, however, a solution was found in which companies owned by local authorities and co-ops will be relieved from any debt exceeding DM 150 per square metre provided that they sell 15 per cent of their stock, preferably to the present tenants, within the next ten years. A proportion of the proceeds goes into a special fund, and there are incentives to sell quickly (Hubert, private communication). The federal government has provided considerable funds so far for rehabilitation of the stock. Together with contributions from the *Länder*, Kohli (1993) estimates that this will be sufficient to modernise and repair a quarter of the stock.

The second main strand of policy is in regard to rents, with a goal of raising rents gradually to West German levels. The first stage was in October 1991, when basic rents were raised by DM 1 per square metre per month, and DM 3 per square metre per month in payment for utilities. From 1 January 1993, there were further rises of between DM 1.20 and 2.40 per square metre per month (Dick, 1993; Kohli, 1993). These rent rises were accompanied by an extension of the housing allowance system to the new *Länder*; indeed imposing these rent increases would have been politically impossible without this. Housing allowances are currently more generous in the new *Länder* than elsewhere (e.g. they cover heating and hot water costs) but this difference is being phased out and will disappear from 1995. By June 1992, there were 3.2 million housing benefit claims, 80 per cent of which were made on 1 October 1991, when the first stage of the rent increase was implemented. Nearly two million households receive housing benefit, almost 30 per cent of households in the new *Länder*. This comprises 31 per cent of tenant households (compared with 10 per cent in the West) and 20 per cent of owner-occupiers (1.2 per cent in the West).

As far as sales to tenants are concerned, there are, not surprisingly, differing potentials within the stock. The pre-war stock is probably the most attractive, but subject to former owner claims. Post-war but low-rise stock is probably the most viable for sales to sitting tenants, and Kohli (1993) estimates that perhaps 1 million of the 2.7 million stock could be sold to tenants. The federal government has brought in special measures, including a 20 per cent subsidy of the purchase price to tenants, up to a maximum of DM 7,000 for the first and DM 1,000 for each subsequent family member. These subsidies are in addition to the normal help to owner-occupiers discussed above. However, tenants often have little equity and are either affected by or worried about the rise in unemployment. Also, many of those who could buy do not want to buy their current flat – which is often poorly designed and too small for present family size. The federal government is sponsoring a number of model schemes, involving some 6,500 units, as a form of demonstration project (Kohli, 1993). Sales totalled 2,500 in 1991 and possibly 18,000 in 1992.

Output is increasing in the new *Länder*. Hamm (1993a) finds evidence of a strong growth rate in house-building activity in 1992, and argues not only that there is a good chance that house-building will get going on a large scale, but also speculates that it will act as the engine of recovery in the East. Social output was 18,000 units in 1992, and was expected to rise to 30,000 in 1993 (Hamm, 1993b). This has to be seen against the background of the poor starting position of housing conditions in the East, and the new needs that are thrown up by rapid economic change, and the associated rise in unemployment. According to Buskase (1992), there are about 500,000 households in East Berlin, Sachsen-Anhalt, Saxony and Thuringia looking for accommodation, of which more than 100,000 are classified as in urgent need. Homelessness did not previously exist in the GDR, a consequence partly of low rents and protection from eviction, and partly of the legal impossibility of such a state – people found homeless could be charged with being 'outcast' (*asozial*) and sent to prison (Osenberg, 1993). With the changes, homelessness is rising and is a particular problem for the young, and for those previously living in company housing who lose it if made redundant (Osenberg, 1993).

Prospects for the 1990s

The housing system in Germany is undergoing a considerable amount of change. New pressures come from without – the impact of EU integration, and the waves of migration from the East; and also from within – the social and economic costs of unification, and the rise in both inflation and unemployment.

European economic integration will have important effects, both direct and indirect, on the national housing policies of the individual EU member-states (for a discussion see Priemus *et al.*, 1993, 1994). There will be direct effects through increased capital mobility. Tomann (1993) sees two important consequences for German housing finance of the opening up of financial services in the Single European Market. First, mortgage lenders from elsewhere will come into the domestic market, either by cross-border trading or through the establishment of branches; second, the integration of the securities market will offer new opportunities for securitisation, although Tomann argues that a European market for mortgage-backed securities is still a long way off. In a more competitive market, current providers of second-lien mortgages, which are relatively expensive in Germany, could be vulnerable to British-style providers of 90 per cent+ mortgages including mortgage insurance. *Bausparkassen* in particular might be thought to be under threat in this way, although Tomann concedes that they do have a specific niche in the market.

Freedom of movement in the single market will have rather less of an impact in Germany as the main migratory pressures are from outside the EU. The migration issue will continue to be important in the housing policy sphere. The impact is two-fold. First, there is the issue of responding to need and demand for housing, both quantitatively and qualitatively. Second, and more fundamentally in the long run, is the question of the adaptation of German housing policy and practice to the fact that Germany is now a country of immigration, and is becoming a multi-ethnic society. Issues such as equal treatment and equal access and how to deal with racial harassment and xenophobia will become more important, although the extent to which policy will respond to this new agenda is not yet clear. Third, there is the continuing imbalance between demand and supply in the market. Access difficulties and homelessness will ensure that housing remains a politically salient issue in the 1990s. Allied to this is the fate of social housing. Despite the recent partial revival of federal subsidies to social housing, the sector will continue to decline as a proportion of the stock. Whether the private market will be able to cope with the new and in many ways different housing pressures of the 1990s remains to be seen. Fourth, there is the privatisation and modernisation of the housing stock of the new *Länder*. There are many legal and administrative issues still to be solved, as well as the continuing question of how the costs of this process should be apportioned between the federal government, the *Länder* and the tenants or owners.

More fundamentally, what will be the long-term effects of privatisation and higher rents, particularly in the context of rapid economic and social change? Will the housing system in the East come to resemble that in the West, or will there continue to be 'two Germanies' in housing terms, despite there formally being only one system? Finally, will owner-occupation rise to 'Anglo-Saxon' levels, or will the traditional dominance of the rented sector continue? For some, the growth of owner-occupation is a natural and universal phenomenon, and hence it is Germany's laggardly behaviour which requires explanation. For others, the German experience shows that the Anglo-Saxon obsession with promoting owner-occupation and comprehensive deregulation are not the only ways to run a modern capitalist housing system. In the 1990s, the issue will be the degree to which the specificities of the German system survive in a more integrated Europe.

German housing policy over the last forty years has been characterised by a high degree of political consensus about the boundaries of state and market, and about the extent of the state's responsibilities for different types of need. In the future, many of these constants will be called into question: what types of need from which types of household have a claim on the state and what sorts of policy mechanisms are appropriate to try to deal with them? Housing policy in the 1990s will probably be more difficult and more volatile than it was in the 1970s and 1980s.

Guide to further reading

Hills *et al.* (1990) provides a clear introduction to a comparative study of housing subsidies and housing finance in Britain and Germany. Other useful articles on German housing finance are by Tomann (1990, 1993) and Hubert (1993). A description of the German system of financing owner-occupation can be found in Council of Mortgage Lenders (1990) and problems of repossessions are discussed by Potter and Drevermann (1988). Norton and Novy (1991) contains a range of essays on low-income housing in the two countries; the chapter by Kreibich is especially useful. Power (1993) gives an account of the development of, and current issues in, social housing in five European countries, including Germany, with an emphasis on housing management issues. Emms (1990) covers similar ground, concentrating on policies for the regeneration of deprived social housing estates.

The number of comparative studies of housing policy has increased greatly in the last few years. Boelhouwer and van der Heijden (1992) provides a detailed study of housing systems in seven European countries (Netherlands, Belgium, Germany, Denmark, United Kingdom and France). Kleinman (1992) and Priemus *et al.* (1993, abbreviated version is 1994) discuss the role of the EU and the possibility of a European housing policy. Ghekiere (1991) provides a comprehensive study of housing policies in all twelve European Union countries, while Ghekiere (1992) discusses the role of the European Union in housing policy. Note that these two latter texts are in French. Ball *et al.* (1988) discuss a range of housing issues in a comparative framework. Useful material on the theoretical and methodological problems involved in comparative housing research can be found in Harloe and Martens (1983) and the special edition of *Scandinavian Housing and Planning Research*, 8 (2), May 1991.

Comparative articles on housing policy appear regularly in the journals *Housing Studies*, *Urban Studies* and the *International Journal of Urban and Regional Research*.

Acknowledgements

I would like to thank the following for comments and advice on the text: Franz Hubert, Gunter Krebs, Volker Kreibich and Philip Potter. I would also like to thank Monika Zulauf for research assistance and Andrea Hofling for translations.

Chapter 6

Education and training

Claire Wallace

There has been remarkable continuity in the development of the German education and training systems this century, despite considerable discontinuities in German history. As a result, a very complex and elaborate system linking vocational to academic education has evolved which is an essential component of contemporary German society. By understanding this system many aspects of German society and policy become clear. By virtue of its high-quality training for the majority of German young people, which results in a generally very highly skilled workforce, the education and training system is often looked upon as holding the key to the success of German industry (Rose and Wignanek, 1990). However, such developments have to be seen in the context of the development of German social policy more generally and of the way in which 'youth' has been identified as a target for intervention within it. These policies have not been without problems as worldwide recession and, more recently, the problems of German unification have posed challenges for education and training as they have for other areas of German social policy. Other problems coming to light are the disadvantaged situation of 'foreign' youth, recent immigrants and young women within education and training. Finally, the very success of the educational and training expansion has in itself produced a transformation of German society, including family and life-course patterns as well as wider expectations and values.

This chapter will begin by briefly considering the historical roots of education and training and will go on to describe the different parts of the contemporary system of education and training in more detail. It then looks at the consequences of recession and unification and at the way in which education and training have responded to them. In a final section, it discusses the situation of young women, 'foreigners' and recent immigrants within the system.

The early roots of education and training

As early as the late nineteenth century, young people were identified as an important group in need of protection and control. This needs to be seen in the context of the industrialisation of Germany during that period and the migration, particularly of young people, from the countryside to the industrial urban regions. At the time, this raised the spectre of uncontrolled youth on the streets causing social unrest, and legislation was consequently introduced from the 1870s onwards to control the work, living conditions and behaviour of young people. The churches in particular provided hostels for young people in the urban areas, although most lived in ordinary dormitories. They were assisted by the 'youth savers', whose campaigns for the establishment of educational services were successful particularly after the turn of the century. In the newly unified Wilhelmine Empire, young people were seen as the promise for the future and therefore in need of moulding to the right image (Linton, 1991).

The campaigns of the 'youth savers' resulted in the ascendance of an educational discourse for reforming youth. The way to control and integrate young people as respectable members of society was by educating them. This was proposed as a solution to delinquency as well as being appropriate for working-class youth in the cities more generally. Here, Georg Kerschensteiner's recommendations for 'civic education' were particularly influential. Kerschensteiner argued that education was necessary not just in order that young people should understand their society but also because it was only through education that individuals could reach their full potential. Along with others, he argued for a broad educational programme in a number of fields to replace a narrow technical or craft focus and to cover topics such as the history and culture of the country, the laws and organisations for young people as well as social insurance and welfare legislation. In this spirit, 'Continuation Schools', based on Sunday Schools, were set up for young working-class people who had left full-time education. Although young people themselves, and especially the casual working class, resisted these attempts to 'improve' them, the prodigiously active youth campaigners were able to get these initiatives institutionalised through imperial legislation in 1908 which provided extended vocational education. In 1920, these 'Continuation Schools' were renamed 'Professional Schools' (*Berufsschulen*), the name which they still hold. In 1938, further legislation was passed to make education of this kind compulsory for everyone up to the age of 18: if individuals left full-time education they were to attend some kind of continuing education. At the same time, more strict criteria for the training of apprentices through 'Mastercraftspeople' (*Meister*) were laid down. In this way, through a series of laws from the turn of the century onwards, a tradition of extended education for all young people was institutionalised, even for those who left school at the minimum age.

This laid the foundations for a particularly important feature of the German system, which was the functional integration of extended education and training into the transition process from school to work. What became known as the 'dual system' meant that those who left full-time education continued in part-time education, which could form part of a vocational training programme or 'apprenticeship' through a combination of work experience and continued specialist part-time education, and also had a general educational component.

In the aftermath of the Second World War, Germany's education and welfare systems were in disarray and youth unemployment rampant. Many young people lived as vagrants, existing through crime or black market trading. However, following currency reform and the establishment of an elected government, the situation began to improve. Education and training were seen as key planks of reconstruction policy. The de-nazification of German society required a reconstruction of its education system, while the high-technology, export-driven style of post-war German industry required a highly skilled, high-quality workforce. However, the *Wirtschaftswunder* (economic miracle) which then followed produced new demands for education and training and some new rifts between the generations. This chapter will now describe developments in education and training in Germany since the Second World War in more detail.

Secondary education in Germany

There is virtually no private sector in education in Germany. The state sector is stratified and has been so since its inception in the late nineteenth century. There are three main layers, rather resembling the old British tripartite system. The *Gymnasien* (grammar schools), which take the top quarter of the young population, prepare people for university entrance through the *Abitur* in a strictly academic curriculum. *Realschulen* (intermediate technical schools), prepare young people for a matriculation exam called *Mittlere Reife*, which qualifies them for clerical and technician training. The *Hauptschulen* (general secondary schools) at the bottom end of the educational ladder provide a leaving qualification (*Hauptschulabschluß*) which enables its holders to apply for manual apprenticeship training. Selection in this highly stratified system takes place at age 10 or so during one or two 'orientation years'. There is intense competition to enter the highly prestigious *Gymnasien* because a young person's level of schooling will determine his or her occupational prospects. A few experimental comprehensives were set up in the 1960s but were never widespread. Compulsory full-time schooling normally lasts ten years and ends at age 15 or 16, although this varies between different regional educational authorities.

Figure 6.1 sets out the educational system in Germany, illustrating the many routes through it. In principle, it is possible for a child to move between the three levels of schooling depending upon his or her ability and performance, although in practice this happens rather rarely. On the right-hand side of the diagram the academic track is clearly marked out. However, people who go through the vocational route on the left-hand side are able to improve their chances by taking a 'technical *Abitur*' at a full-time vocational school and then going either to a university or a polytechnic. Students can also transfer between a polytechnic and a university after their first year. This means that there are many connecting bridges across the system as well as routes up. Recent research suggests that it is quite possible for young people in Germany to undertake an apprenticeship to begin with, then to go to a full-time vocational school, then to a polytechnic for a year and then on to university. This option of 'drifting up' the system seems to be taken particularly by young men, who do not always set out with a very clear career orientation; young women seem less likely to take advantage of such opportunities for social mobility (see Evans and Heinz, 1994).

Policy and administrative responsibilites for education in Germany are decentralised, held by the *Länder*. The individual *Länder* have introduced different educational policies over the years, resulting in considerable regional variations. For example, in some *Länder* there are ten years of compulsory schooling and in some only nine. Some have introduced a number of comprehensive schools and others almost none at all. Even the requirements of teacher training can vary between *Länder*. However, some homogenisation is brought about by regulatory bodies at the federal level.

Although the basic structure of the education system in Germany has remained remarkably stable, it has been considerably expanded in the post-war period with new branches, layers and connections being added. Following the *Wirtschaftswunder* of the 1950s and 1960s, it was felt necessary to expand the education and training system to prepare for what was thought to be the new technological future. By the end of the 1960s and the formation of an SPD government, there was an attempt to introduce a more egalitarian system offering increased opportunities to a greater range of social classes. These factors culminated in a number of reforms which were introduced during the period 1969–71 by the Federal Ministry for Education, though it should be remembered that there was considerable variation in the ways they were implemented by the various regional educational authorities. The reforms introduced some comprehensive schools but also extended the 'dual system', making it part of an integrated education and training scheme. One of their aims was to provide comprehensive financial support for

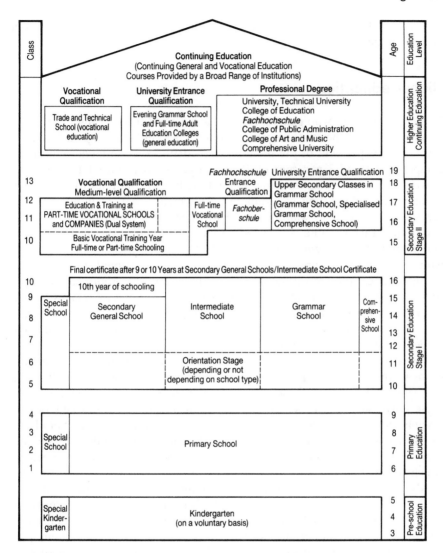

Figure 6.1 Basic structure of the education system of the Federal Republic of Germany, 1992

Source: taken from Federal Ministry of Education and Science (1993).

students, rather like a British mandatory grants system, although in practice little of this was forthcoming because of many subsequent amendments. Nevertheless, the reforms made it possible later for larger numbers of young people to stay in education for longer periods of time: 'youth' came to be viewed as an extended moratorium period during which people pursued education or training. Before explaining this more fully, it is necessary to look first at the different components of the education and training system in more detail.

Higher education

In theory, all those who gain an *Abitur* have a constitutional right to a place at university and the vast majority (about 95 per cent) take up such places. Twenty-three per cent of the population aged 19–26 are in higher education compared with 17.3 per cent of 18- to 25-year-olds in Great Britain. The university degree begins for many students at 19 and continues for about five to six years, culminating in a diploma. This means that, including military service and a possible waiting period for a place in a university, students taking this track spend a protracted period in education: the average age of completion of a first degree in 1990 was 28.4 years for men and 27.5 years for women. Even so, the university intake has more than tripled since 1970. As a consequence, the constitutional right of those with an *Abitur* to take up a university place was modified through a system of *numerus clausus*, which meant that places on popular degrees such as medicine and law were rationed according to grades achieved in the *Abitur*. In practice, this means that some students wait a year or two until a place becomes available.

The shape of higher education changed in the 1970s with the founding of new universities in places such as Bremen, Oldenburg and Bielefeld (to name but three of those well known in social science disciplines). In these universities in particular, new styles of management and new degree disciplines were introduced. However, universities still tend to be very large by British standards, with between 40,000 and 50,000 students. Students themselves can determine how many courses they will take each semester, which means that the university degree can be lengthened to suit personal needs and circumstances. Since student grants are low, a large number of students work part-time (see Chapter 3). Roughly one-third of students are supported at least partially from grants, one-third mainly support themselves and one-third rely on parents, who are legally obliged to support them until the age of 27 (Bargel, 1985). Increased demand has resulted in pressure on the higher education system to deliver a 'mass' rather than an élite education. In addition to the universities, there are also music and art colleges and polytechnics. Polytechnics offer degrees, although not of the same level as a university degree (rather like the difference between an ordinary and an honours degree in Britain), and tend to offer technical rather than academic subjects. They are particularly geared towards the needs of those working their way towards qualifications through the vocational route (see Figure 6.1, above).

In addition to the full-time institutions described so far, there are a number of 'open learning' possibilities. People can study additional subjects through a scheme similar to Britain's Open University, and in addition there are adult education centres and university extra-mural courses which offer an expanded number of places each year. The churches are also active in adult continuing education. For those who wish to improve their education and training there are a variety of part-time and evening study possibilities: this would be the normal way of obtaining a *Meister* qualification, for example (see below).

One very important factor in the development of German higher education was the student revolts of the late 1960s, in which students demanded various university reforms. A more informal atmosphere was introduced: there is relatively little formal ceremony in German institutions of higher education compared with British universities. Some universities became labelled 'red universities' as a result of student activism, which prejudiced the reputations of many of their students in finding positions later. The radical left-wing culture in some institutions drew a strong response from the authorities in the form of the curtailment of some activists' freedom of employment (*Berufsverbot*) in respect of positions in the civil service and some private enterprises. Nevertheless, the student experience of the late 1960s continues to be influential in shaping some middle-class cultures, in ensuring a very strong socially critical voice in Germany and in providing the foundations for the Green and other alternative social movements.

Although there is still a tendency towards class reproduction in the German education system – while 80 per cent of working-class parents wanted their children to continue in education, only 20 per cent obtained access to universities (Bargel, 1985) – there is nevertheless some evidence that educational reform changed the class balance in universities, as illustrated in Table 6.1. However, in interpreting the figures in this table we have to bear in mind the decline in the total number of blue-collar workers during this period, as well as the large numbers in the 'other' category in 1990. Universities remain very middle-class institutions; the erosion in grants along with steeper competition in the 1980s has further discouraged many working-class aspirants.

Since students qualify in largely academic subjects, they tend to be rather unsuited for entry into the labour market. Employers complain that graduates are not the best material for training after having spent so many years in education. Former students face competition from those with more applied skills who have worked their way through higher education by alternative routes. Nevertheless, a university degree remains a necessary qualification for certain occupations such as teaching, law and medicine.

The main problem with this system of higher education is that it takes a very long time for people to complete their degrees, especially if they change courses part way through. The federal government has considered ways of trying to shorten the degree programme by introducing intermediate degrees more like a British or American Bachelor's degree. However, such

Table 6.1 First semester students in higher education according to father's occupational status (percentage), universities and colleges of art and music, former West Germany, 1970 and 1990

Year	Self-employed	Father's occupation Civil servant	White collar	Blue collar	Other*
1970	26.4	25.2	34.0	11.9	2.4
1990	15.3	17.9	34.4	9.3	23.1

Note: 'Other' includes those for whom there are no data available.
Source: Federal Ministry of Education and Science (1993).

suggestions have met institutionalised resistance from the universities, which retain a high degree of autonomy, guaranteed by the constitution, and whose professoriat remain a very prestigious and influential social group.

Vocational training

The vast majority of German school leavers – about five out of six – enter the integrated vocational and educational system, either through extended full-time vocational training or through what is known as the 'dual system'. This means that they work as apprentices for an employer for most of the week and spend a proportion of their time in a vocational school where they learn the theoretical aspects of their trade, along with law, accountancy and a generalised civic education. Nearly all of those who are qualified and who want an apprenticeship place eventually find one, although not necessarily in the trade they were seeking. The dual system is based on the fact that all school leavers are required to undertake two more compulsory years of education of at least eight hours per week after the minimum school leaving age. This is undertaken as day release training in special vocational colleges. Even the unemployed or those going straight into employment without training should do this continuing education, although in practice many of those in these groups disappear from the system.

In addition to the 'dual system' there is another layer of education which has been expanding over the last ten years, that of full-time vocational education for which there is a variety of colleges and establishments (see Figure 6.1, above). Some institutions also offer part-time courses. These arrangements form additional steps upwards or across the education and training system at every stage of a young person's career, by means of which they can improve their theoretical or practical training or continue their more academic education.

The comprehensive apprenticeship system, regulated by the 1969 Vocational

Training Act which was based on legislation introduced in the 1930s, is controlled and provided mainly by employers but regulated by the state in what might be termed a 'corporatist' model (see Chandler and Wallace, 1990). There are over four hundred approved occupations all monitored by a central training institution in Berlin, the *Bundesinstitut für Berufsbildung* (BIBB). The BIBB convenes regular meetings between employers, trade unions and federal agencies, including the education establishment, to decide what is required for a particular profession. The BIBB is also responsible for reclassifying, realigning or even abolishing crafts and trades deemed to be obsolete in line with the changing requirements of industry. Each craft and trade is examined by the legally constituted guilds or associations for commerce, trades and professions. This system has developed over a century and so has inherited a high degree of legitimacy. It is secured through a set of legal regulations which mean, on the one hand, that no one can practise a craft or trade or train an apprentice without the appropriate qualification, and, on the other, that the status and legitimacy of qualifications obtained are guaranteed.

In order to understand the importance of this, it is necessary to know that in Germany someone who has learned a trade or occupation and passed the required examinations carries a far higher status than someone who has not. Those with further qualifications such as that of *Meister* or Mastercraftsperson carry correspondingly higher status and rewards. One can be an ordinary bricklayer, for example, or a *professional* bricklayer, which carries a certain authority and status. Trained craftspeople also receive better salaries and with them come other benefits such as better social insurance conditions in respect of unemployment, health and pension benefits. Since social provision in Germany is broadly linked to occupational position, the training system constitutes part of the foundation for social stratification more generally.

What remains distinctive about this integrated educational and training system compared with Britain's is that Germans are able to continue their education and training throughout their working lives. Once they have finished their apprenticeship they can attend part-time or evening classes in order to improve their qualifications (there are many vocational schools catering for this demand). Nine per cent of newly qualified apprentices go into part-time education after finishing their first qualification, and 11 per cent go on into full-time education (Rose and Wignanek, 1990). Some train as Mastercraftspeople and even go on from there either to a polytechnic or to a full-time vocational school (see Figure 6.1, above). Much employment promotion has traditionally been through internal labour markets to which apprenticeship training provides access. In this way, the West German system has been very successful both in legitimating itself and in providing routes for mobility.

There are two stages to the basic apprenticeship, the first being a two-year course in general training and the second being more specific training. The trainee enters into a contract with an employer which may or may not include the second stage, depending on the trade. For example, nearly all those in the building trade went on to 'stage 2' training whereas only about one-third of those in textiles did so. The costs of apprentice training are paid largely by industry and partly by the educational system in providing the off-the-job element. It has been estimated that the costs are split 60:40 between business and the regional authorities who provide the educational component. The employers gain low-paid workers even if they lose them for a day or so each week to the local professional school. Small employers, who provide approximately 70 per cent of places, are the main people to benefit from this system, even though they are not the ones most likely to employ apprentices afterwards (Casey, 1983).

Allowances are low, which means that trainees themselves – and perhaps their parents – bear some of the costs. Recent research carried out in West Germany indicated that although young people there received much lower incomes from their apprenticeship training than was the case for young people of the same age in England, they saw this as a worthwhile sacrifice in order to gain access to much higher wages later on. The importance of a 'profession' is so ingrained that those who did not pursue one felt it necessary to account for themselves rather than vice versa (Evans and Heinz, 1994).

The large numbers of young people in low-paid or unpaid positions as students, apprentices and trainees are explained by the fact that, under the subsidiarity principle, parents are obliged by law to support their children through training. Most parents tend to see this as a worthwhile investment to secure their children's future. But what happens to those who do not successfully pass through the system? It is estimated that about 12 per cent of the age cohort fail to complete an apprenticeship (Lex, 1990). These are most likely to be children of unskilled or semi-skilled manual workers. Over-represented among them are the children of 'foreign' workers, those who did not get a school leaving certificate, recent immigrants and those who left special schools for the handicapped and socially deprived. In eulogising the successes of the German education and training system, many authors forget this significant minority. The 'success' of the system is dependent on low-paid, insecure and unskilled jobs being carried out usually by immigrant workers, who constitute some 8 per cent of the labour-force, or about five million people. The stigmatisation of work without training is reinforced by the fact that these marginal social groups are the ones most likely to do it.

Other problems identified from the 1970s onwards were that there was considerable stratification *within* the apprenticeship training system. Some employers took advantage of the fact that there was an oversupply of apprentices in the trades (bakers, hairdressers and so on) to acquire trained workers who were nevertheless excluded from a full skilled status in other industries (Lex, 1990). Critics have also argued that the system is overly rigid and bureaucratic. More trades can be classified as 'skilled' than in Britain, which makes the construction of skill heavily formalised. The BIBB, too, can sometimes take several years to agree on the reclassification of a profession. Certainly, the system of vocational training rests upon a highly stratified educational system. In practice, however, it also tends to be very flexible. Recent research has shown that young people had little difficulty in moving up the system through a variety of different routes, while some sort of educational or training option was provided at every stage of their careers (Evans and Heinz, 1994). Although trade unions complain that the dual system of apprenticeship training is too heavily controlled by employers, the evidence suggests that German employers have responded creatively to recession by offering more training places rather than less, as has been the case in England.

The consequences of recession

Germany suffered from the consequences of the world-wide economic recession from the mid-1970s onwards. This coincided with the 'baby boom' cohort entering the labour market, so that youth unemployment rose from 0.7 per cent in 1970 to 4.7 per cent in 1980, reaching a peak of 9.3 per cent in 1985 before dropping off slightly to 6.3 per cent in 1991. At the same time, however, educational reform had encouraged more people to remain in education for longer periods of time. The government's response to recession was to expand the training and education system still further in order to absorb the 'baby boomers' of the 1980s and to hope that an upturn in the economy would have taken place by the time this cohort eventually left the system. The employment of apprentices was made more attractive to employers through the lifting of some protective legislation and imposing a payroll tax on employers who did not recruit sufficient apprentices. Employers responded by providing 47 per cent more apprenticeship places over the 1980s in the belief that they would be stockpiling trained workers for the future (Rose and Wignanek, 1990).

A number of 'special measures' were also introduced, including the addition of extra stages in the transition from school to work. In some *Länder*, an extra year of schooling was added to keep young people in education until the age of 18 (Koditz, 1985). A period of basic vocational education (*Berufsgrundbildungsjahr*, BGJ) which was of six to twelve months' duration was introduced, as well as a year of preparation for work (*Berufsvorbereitungsjahr*, BVJ), intended for those who could not immediately begin apprenticeships. This was to count as a year of the apprenticeship. Although these measures began partly as an attempt to create a more comprehensive and unified training system, they soon came to constitute 'warehousing' for young people who might otherwise have been unemployed. In 1987, some 112,000 people joined such programmes, although they never gained much legitimacy with employers who saw them as 'make work' schemes.

One of the consequences of these measures was to increase greatly the competition for apprenticeship places. Popular apprenticeships became oversubscribed, and this led to an escalation of the qualifications necessary to enter them. A *Hauptschulabschluß* was no longer sufficient for some professions, which now demanded at least *Mittlere Reife*. A new development was that some young people with an *Abitur* chose to do an apprenticeship before starting university in order to insure themselves against possible unemployment in the future. This resulted in a situation of rapid 'qualification inflation'. The increasing demand for university places in Germany is indicative of a qualification upgrading throughout the education system, with 88 per cent now leaving with some qualification as against 75 per cent in 1965. More people stayed on in education to improve their qualifications and the additional vocational preparation years added to the amount of time people could spend in extended education. Some who were not able to enter the apprenticeship of their first choice trained first in something else and then retrained in another apprenticeship having completed the first one, or even before they had completed it. By the mid-1980s, some two-thirds were changing courses in this fashion. In the words of one sociologist, education and training became like a 'carousel', with people stepping on and off to improve their opportunities or as their aspirations changed (Krüger, 1990).

The effect of this for the secondary school system has been a general shift upward of the kind illustrated in Table 6.2: more people are now going into grammar and intermediate technical schools and less into the general secondary schools. The result was that young people needed to stay longer in education and become more qualified in order to find good training

Table 6.2 Population in different types of school (percentage), classes 7–9, former West Germany, 1960 and 1991

Type of school	1960	1991
General secondary school (*Hauptschule*)	63.9	33.4
Intermediate technical school (*Realschule*)	15.6	28.7
Grammar school (*Gymnasium*)	20.5	31.1
Comprehensive school (*Gesamtschule*)	3.4*	6.8

Note: *1975 figure.
Source: Federal Ministry of Education and Science (1993).

places: the mean age of starting an apprenticeship rose from 16.5 years in 1980 to over 18 in 1988, while the proportion taking apprenticeships rose from 55 per cent to 75 per cent of the age group under 19 between 1960 and 1985. This then postponed young people's entry into work, causing what has been identified as a 'second stage' transition problem, and indeed in 1982 it was estimated that 13.4 per cent were unemployed after finishing their apprenticeships (Heinz *et al.*, 1987). The same study found that not all got the apprenticeships they wanted: in 1985, 55 per cent did not get into the firm they wanted, 42 per cent needed to travel more than two hours daily to get the training they wanted, while 31 per cent gave up their chosen career altogether and did something else.

Many have argued that Germany has coped far better with rising youth unemployment than other countries in Europe. The problem is far less conspicuous there given that the system has seemed able to absorb surplus numbers. Nevertheless, a problem of hidden unemployment persisted as an estimated 100,000 young people were not registered for work and therefore did not count as unemployed. Many of these were the children of foreign workers (Dehnbostel and Rau, 1986). Others lingered on pre-vocational and other courses since they were not eligible for most benefits until they were over 18 in any case.

The overall consequence of changes to the system of education and training over the last decade has been to create an extended period of adolescence, sometimes called 'post-adolescence', during which people move around the education and training system without necessarily settling on any specific career (Gaiser, 1991). As well as offering more opportunities to young people, these changes have also increased their sense of insecurity since there is no certainty that education or training will lead to a job. Young people have to be more self-aware and make more decisions at all stages of their lives than before. German sociologists theorise that this contributes towards the 'individualisation' of life-styles more generally (see Chisholm *et al.*, 1990; Evans and Heinz, 1994). Some have interpreted the phenomenon as part of a 'de-standardisation' of biographies, as it seems to be linked to a search for individual autonomy and less conventional patterns of family life, such as repeated moving in and out of the parental home (see Jones and Wallace, 1990). In addition, this lengthening period of preparation for work means that young people have to survive for longer on different grants, bursaries and training allowances, or on support from their parents. This disadvantages them in the housing market: in consequence, most have to live with their parents involuntarily for some years. Individuals also face the increasing stress of competition for qualifications and employment or training places (Gaiser, 1991). From this, it might be said that the system of education and training has produced something of a transformation in the way in which people see their lives.

The consequences of unification

The former East Germany had an educational and training system analogous to that of the West – and a very successful one, albeit geared to a different kind of economy. The majority of East Germans went to polytechnical schools, which provided an all-round comprehensive education. Their routes through education and training were shorter: they could leave school from the age of 14; they did a two-year apprenticeship and a four-year higher educational degree. They established families and became independent at an earlier age than West Germans (Dennis, 1985; B. Bertram, 1992; Schober, 1992). Like their West German counterparts, the majority were qualified (85 per cent left school with a certificate), and the majority (85 per cent) had experienced some kind of skilled training (B. Bertram, 1992).

However, there were also important contrasts between the two systems. Education and training in East Germany were oriented towards an economy based on engineering, arms production and heavy industry, with a heavy emphasis on blue-collar work. Work experience was integrated with the school curriculum: young people were encouraged to develop links with local enterprises and agricultural co-operatives or state farms from very early in their school career (Dennis, 1985). In the later stages of their schooling they would spend one or more days a week on work experience. Only one-third of 16- to 20-year-olds worked in the service sector, compared with nearly half of the same group in the West. Furthermore, 75 per cent of young East Germans worked in industry, and their training may have involved being resident in one of the larger enterprises for the duration of their apprenticeship. Only very small numbers served apprenticeships in trades or small businesses, which were a very minor part of the centrally planned economy. While in West Germany 36 per cent of young people served apprenticeships in trades, in East Germany this proportion was only 5 per cent. However, like their West German counterparts they would have spent part of this in a state-sponsored general educational school (Dennis, 1985; Burkhardt, 1992; Schober, 1992). Between 5 and 7 per cent failed to secure apprenticeships; including later dropouts (there was a very high turnover in the youth labour market), about 14 per cent ended up with no trade at the end of their training period (B. Bertram, 1992). Thus, although there was a highly skilled workforce and an extensive training and education system, this was linked to giant, obsolete industries which depended very heavily on trade with the East.

After unification, this trade collapsed and the large industries became industrial dinosaurs. The old industries began to fail or were closed, which made for a shortfall in apprenticeship places. In any case, young people did not want to take apprenticeships in older industries such as metals and chemicals which had no future. Instead, they sought training in new areas such as banking, retail and hotels, although these under-developed sectors provided very few places in the East. Despite a variety of job creation and job retention schemes, unemployment soared, with a real rate of up to 40 per cent in some regions. This included about one in three young people, the most disadvantaged being those with the least qualifications. Consequently, when in 1991 the government promised a training place or a place on a scheme for every school leaver, there were 160,000 young people seeking work and only 53,000 places available (Schober, 1992). Altogether, 40,000 of these places were offered by the Federal Labour Office, the *Bundesanstalt für Arbeit*.

In addition to the special measures for West Germany described earlier, others were introduced in the eastern *Länder*. In order to compensate for the disappearance of firm-based training as larger companies closed or were significantly pruned, the government offered a pooled system of training in outside institutions which could benefit a range of businesses in the area. *Berufsbildung in überbertrieblichen Einrichtungen* (BüE) was paid for by the Federal Labour Office and offered 37,000 places. Another scheme to promote training in small businesses (*Förderung von Ausbildungsplätzen in Kleinbetrieben*) tried both to create training places and at the same time to encourage the development of a small business sector by paying a subsidy of DM 5,000 for each place offered. Although it was anticipated that 50,000 new places would be created, only 10,000 had materialised by the end of 1991. In West Germany, meanwhile, there was a surplus of training places over trainees, due to the demographic decline in the number of school leavers. Consequently, a number of young people commuted to the West to find training places. This was the more desirable option for young people because it represented a way of obtaining training in one of the more modern and future-oriented industries which were missing in the East. One survey found that 43 per cent of young people in the East were definitely prepared to move West for training and 41 per cent said 'maybe' (Schober, 1992).

These developments have changed the career circumstances of young people in eastern Germany. From conditions of labour shortage, there is now a labour surplus. The period of transition from school to work has become more protracted, and its outcome more uncertain: whereas in the past training led definitely to a work placement, now it no longer does so. Whereas in the past most were able to do the jobs they wanted, now they are unlikely to find their first choice of training. At the same time, a study in Leipzig repeating the same questions to different cohorts of school leavers since 1972 has found that young people have become more career-oriented and more concerned with the prestige of the career they pursued (B. Bertram, 1992). Perhaps as a corollary of this, they have lost their concern with doing socially useful work and have become more individualistic and more materialistic in their goals.

Gender divisions

There are important differences between young men's and young women's patterns of education and training in Germany. Those least likely to find an apprenticeship place, for example, are girls and the children of migrant workers. There are very marked lines of occupational segregation according to gender, with some two-thirds of young women concentrated in retail, clerical and hairdressing training. In the early 1980s, while young men were far more dispersed through a variety of trades, these still tended to be in more recognisably technical or craft training (Federal Ministry of Youth, Family Affairs, Women and Health, 1984). Furthermore, whereas 73 per cent of males went on to complete second-stage training, only 27 per cent of females did so. The sorts of schemes taken by young women were the ones most likely to last two rather than three years and to lead to lower status, lower paid jobs (Mayer *et al.*, 1983). In pay terms, too, women apprentices fared comparatively worse, getting only about one-half to one-third of the pay of those in male-dominated occupations.

These gender differences did not just emerge in the 'dual system' of apprenticeships described above; they were an integral part of the structure of education and training more generally. Krüger (1989) has argued that in fact only a minority of girls go into the apprenticeship system – the majority stay in education. Here they enter what she terms the 'moratorium' sector, taking vocational training courses of various kinds and preparing for work through education rather than through apprenticeships. Young men, by contrast, are more likely to take up apprenticeships in the dual system or, less often, to go through the full-time vocational schools. Young women are also more likely to be staying at school to take academic qualifications. However, this greater educational orientation on the part of young women does not necessarily advantage them in the labour market. The courses they take lead either to stereotypically feminine occupations or to no clear vocational goal. This is also a longer process; although young women invest more of their own time and effort in preparing themselves for work than do young men, they have less secure occupational outcomes (Krüger, 1989). Other research indicates that while the multi-route vocational education system encourages young men to raise their aspirations at each stage, it appears to have the opposite effect on young women, perhaps because they have more barriers to cross at each stage (Wallace, 1994).

Young women in West Germany have tended to plan their future employment careers around anticipated domestic responsibilities (Wallace, 1994). A conservative family policy supported by a lack of part-time jobs and the tendency for school to end at midday means that women with children are less likely to go out to work than in Britain. Furthermore, the competition for educational places puts pressure on women to stay home and coach their children in the afternoon. In East Germany, by contrast, the tradition was for women to work full-time, supported by nursery and other provision. However, these facilities have been lost as enterprises have closed and women have found themselves the first to be made redundant (Einhorn, 1992).

The abolition of gender differences was a proclaimed goal of the socialist society of the former East Germany and yet, despite offering similar educational and training opportunities to young women, the workforce was divided on gender lines between women's and men's jobs. Although boy and girl pupils covered the same school curriculum, it is evident that young women entered feminised occupations on leaving school. In 1987, 60 per cent of women school leavers entered just 16 of a possible 259 occupations (Nickel, 1990). During the 1980s, gender differences seem actually to have widened as new technologies displaced women workers from the better jobs and higher levels of pay.

Minority youth

Young people from ethnic minorities have been something of a neglected problem in Germany until very recently. They include children of guest-workers invited over in the 1950s and 1960s, those of ethnic German migrants, those of refugees, migrants from other EC countries and the children of seasonal workers (Bendit *et al.*, 1993). It is estimated that 65 per cent of the 15- to 19-year-olds in this group have no training (Bendit, 1985). They are more likely to attend general secondary schools, to leave without qualifications or to drop out of the educational system early, and are less likely to find apprenticeships. They are also over-represented in special schools for disabled and disadvantaged children. Despite greater recognition of the situation of young people from ethnic minorities in recent government reports, youth services barely reach them, particularly young women. A comparison of the educational qualifications of young people from ethnic minorities with those of all Germans is given in Table 6.3.

Although official policy is one of 'integration and normalisation' (see Federal Ministry of Youth, Family Affairs, Women and Health, 1990), it has been argued that disadvantage is reproduced between generations by the education and training system (Bendit, 1985). In 1981, special measures were introduced to help integrate young people from ethnic minorities into the system of vocational training, known as *Maßnahmen zur beruflichen und sozialen Eingliederung junger Ausländer*. Altogether 15,000 places were offered, with the result that more gained apprenticeship places by 1983. At the same time, however, the federal government put pressure on ethnic minority populations to return to their countries of origin.

In the 1990s, the children of migrant workers have been joined by new groups of asylum seekers, ethnic Germans from the former Soviet

Table 6.3 Qualifications of ethnic minority groups compared with all Germans (percentage), former West Germany, 1988

Type of qualification	Ethnic minority groups[1]	All Germans[2]
Basic secondary school certificate	44	25
Intermediate secondary school certificate	26	37
University entrance certificate	9	32
No certificate	21	6

Source: [1]Bendit *et al.* (1993).
[2]Federal Ministry of Education and Science (1993).

Union, Romania and Poland (many of whom do not speak German), and refugees. As yet there is little information about the experiences of these groups, but their presence is likely to pose new problems and challenges for the education system as a vehicle of their integration into German society.

Conclusion

This chapter has shown that education and training form an essential element not just of German social policy, but of the structure of German society more generally. The very high regard accorded to the development of skills and expertise, along with later rewards in terms of status, security and other benefits, form an integral part of contemporary German culture. Education and training can be seen in the context of the development of youth policies in general, in which young people have been regarded as an official target of intervention within the creation and elaboration of the modern German state.

Following unification, Germany has faced new problems which have impinged very directly upon the otherwise rather stable and secure education and training systems. The rise of unemployment has brought extensions to provision, though these have still not been able to prevent a dramatic rise in unemployment in the East. The new influx of immigrants has increased awareness of the problems of assimilating young people from other ethnic minorities. Finally, there is increasing awareness of the disadvantaged situation of young women, a problem which is particularly acute in the eastern *Länder*. These emerging problems of gender and ethnicity seem likely to lead to new policy debates and developments in the future. Despite Germany's current economic problems, however, their legitimacy among employers, policy-makers and the general population means that a basic commitment to education and training remains.

Guide to further reading

A general guide to systems of education and training in Europe can be found in Chisholm (1992), who also gives a good coverage of the German one. A number of studies have been carried out in recent years which compare British and German education and training: results can be found in Bynner and Roberts (1991) and Evans and Heinz (1994).

The Federal Ministry of Education and Science produces booklets giving up-to-date educational statistics each year in English and in German and these can be obtained free from the Ministry in Bonn. The Federal Ministry of Women and Youth funds a Youth Institute in Munich which carries out regular research on youth issues. Highlights of this can be found in the new journal *Diskurs*. The Ministry also produces bi-annual reports on aspects of youth affairs which are a useful source of information, but a more accessible and lively summary is provided in Gaiser *et al.* (1985), produced by the researchers at the Youth Institute.

Note

All the statistics used in this chapter, except where otherwise indicated, are taken from Federal Ministry of Education and Science (1993).

Acknowledgements

I would like to acknowledge the help of the *Deutsches Jugendinstitut* in producing this chapter, and of Wolfgang Gaiser and colleagues from Leipzig in particular, who supplied me with material and answered my questions. Many of the background ideas are based on research in which I was involved between 1990 and 1991 and which surveyed young people in education and training in the United Kingdom and West Germany; this was funded by the Anglo-German Foundation and formed an extension of the Economic and Social Research Council's 16–19 Initiative. I am indebted to all who worked on those projects. Finally, I would like to thank Lynn Hayes for her encouragement and comments.

Chapter 7

Personal social services

Walter Lorenz

Personal social services in Germany reflect the character of the country's social policy structure and general political tradition. Since the 1970s, the term *Sozialdienst* (social service) has gradually found acceptance as comprising two basic types of services, the *Allgemeiner Sozialdienst* (ASD, general social service) and the *Spezieller Sozialdienst* (special social service), but these labels by no means refer to instantly recognisable organisational structures constituting a uniform national pattern. Instead, they refer more to professional principles of social work delivery which slowly became established with the advent of large numbers of professionally trained social workers during the 1970s. The significance of this is that the personal social services as professional social work services have never been given universal organisational recognition in Germany in their own right. They have had to create a space for themselves within the existing institutions of social welfare, which were by no means created on social work principles. Social services exist dispersed over a variety of statutory organisations and departments such as welfare, youth and health departments, and attached to schools, hospitals and family advice services; meanwhile, there are plans to transform the probation service into a social service within the justice departments of the *Länder*. They also operate within the service array of the voluntary welfare organisations. For the purposes of this chapter, the terms 'voluntary' and 'private' for German welfare organisations are used interchangeably and refer to non-governmental, non-profit-making associations which, as *freie Träger* or *private Vereine*, have privileged status in German law. Unless otherwise specified, they are highly professionalised services and may or may not draw on the work of volunteers. To add to this confusion, the administrative position of statutory departments such as youth, social and health departments varies from place to place. An at times very intense debate about a standardised organisational solution to these historically contingent discrepancies has not yet yielded tangible results. Instead, a third factor in service provision gained enormous momentum during the 1980s, probably on account of the inflexibility of the established organisations: self-help initiatives and independent social movements concerned with social issues became a force to be reckoned with in the delivery and transformation of personal social services.

Nevertheless, an elaborate and in most cases well-coordinated network of services does exist in Germany which caters for all personal social needs, prescribed very broadly in paragraph 8 of the Federal Social Welfare Act (*Bundessozialhilfegesetz*, BSHG) as 'help for individuals in special circumstances' ('*Hilfe in besonderen Lebenslagen*'). This reflects a fine tuning of more general statutory welfare provisions to the particular needs of individuals, the aim of which was to individualise and personalise the administration of welfare and to engender a sense of justice and fairness which had originally given rise to the profession of social work. In the 1970s, social policy in West Germany resorted to individualising and personalising its provisions on a large scale. The goal of a *bürgernahe Sozialpolitik* ('social policy brought close to citizens') was pursued not through radical organisational changes but by professionalising and expanding the existing welfare delivery systems of the statutory and the voluntary sector on an unprecedented scale. Both politically and economically, welfare services play a major role in German society, with the voluntary sector employing more staff than the statutory sector by a ratio of about 1.75 to 1. To put this into perspective, the major private welfare associations in 1990 together employed 3 per cent of the German labour-force and more people than are employed by the entire motor industry (Rauschenbach, 1991).

This chapter will first explore the historical background to these developments in an attempt to make visible a service which, from a British post-Seebohm perspective of integrated social service departments, might almost be deemed not to exist. And while the creeping privatisation of social services in the United Kingdom might produce structures which superficially resemble the plethora of German 'contracted out' services, this historical analysis will help to underline fundamental policy differences.

The historical background

During the latter half of the nineteenth century, three characteristic traits of German social services began to take shape which were to assume lasting significance. First, poor relief became a matter of public administration through which the bourgeoisie demonstrated its competence in running the state's affairs at local level and in performing the task of social integration in the new nation-state. The 'Elberfeld system', which made it the duty of citizens to become involved in the delivery of welfare services, was eagerly adopted by other German towns and cities (Chapter 1). Politically, the relationship between local authorities and the central state was regulated by the principle of local self-government (*kommunale Selbstverwaltung*), which became the cornerstone of local democracy and is today anchored in Article 28 (2) of the Basic Law. Local authorities are free to create their own services with the immediate participation of citizens and to take full responsibility for their actions, although they carry out their functions on behalf of the state. The close coordination between (increasingly full-time and paid) 'outreach workers' assessing people's needs and city officials deciding on benefits and entitlements sets a lasting pattern for the distinction in German social services between front-line, outreach work (*Außendienst*) and office-based work (*Innendienst*).

Second, the efforts of the private sector, at least as far as bourgeois initiatives were concerned, were also largely geared towards supporting the 'national cause' and furthering the micro-level integration of Germany which had been achieved at the macro-level through the founding of the German Reich in 1871. The organisational and legal structure of the *Verein* (a term which carries the English meanings of a society, association or club but which in German has a distinctive legal status) became a central component in this process of nineteenth-century German integration. It 'served new classes and groups to emancipate themselves from bourgeois society as well as stabilising and safeguarding conversely the bourgeois society against disintegration into classes, against the rise of class society' (Nipperdey, quoted in Sachße and Tennstedt, 1980, p. 238). In order to secure their power base, German charitable organisations formed large umbrella organisations as the fora in which spheres of influence could be delineated. In addition, a central 'broker institution' was founded to promote efficiency and achieve national uniformity in approaches to the poor. The German Society for Private and Public Welfare (*Deutscher Verein für öffentliche und private Fürsorge*) represented both sectors, which jointly determined the course of social policies and of service delivery systems. The balance between the autonomy afforded to these private entities and their firm, legally protected and official place in the national agenda of the state mirrors the delicate balance of responsibilities between local authorities and the state. Both relationships can be regarded as setting the pattern of subsidiarity which came to be the key principle of German welfare delivery (see the Introduction).

The third characteristic of German personal social services, which again has its roots in developments of the late nineteenth century, is the idea that social problems are amenable to educational measures and that education in its broadest sense can transform and reform society. The conceptual heritage which accounts for social pedagogy being the distinct professional orientation of German social services can be traced back to the movement of 'reform pedagogy' as well as to the autonomous youth movement of the turn of the century which revitalised the reform spirit. Educational reformers like Diesterweg and Natorp widened the scope of the educator/pedagogue far beyond the narrow confines of the school: society as a whole needed educating so that its members could learn to function as a society (Lorenz, 1994). Social pedagogy was conceptualised as the practical, methodical counterpart to social policy: it represented a means of helping individuals to become truly members of society, to fully realise their social nature. Its aims were to transcend the destructive, anti-social limitations of individualism without falling prey to the 'lure of socialism'. While education in this sense is certainly a life-long process, youth nevertheless remained the focal point of social pedagogy both as the object of the reformist aspirations of the liberal bourgeoisie, which promoted a range of measures under the heading of *Jugendfürsorge* (youth welfare, which included *Fürsorgeerziehung*, literally 'care education' or residential care), and as the subject of the autonomous youth movement. The *Wandervogel* movement (the 'wandering birds') became a rallying point for the latter, subjective aspect of the significance of youth. It represented a collection of romantic, anti-modernist and to some extent anti-authoritarian sentiments which the state was anxious to incorporate and neutralise. The typically Prussian response was to prohibit all political activities by young people under the age of 18, but at the same time to instigate official youth policies which, as *Jugendpflege* (youth work, in contrast to *Jugendfürsorge*), can be regarded as the beginning of a statutory youth work policy and which, in turn enlarged by family support measures, remains a main plank of German social services.

These three characteristics – the central welfare responsibility of the state as a guarantee of national unity and cohesion, the acknowledgement of the importance of civil society in welfare matters through the principle of subsidiarity, and the both conceptually and professionally unifying notion of personalised welfare services as pedagogy – shaped the welfare legislation of the Weimar Republic, laying the foundation for a coherent and progressive structure of personal social services (Landwehr and Baron, 1983). Developments during the Weimar period reflected the popular will to abolish the poor relief system and its stigmatising effects, even if the constant economic crises of the 1920s never allowed the new system to become fully operational. Responsibility for the welfare of citizens was brought in from the margins of stigmatising poverty relief departments and located in new, centrally important local authority departments for welfare (*Wohlfahrtspflege*), youth support (*Jugendfürsorge*) and health (*Gesundheitsfürsorge*).

The social policy of the Weimar Republic affirmed the principle of subsidiarity in all aspects of welfare. The state was limited to offering direct services only when the voluntary sector was not capable of delivering them. A *de facto* division of labour ensued in which the public sector became responsible largely for material benefits and core areas of health care while the voluntary sector tended to take on personal care and preventive responsibilities (Buck, 1983). Opportunities for collaboration between representatives of both sectors were created in the form of legally constituted expert committees (*Fachausschüsse*) and local, regional and national working parties (*Arbeitsgemeinschaften*). These principles and patterns of cooperation negotiated during the Weimar period were adopted almost unchanged in the construction of welfare services and legislation in post-war West Germany.

Within this organisational context and its reliance on volunteers, professional work practices were only gradually able to gain acceptance. By the late 1920s, social work educators like Alice Salomon and Siddy Wronsky had developed a comprehensive methodology of 'social therapy', based in part on their American colleague Mary Richmond's 'social diagnosis', which aimed at a holistic view of clients' total situation. However, practitioners' growing caseloads foiled the systematic introduction of such concepts into the everyday reality of welfare institutions. Equally, the reformist ideas of 'cultural renewal' which the tradition of social pedagogy, revived by the experience of the youth movement, had sought to introduce into the public life of the Weimar Republic had only a marginal impact on the practice of personal social services in the narrower sense, although youth services and community and adult education initiatives were inspired by pedagogic ideals. In a seminal textbook of 1929, Gertrud Bäumer, assistant secretary at the Ministry of the Interior, defined social pedagogy as all assistance towards the successful socialisation of young people which public and private organisations can offer outside and beyond the organisational confines of the school. In her view, social pedagogy (and thereby social services) should become an instrument of social policy equivalent to and parallel with the education system, albeit dispersed over various types of agencies and settings, mediating between schools and families and supplementing the educational endeavours of the latter (Lorenz, 1994).

The vision of an all-encompassing, tightly coordinated social service network became a reality only a few years later, when the Nazi regime usurped social services and welfare agencies for its political ends. The *Gleichschaltung* (forcing into line) by the Nazis of all existing statutory and voluntary welfare agencies was ethically and socially more destructive than the setting up of a new party-led welfare organisation, the *National-sozialistische Volkswohlfahrt* (NSV), which explicitly dealt only with 'deserving' cases in fulfilment of its racist principles. Personnel in the traditional services also became implicated in the racist aims and activities of the state. For members of minority groups labelled 'inferior', any contact with the welfare machinery became potentially life-threatening since the state instigated and exploited an elaborate system of recording, reporting, classifying and segregating in its fanatical pursuit of genetic superiority. Local youth departments changed most profoundly: they had to transfer all their youth work activities to the Hitler Youth organisation, their responsibilities for preventive health (health education and services for mothers and their babies) to the newly standardised health departments, and all other non-control functions like fostering and pre-school education to the NSV. This left them with a hard, punitive core of social control tasks which gave them the reputation of 'youth prosecution departments' (Kühn, 1986). The subsidiarity principle proved to be no guarantee of the autonomy of voluntary organisations and became instead a vehicle for central state blackmail both of organisations and of individuals. Political pressure demanded not just a return to the discriminatory practice of nineteenth-century poor relief but ruthless violations of human dignity and rights such as forced sterilisation, incarceration and murder of people pronounced 'unworthy of life', in which many 'reputable' charities became the unwitting or even deliberate collaborators (Klee, 1985).

Welfare services in the German Democratic Republic

After the defeat of Germany and of National Socialism the two German states developed very different approaches to welfare and particularly to personal social services. The communist ideology of the German Democratic Republic insisted that socialism would obviate the need for separate welfare services. There was no place for the principle of subsidiarity within this political framework. Employment, housing, health and childcare facilities in particular carried high priority as universal entitlements to be provided directly by the state, as spelled out in the pronouncements of the 8th Party Congress of 1971 (Ford, 1987b). These policies did indeed provide a safety net of basic social security, which helped to prevent the widespread social problems arising from poverty, unemployment, destitution, homelessness or unsupported parenthood which form the bulk of the case load of capitalist social services.

Personal social services as such manifested themselves at the official level largely as services incorporated into the functions of local health departments. In 1952, *Sozialämter* were dissolved and cities, districts and regions created Offices for Health and Social Affairs (*Abteilungen für Gesundheits- und Sozialwesen*). Their responsibilities covered allocation of employment and accommodation, retraining of people with disabilities, assessment of special needs and payment of financial benefits, organisation of crèches and residential centres and, in later years, support for elderly citizens and for large families (Weiss *et al.*, 1990). This service operated on the principle of rehabilitation, not just in relation to disabilities but also for people with problems of addiction and delinquency. *Fürsorgerinnen* (who maintained this traditional title to distinguish them from the western *Sozialarbeiterinnen*) employed in these departments and at *Polikliniken* had a mixed educational and social control role in matters of childcare, preventive hygiene, mental health and personal relationships. Some of the 652 *Sozialfürsorgerinnen*, according to GDR statistics of 1988, worked in centres on housing estates, mainly in the bigger cities, although they were far outnumbered by the 6,061 *Gesundheitsfürsorgerinnen* (medical care workers) (Weiss *et al.*, 1990).

At the semi-official level (as the term 'voluntary' can hardly apply to these entities), several organisations were involved in providing social services in the broadest sense. The Red Cross of the GDR played a significant role in rehabilitation, home help and meals on wheels, while a more low-key neighbourhood support organisation, *Volkssolidarität*, which was formed in the immediate post-war period, concentrated on work with elderly citizens. But perhaps the bulk of informal welfare work was done at the workplace through the official trade union (the *Freier Deutscher Gewerkschaftsbund*), whose officials frequently concerned themselves with welfare matters, including alcoholism counselling, as well as through the official youth organisation, *Freie Deutsche Jugend*, and its *Pioniere*.

Welfare activities by the churches were approved by the state in limited areas such as general hospitals, homes for elderly people or people with disabilities, where fees could be claimed from the state insurance system. Other welfare activities such as kindergartens, advice centres and home help services were mainly parish-based and had to be financed from the churches' own funds. The churches received subventions from western partner churches of about DM 160 million annually, a considerable influx of funds which helped to secure the tacit approval by the state of these activities. In 1989, the *Diakonisches Werk* was operating 1,333 and *Caritas* 505 centres and institutions (Blandow and Tangemann, 1992).

Developments in the Federal Republic of Germany

The reconstruction of West German welfare services after the Second World War built on the key principles which the social policy of the Weimar Republic had attempted to integrate. Within this policy framework, the Allied powers emphasised two measures in particular as safeguards against any relapse into totalitarianism: a consistent decentralisation of all services and a strengthening of the ideological diversity of voluntary services.

In the immediate aftermath of the war, Germany experienced social problems on an enormous scale: in the early 1950s, some 10 million refugees and 'displaced people' were to be found on the territory of West Germany; 75 per cent of homes in the cities were destroyed or damaged; unemployment rose to 15 per cent; 600,000 men were invalids as a result of war injuries; and 1.75 million young people had lost one or both parents (Nootbaar, 1983). In these conditions, securing a material basis of existence for the population at large became a priority. The Christian Democrat government thought it preferable to achieve this by covering as many eventualities as possible in the form of legal entitlements rather than through discretionary benefits, a policy which was initially strongly opposed by traditional welfare organisations, which feared for their survival. Achinger, a leading figure in German academic and applied social policy, pondered that 'Social work is in danger of losing financial support as a natural point of entry to dealing with wider aspects of the situation of persons in need', while adding that 'Instead, social work gains the freedom of a true helper who does not have to snoop around before being able to offer money' (quoted in Nootbaar, 1983, p. 260). In contrast to the Weimar period, the unprecedented economic prosperity of Germany's social market economy proved more successful in moving away from poor relief principles, inasmuch as the insurance system was now financially capable of covering most eventualities. By securing these arrangements, the 'social state' (*Sozialstaat*) confirmed its central and explicit role in welfare matters. Just as private insurance played an essential part in providing overall social security, so the voluntary sector managed to strengthen its position in relation to personal social service delivery at all levels. The leading welfare associations were reconstituted and developed elaborate organisational structures which gave each of them a nationwide presence.

The attention of public and private agencies alike was focused on the problems of young people who had been set adrift by the collapse of fascism (which had been the formative influence on their socialisation), by the experience of war itself and by the ensuing economic difficulties which hit young people particularly harshly. In this regard, social workers in the German tradition of social pedagogy had much to offer, both as youth workers promoting democratic political and cultural values in the area of *Jugendpflege* through clubs, leisure activities and cultural programmes, and as educators, counsellors and social therapists in the area of *Jugendfürsorge* for young people with specific social problems.

The German pedagogical tradition itself received a new impetus. 'Re-education', in the sense of a critique of authoritarian styles of leadership and youth organisation, played an important part in early post-war programmes instigated with the support of the Allies, who had sponsored specific training programmes in group work. Training centres such as *Haus Schwalbach* and *Jugendhof Votho* became symbols of a new era in social pedagogy, which nevertheless endeavoured to connect to the concepts and approaches pioneered in the 1920s. Many of the American and British trainers were indeed German refugees like Gisela Konopka, Hertha Kraus, Annemarie Schindler and Magda Kelber, who had integrated their German traditions of social pedagogy with the social work and social group work concepts of their host countries (Lorenz, 1994).

With these modifications, the three traditional key characteristics of German welfare fitted into the Allied blueprint for the social reconstruction of Germany, and indeed into the Cold War agenda of making Germany a front-line paragon of freedom and democracy. Personal social services once more came to play an important part in this wider political agenda, which was later reactivated forcefully in the process of German unification.

Main services and service providers

As stated at the beginning of this chapter, personal social services in Germany do not follow a uniform organisational pattern, but are distributed across several types of public and private or voluntary service providers (*Träger*), with the private, non-profit-making sector being particularly strong. The responsibilities of the public sector are divided between statutory administrative bodies for a particular area (*öffentlich-rechtliche Gebietskörperschaften*), which means departments of local or regional authorities which carry out those functions prescribed by legislation in the areas of youth support (*Jugendhilfe*), social assistance (*Sozialhilfe*) and health (*Gesundheitshilfe*). Depending on the legal framework, these departments distinguish between federal, state (*Land*), district (*Landkreis*) and local levels. These usually very large administrative structures are organised in sections (*Dezernate*), each dealing with a cluster of local policy issues (culture or environment, for example), of which 'social affairs' normally forms a separate unified *Dezernat*. This section is in turn made up of separate departments, such as the welfare department (*Sozialamt*), the local youth department (*Jugendamt*) and the health department (*Gesundheitsamt*).

This structure is replicated at the different administrative tiers. Youth authorities, for instance, are to be found at every level of public administration. Youth departments (*Jugendämter*) constitute the immediate local unit which ensures the provision of a variety of appropriate services for children and young people in accordance with the 1991 Children and Youth Services Act (*Kinder- und Jugendhilfegesetz*, KJHG). The regional youth department (*Landesjugendamt*) represents an intermediary level and can take the organisational form either of a state (*Land*) authority or of a local authority (statutory body established by associations of local authorities), depending on the constitution of the respective *Land*. Above them are the higher regional youth authorities (*oberste Landesjugendbehörden*), charged with administrative and planning responsibilities for the entire *Land* with respect to both statutory and voluntary youth provision. Finally, the Federal Ministry for Women and Youth fulfils an overall coordinating and planning role, without however interfering in the autonomy of the regional governments (Köhnen, 1992).

In practice, this means that social services (*Sozialer Dienste*) may be part of any one of these departments, for instance the *Sozialamt*. In this case they would function parallel with a sub-section dealing with social assistance

(*Sozialhilfe*), for example to unemployed people, war veterans or people in special financial crises, and another section responsible for residential and day care. The services of the welfare department would then include counselling and advice centres, work with elderly people and people with disabilities, hospital social work and a range of specialised services (*Hilfe für Personen mit besonderen sozialen Schwierigkeiten*), such as those for homeless people.

Alternatively, social services may be part of the youth department, as an expression of the high priority of youth welfare in preventing other social problems. These arrangements also seem best suited to the training and expertise of front-line social work staff in social pedagogy. The Children and Youth Services Act again mentions two broad areas of work as constituting the overall duties of the youth departments: 'remedial' responsibilities (traditionally *Jugendfürsorge*) for young people and their parents in the form of counselling (*Erziehungsberatung*), family work, day care, residential care and fostering, and the preventive-universal activities traditionally associated with youth work (*Jugendpflege*) in youth centres such as leisure pursuits, play and holiday schemes, cultural and educational programmes and youth exchanges (for detail and discussion, see Lorenz, 1991). Staff in both sectors usually have a social work or social pedagogy qualification, although the title used in the preventive field is *JugendpflegerIn*. According to the Act, youth departments consist of professional and administrative staff, and a youth welfare committee (*Jugendhilfeausschuß*, JHA), which is composed of local council members, representatives of statutory bodies, youth associations, voluntary organisations dealing with young people, as well as of other individuals with expertise in the field of youth work (Köhnen, 1992).

A third administrative model, not as frequent as the first two, allocates social services to the public health department. This is only possible in *Länder* where public health services have become the responsibility of the local authority or *Kommune*. Health departments were standardised in the early years of the NS regime and given a domineering role; owing to the lack of fundamental legal reforms in this area after the war they still carry wide-ranging social control functions. While in the early 1950s the majority of *Fürsorgerinnen* were employed by the public health departments of local authorities, the welfare function of these statutory departments declined during the 1960s as medical services boomed. However, many specialised social work services have been developed within the health field such as those in social psychiatry, family planning, addiction counselling and preventive medicine.

In a fourth model, the social services form their own separate department (*Amt für Soziale Dienste*, traditionally also called *Amt für Familienfürsorge*) at the same administrative level as the welfare, youth and health departments. This structure was advocated in 1983 by the *Deutscher Verein*, the body representing both public and private sectors of welfare (above), and has since been the subject of much debate and experimentation. Its main advantage lies in the greater immediacy with which it is accessible to clients and with which it can, in turn, be oriented towards a particular neighbourhood or district (*Sozialraumbezug*). The fact that with this model various welfare departments can use the same social work staff for information and consultation on families both helps to avoid clients being inundated with a number of different 'official visitors' and provides a basis for networking among client groups, as well as allowing for various crises and difficulties in the life of clients to be seen in a wider, 'holistic' context. In this way, the department can make an important contribution to area-specific social planning as the cumulative effects of different causes of social stress and their structural origins become more readily visible to front-line workers. However, the experience of some local authorities operating this model has also shown that the major reorientation of social work from 'cases' to 'neighbourhoods' has not in fact happened. This is partly due to the generic staff's heavy load of assessment and counselling work on behalf of other departments and partly to financial restrictions impeding the development of a truly comprehensive service. Social workers within this organisational framework are on the whole as much restricted by procedural regulations, assessment duties and the need to provide 'sticking-plaster' assistance as in the other organisational models.

Irrespective of where they belong organisationally, these 'generic' front-line services (*Allgemeine Sozialdienste*) cover a wide range of duties in relation, potentially, to the whole of the population. In a sense, their actual political mandate is to put into practice the concept of the social state, the caring state that integrates society by implementing and personalising its complex legal provisions. Social work in these services characteristically includes the assessment of the material conditions of applicants for welfare benefits and assistance, psycho-social family assessments in matrimonial and juvenile court cases and the preparation of recommendations relating to care procedures for children and juveniles (including the approval of foster families), as well as many other legally prescribed responsibilities. In the German context, such work always requires a detailed knowledge of legislation, since all these functions are minutely prescribed by law, both in terms of the scope of the services and in terms of the legality of the actions of the workers themselves as 'servants of the state'. Work in statutory settings is therefore not a preferred career option for German social workers trained in the social pedagogy tradition and is considered to be more suited for those trained as *SozialarbeiterInnen*, despite the general blending of both traditions.

This is indicative of the tensions each of these organisational patterns of social services creates between the bureaucratic and the professional objectives of the agency. Their statutory responsibilities concerning the assessment of material and social circumstances (and, in some local authorities where the distinction between office work and field work has been abolished, their powers to make decisions) bestow on social workers a reputation as state officials with limited professional autonomy. In addition, the effects of subsidiarity and the prior options it affords to voluntary agencies tend to turn state services into agencies of last resort, dealing with situations for which the voluntary sector is not prepared to make provision or take any other kind of responsibility. The division of services along administrative lines and between public and private agencies narrows the scope of professional social work considerably.

It must be borne in mind, too, that while these departments have an overall statutory responsibility to ensure that appropriate services are being provided, they need not necessarily provide those services themselves, apart from the specific statutory functions mentioned above. According to paragraph 10 (ii) of the Federal Social Welfare Act, the statutory social service departments are obliged to collaborate with the voluntary sector and to support their work. This collaboration can reach as far as the total delegation of functions to recognised voluntary organisations. This is usually the case with specialised social services, of which the majority have to be delegated in this way and which therefore have much more potential for developing a higher professional profile. These specialised services (*Spezielle Sozialdienste* in contrast to the *Allgemeine Sozialdienste*) exist mainly as multi-disciplinary agencies combining medical, psychological and social work expertise and dealing with specific client groups or problem areas such as disability, homelessness and substance dependency. On account of these specialisations the administrative and organisational allocation of such services to appropriate government departments is far less problematic than that of the generic services.

The 'dual welfare structure' of statutory and independent agencies is a peculiarly German phenomenon without parallel in Europe (Tennstedt, 1992): it gives the major voluntary organisations wide scope to develop a comprehensive range of personal social services. In 1962, in what has become known as the *Subsidiaritätsstreit* (dispute over the interpretation of subsidiarity), some of the *Länder* launched a constitutional challenge to the emphasis on the principle of subsidiarity which had been written into the newly enacted social and youth welfare legislation of 1961. This went as far as stating that whenever possible the work of the voluntary welfare agencies had to be given priority, to the extent that local authorities should desist from developing youth services, for example, if the voluntary sector were capable of providing them. The grounds for the challenge were that the obligation to give priority to voluntary agencies negated the concept of the German state as a *Sozialstaat*, as defined in Articles 20 and 28 of the Basic Law, and infringed the administrative autonomy of local authorities. These arguments were refuted by the Constitutional Court in its decision five years later, which became a landmark in German post-war social policy. The essence of the judgment was that while the state did indeed hold the sole and ultimate responsibility for the goal of providing comprehensive welfare measures for all its citizens, this did not imply a state monopoly on the means of achieving it (Orthbandt, 1980). This judgment confirmed the practice of collaboration between public and private welfare organisations, and gave the established private, non-profit sector (referred to as *gemeinnützig*, 'for public purposes') an unassailably privileged position. Not only did the private sector hold precedent over the public in setting up services, it could call upon public resources as a right once it could demonstrate an existing need for which there was a statutory framework and could vouch for its ability to provide an appropriate service.

This principle was reaffirmed in the 1991 Children and Youth Services Act, which gives high priority to users of services having a voice in the planning and delivery of services. Under section 75 of the Act, 'recognised' private youth organisations have a privileged position in terms of their right to permanent public funding and their participation in working and planning committees. The status of 'recognised' association is conditional upon a proven record of non-profit-making, professionally led activities with children and young people over at least three years, the ability to contribute 'substantially' to the delivery of youth services and an ideological orientation in conformity with the constitution. Church organisations and agencies of the major welfare associations receive automatic recognition (Krüger and Zimmermann, 1991).

Such privileges and the practice of collaboration between the major voluntary organisations brought about the virtual cartel of the six leading welfare associations or *Spitzenverbände*: those of the churches (the Catholic *Deutscher Caritasverband* and the Protestant *Diakonisches Werk der Evangelischen Kirche in Deutschland*), the Jewish community (*Zentrale Wohlfahrtsstelle der Juden in Deutschland*), the labour movement (*Arbeiterwohlfahrt*), the Red Cross (*Rotes Kreuz*), and the association of independent organisations, the *Deutscher Paritätischer Wohlfahrtsverband*. All of these had played important roles during the Weimar years. They are organised at local, regional and federal level as *Vereine* with various forms of affiliation. About 62,000 legally independent organisations are affiliated to the peak associations or *Spitzenverbände*, and between them they maintain approximately 68,500 institutions and employ some 750,000 workers, with *Caritas* being the largest association among them. The voluntary sector's 'market share' of all social services is estimated at around 65 per cent, with public services making up no more than 20 per cent, commercial services 10 per cent and self-help initiatives and independent groups the remaining 5 per cent (Oppl, 1992a).

The financial affairs of these private non-profit-making organisations are largely a matter of conjecture, and only the publicly financed part of their operations is open to public scrutiny. The annual financial turn-over of their operations is estimated at DM 45–70 billion and their total capital investment at DM 153 billion, but no statistics are kept on the volume of donations (Christa and Halfar, 1992). Their income consists predominantly of state grants and service charges (either from insurance sources or from public funds), with no more than 10 per cent derived from fundraising, property and subscriptions (Oppl, 1992b). Welfare organisations affiliated to the churches benefit from the German system of deducting ecclesiastical membership contributions from individuals' salaries in the form of a 'church tax'.

Public finance of social services is shared between the federal government, the *Länder* and local authorities. In relation to the costs of services for children and young people, which form the largest sector of personal social services that can be accounted for separately (the budgets for other sectors include the cash benefits for whose distribution they are responsible or general spending on public health), about 60 per cent to be raised by the local authorities, the *Land* contributes about 30 per cent and the federal state 10 per cent. About 20 per cent of these resources get allocated to the voluntary sector as direct subventions (BMAS, 1990). The main instrument through which the federal state supports youth services is the Federal Youth Programme (*Bundesjugendplan*), which allocates specific priority tasks in the course of political consultations.

The dominant position of the large voluntary organisations can be understood as a typical example of neo-corporatism, which in practice negates the pluralism it seems to enshrine. Rather than competing among themselves to develop a pluralist diversity of approaches, the major organisations have established an elaborate system of mutual consultation on how areas of responsibility are to be divided. For instance, in relation to service initiatives both for and with people of foreign origin, the *Deutscher Caritasverband* took responsibility for Italian, Spanish, Portuguese and former Yugoslavian national groups, the *Diakonisches Werk* for those from Greece and the *Arbeiterwohlfahrt* for people with predominantly Muslim backgrounds from Morocco, Turkey and Tunisia as well as Yugoslavia. This cooperative arrangement also allows them to present a united front as they negotiate with the state over allowances for the services they provide. What is more, the state is obliged to consult the major organisations extensively in the planning stages of new legislation and to programme initiatives in order to anticipate and incorporate any possible objections on their part. The organised, comprehensive and plural appearance of service coverage belies the underlying inefficiency and monopolistic structure of practical arrangements, which have come in for growing criticism. Not only is the voluntary sector able to choose the most 'profitable' areas of work (Heinze and Olk, 1991), leaving it to the state to fill gaps in service provision, there is also evidence that economies of scale exert pressures on 'problem definition' so that existing places in institutions are always filled to capacity (Oppl, 1992a).

Policy developments in the 1970s and 1980s

With regard to personal social services as to social policy in general, the decades since 1970 have brought profound and heterogeneous changes in Germany. The 1970s were strongly influenced by the social sciences inspired critique of capitalist, authoritarian society which swept most of the western world in the late 1960s. The rapid expansion of social services and the vigorous recruitment of personnel in the ensuing years can be seen as an attempt by the Establishment at soaking up unrest through social investment, while leaving basic structures of power unchanged. The welfare professions expanded more rapidly than any other occupational group to reach an employment level of over half a million by the early 1990s. Seventy-five per cent of these posts have been created since 1970. A steady, though varying, rate of increase persisted even during years of severe restrictions on public expenditure; since 1989 yearly increases have doubled by comparison with the early 1980s (Rauschenbach, 1993).

This expansion was accompanied by a further strengthening of the étatist character of German welfare provisions and its formal manifestation through detailed legislation. Its cornerstone is the Social Code (*Sozialgesetzbuch*), the first section of which was enacted in 1976 and into which successive welfare legislation has become incorporated. The phenomenon of *Verrechtlichung*, meaning that procedural matters are turned into legal questions, affected social workers in both public and private settings who now had to watch ever more carefully to see that their actions and decisions conformed with statutory regulations. The limitations *Verrechtlichung* imposes on professional autonomy and on the creative use of new forms of practice are a matter of ardent debate in Germany. In terms of administrative reform, patchy attempts at a fundamental reorganisation of local government managed to reduce and concentrate the number of districts (*Kreise*) and of *kreisfreie Städte* (municipalities equivalent to *Kreise*), but did little to resolve the complexity of relationships between the various local, *Land* and federal state levels, all of which have a direct bearing on the delivery of social services.

At the same time, the degree of professionalisation of social services increased markedly. Social work training had undergone a profound change at the beginning of the 1970s, and newly established courses at *Fachhochschulen* (higher vocational schools) produced large numbers of graduates. More specifically, within the field of youth services the proportion of staff trained in social pedagogy in the widest sense (which includes nursery nurses and educators as the largest groupings) went up from 47 per cent to 58 per cent over the two decades in question, while most of the other 42 per cent are accounted for by equally well-qualified professional groups such as teachers, psychologists, therapists and administrators (Rauschenbach, 1990). Training patterns in the subject area of social work as such maintained the traditional dualism between *Sozialarbeit* and *Sozialpädagogik*, although the differences in training and in the reputation of the two qualifications became ever more relative and nominal. The main distinguishing feature that remained was that *Sozialarbeit* still required a more detailed knowledge of legislation and of administrative structures and procedures, while *Sozialpädagogik* allowed more scope for creativity.

But as the social professions began to consolidate their position and to gain official recognition and higher status, their standing in the eyes of the public also became the subject of profound criticism. Their very expertise, often couched in elaborate technical language and set in cumbersome procedures, distanced them from ordinary citizens who were afraid of becoming increasingly dependent on professional gate-keepers for access to information and resources. Even where these professionals were employed by non-state agencies, their way of operating was seen to be no different from the labyrinthine inaccessibility of state bureaucracies. Both were exposed primarily as bastions of power and only secondarily as serving the public.

During the 1970s, a noticeable rift between public and private services developed as a result of the reversal of expansionist social policies. The public expenditure proposals (*Haushaltstrukturgesetz*) of 1975 initiated a period of fiscal restrictions, a signal that the German welfare state also had reached crisis-point. As in other countries, this ushered in an ideological hunt for 'scroungers' and stigmatising pressures on welfare recipients. The achievements of the 'social state' came in for questioning from both the political right and left.

These developments had an ambiguous effect on the voluntary agencies. First of all, as they were largely dependent on state subventions, they were also affected by the financial restrictions. This reinforced the impression held by users of their services, and confirmed by surveys in the 1980s, that the leading voluntary agencies of the *Spitzenverbände* really had very little autonomy and were instead an 'integral part of the social state' (Olk, 1987, p. 148). The gulf of scepticism and mistrust between services and users widened and some of the established welfare organisations lost their appeal to voluntary donors (Christa and Halfar, 1992).

These trends point towards the growing significance of a different kind of organisation located between the state and the established private welfare organisations. While the idea of self-help has a long and important history in the form of the co-operatives, friendly societies and mutual aid associations of the labour movement, there is something very different about the renewed and vigorous appearance of self-help initiatives in the midst of elaborate and sophisticated public and semi-public support systems. Their rise in Germany during the 1970s and 1980s was closely associated with the emergence of new social movements. With their critique of established bureaucratic and neo-corporatist structures and their challenges to positions of power, including those of the professions, social movements have become a considerable force in Germany as in other societies. Spearheaded by the women's, ecology and peace movements, local initiatives and self-help groups began to question the authority of the state and to speak and act on behalf of all sectors of society. In Germany, the critique voiced by self-help movements in the welfare arena targeted not so much the absence of services but the inefficiency and self-interest reflected in existing provision. This included a critique of the cosy arrangements between the state and large private organisations which profess to represent the interests of service users but which in fact have become impervious to minority views and interests (Grunow, 1986).

The rise of self-help movements in Germany was also influenced by changes in demography and life-style in what had become a highly affluent, mobile and goal-oriented society. The coincidence of a sharp decline in the birth rate with a much higher life expectancy further weakened family cohesion, which had already become tenuous through the individualisation of life-styles. Self-organised mutual support and assistance in loosely organised communities of people facing similar challenges were able to offer alternatives which fulfilled a need for direct, personal contact, for control over change and for a vision – however vague – of a better society. Having originated in relation to physical and mental health problems, self-help initiatives soon spread to people experiencing homelessness, unemployment, release from prison, the threat of racist attacks or deportation. Their close proximity to other social movements widened the scope of participants in such initiatives, many of which can no longer be described as 'self-help' groups in the strictest sense.

The 1980s brought about an unprecedented rise in such organisations. Their estimated number around the middle of the decade was 40,000, with about 10,000 groups in the health field, 2,000 in unemployment and about 400 in housing and homelessness (Nowak, 1988). However, for many of them, expansion and the need to gain access to financial resources in particular led paradoxically to a rapprochement with the traditional major voluntary organisations. These established bodies, in turn, were keen to utilise the trend as a boost to their own image, pointing out that their extensive use of volunteers in certain areas of work had traditionally counter-balanced the influence of experts and professionals and had in a sense anticipated the demands of the self-help movements. Self-help initiatives also began to establish networks among themselves as a kind of 'self-help infra-structure'. The aim was to systematise user information and to offer support and training to new groups. The *Paritätischer Wohlfahrtsverband*, the most vociferous exponent of the principle of self-help and of devolved organisation among the large welfare associations, provided support to many such local information centres for self-help groups (*Selbsthilfe-Kontakt- und Informationsstellen*) and to a national support centre, NAKOS (*Nationale Kontakt- und Unterstützungsstelle für Selbsthilfegruppen*).

The sudden popularity of volunteers and private initiatives was seized upon by conservative political circles eager to exploit the self-help movement, for their own ideological purposes, as a popular endorsement of their policies of 'rolling back the state' and especially of dismantling public social services (Grunow, 1986). Ideological positions from the political right and left began to cross over, adding to the traditional blurring of service boundaries an ideological mix that mirrored the emerging 'welfare mix' (Evers and Wintersberger, 1988). In consequence, the entire social service field in Germany is in a state of flux, instability and uncertainty, particularly if the gradual influence of the commercial sector is also taken into consideration. Most pronounced in relation to the care of the elderly and in nursing and rehabilitation, the creation of market situations is noticeable and will become more pronounced. Pressure derived from the European concept of the *économie sociale* could, in the views of some commentators, amount to a profound challenge to the privileged position of the big German voluntary organisations (Oppl, 1992).

The uncertainties created as a result of these complex developments have had some positive effects on the work of statutory agencies, and of youth departments in particular. There are indications that at least some of the central principles propounded by the social movements are beginning to affect the approaches being developed by youth departments. Research registers a shift from reactive towards preventive measures, from bureaucratic rigidity towards flexibility, and from authoritarianism towards consultation and cooperation with service users (Lukas, 1991). 'Transparency' and accountability in both public and private sectors have become demands which cannot be satisfied by designer-made campaigns proclaiming the *Bürgernähe* (proximity to the citizens) of services but have to be endorsed by radical changes in practice. It remains to be seen whether the elaborate structure of personal social service delivery in Germany, which shunned radical change and reform for more than a century, will be capable of responding positively and openly to a new environment of articulate and self-organised citizens.

The effects of German unification on the new *Länder*

The greatest opportunity to examine the relevance and efficiency of the traditional service delivery system in the light of changing social conditions and to instigate new organisational and service delivery approaches for German social services came with German unification. First indications are that this opportunity has been missed. Unification meant the dissolution of all public and legal structures in the former GDR. Exactly the same structures of public and private organisations and services which determine the West German social, political and economic landscape were exported wholesale to the East in an attempt to obliterate all traces of the communist regime. As no effective decentralised political structure had existed in the former GDR and no tradition of self-government had been allowed to develop, there were no obvious starting-points for reform. However, the very fact that the changes were decreed by the central state without a meaningful process of consultation and participation 'on the ground' belied its decentralising intentions and tipped the balance in the precariously poised subsidiarity model in favour of large structures. Evidence concerning the implementation of the administrative and legal transformation suggests that it resulted in more difficulties and frictions than had been anticipated. In regard to personal social services, these difficulties relate both to the official denial of the necessity of explicit welfare measures and services under the former communist regime and to the intricate complexity of the West German welfare system.

The new system requires staff who are familiar with social welfare law and, more fundamentally, with new administrative procedures which are based on a civil service ethos of professional accountability diametrically opposed to the 'cadre mentality' of the GDR administration (Backhaus-Maul and Olk, 1992). Additionally, it requires professionals in all fields of social work equipped with specific competences, the relevance of which the former official ideology consistently denied. Many positions in local authority offices were therefore initially staffed by civil servants from West Germany, but the deficit was also addressed by means of an extensive and rapid training and retraining programme at all levels.

At the same time, the new *Länder* of the former East Germany were affected by an unprecedented escalation of social problems, among them problems which had previously been almost non-existent and for which there were neither official services nor personal coping mechanisms. Chief among these is unemployment, which in 1993 nominally reached 16 per cent but which, when figures for early retirement, short-time working and job training were included, in fact amounted to about 37 per cent (Ganssmann, 1993). Similarly, the privatisation of housing confronts both citizens and officials with unfamiliar problems. The new local authority welfare departments have to deal with a growing number of hardship cases, all of which require detailed individual assessment. Officials are also concerned about the low take-up rates of public benefits, which are perceived as intensely stigmatising (Rohde, 1993).

The former GDR had little tolerance for independent welfare organisations. The German Red Cross and *Volkssolidarität* were closely connected to the party machinery, and although the churches had some scope to develop their own services the boundaries within which they were allowed to operate were tightly controlled, being restricted to hospital work and the fields of geriatrics and disability. Their branching out into work with marginalised groups in socialist society or into educational initiatives usually sparked off conflicts with the regime. This meant that, after unification, the idea of private welfare organisations negotiating with the state and being afforded legal autonomy was new for citizens and civil servants alike. Furthermore, the social conditions responsible for the proliferation of social movements and self-help organisations in the West, a post-industrial middle class and a diversity of moral and social milieu, were largely absent in East Germany. Yet in the haste of unification little room was given to a process of reflection and deliberation as to how the tenuous signs of civil society in the East, which after all had been instrumental in bringing down the old system through sustained campaigns and demonstrations, could be encouraged to become a seed-bed in which autonomous projects and initiatives could grow commensurate with local conditions. Instead, as far as private services are concerned, the dominant position of recognised voluntary organisations in West Germany was replicated. Independent initiatives find it difficult to gain access to equivalent resources unless they attach themselves to the large voluntary organisations which command the support of their western central offices (Backhaus-Maul and Olk, 1992).

These recognised voluntary welfare organisations themselves found it difficult to become established in the new *Länder*. Organisationally, there were some rudimentary structures of the denominational associations (*Caritas* and *Diakonisches Werk*) to serve as starting-points, but the declared atheism of the old regime combined with the effects of consumerist secularisation arriving from the West eroded their basis of volunteers to levels that question the viability of local branches. Organisational continuity is particularly problematic for the Red Cross, with its legacy of GDR state support. The activities of *Volkssolidarität*, the other officially sanctioned voluntary organisation under the old regime, were transferred to some extent to the *Paritätischer Wohlfahrtsverband*, which otherwise provides an organisational umbrella for autonomous projects. The *Arbeiterwohlfahrt* had to start from a complete absence of initiatives grounded in the traditions of the labour movement; though untainted by the communist legacy, it nevertheless found it hard to establish either a role or an infra-structure in this vacuum.

German unification provides a test for distinct characteristics of German social services which reveals their strengths and weaknesses. In particular, it exposes the discrepancies between the promise of responding flexibly and imaginatively to changing social conditions and the reality of bureaucratic ossification, between an ideological façade of citizen and user participation and vested self-interest in private and public welfare organisations alike. Politicians are emphatic that the contribution of voluntary organisations ensures pluralism and consumer choice as the emblems of a free democracy. In 1991, the federal government allocated DM 30 million for the development of voluntary agencies in the new *Länder* and a further DM 17 million in 1992, but since 1993 the voluntary sector has been dependent on subventions from individual *Länder* as well as on transfers from parent associations in the West (Gutschick, 1992). The ideological, cost-cutting side of voluntarism has a suspicious ring for the citizens of the new *Länder*, while the very model of subsidiarity in welfare matters meets widespread incomprehension, scepticism and apathy (Feldmann and Kahler, 1992).

Priorities for future developments

Personal social services in Germany, understood as the totality of public, voluntary and self-help organisations, are headed for a turbulent time. Together they represent a measure not only of social solidarity as such in German society but also of the diversity of means and ends of how solidarity is to be achieved. While the demographic trend towards a rapidly ageing population and the fears this evokes about being 'deserted by society' beyond the threshold of one's economic usefulness will keep the central regulatory role of the state on the agenda, there is much uncertainty over the appropriate ownership of social services. The professional dimension of making the best possible expertise available to all users of services has long been superseded by the political dimension which centres on the power to define the content of 'well-being' and the means of securing it. The dialectics of autonomy and mutual responsibility, which have been a constant historical theme of German social services, have once again unsettled the compromise worked out in the decade immediately after the Second World War. German unification, the process of European integration and the worldwide politics of migration will test existing boundaries of solidarity to their limits. New means of defining solidarity and of giving it statutory backing in social and human rights will be judged crucially in Germany of all countries by their ability to combat and overcome racism as the ideological exclusion and physical oppression of people deemed not to belong to one's own nation. German national identity, which has been called into question once again through unification and through European integration, will require a forward-looking community education effort in which personal social services can play a crucial role in breaking with the chimeras of Germany's past.

Guide to further reading

The standard work on social affairs and social work in Germany available in English translation is Flamm (1983). Its vast scope and yet condensed form is impressive, and it provides basic information about political structures and public administration as well as summarising all aspects of welfare legislation and welfare services. Therein also lie its limitations: it can only provide condensed references and requires a deeper knowledge of the context of each field in order to be of real use. It also needs updating urgently in the light of new legislation and of German unification. Munday (1992) is a more up-to-date reference guide to social services in all European Union countries which contains a concise and clearly presented chapter on Germany that includes observations on unification. The information is organised by main client groups and is intended as an overview primarily for practitioners. Köhnen (1992), by contrast, is very specific in dealing only with services for children and young people. Its unique features are that it serves as a specialised dictionary as well as a kind of encyclopedia for key terms in the glossary. Its purpose is to make visible the fundamental differences between German and British approaches to youth work and youth policy and it works well in both directions, not least because of its reliable and expertly translated terminology.

The following monographs on developments in European social work make references to key aspects of the social services in Germany: Cannan *et al.* (1992) focuses on citizenship and participation as a theme in European social work and traces echoes of this in Germany; Lorenz (1994) deals more explicitly with the historical background to the diversity of social work services in Germany, attempting to elucidate the 'pedagogical' tradition and to evaluate the impact of social movements on future directions in social work.

Primary data are best obtained from the official publications of the appropriate federal ministries such as the *Jugendbericht*, published by the Federal Ministry for Women and Youth, and the *Sozialbericht*, published by the Federal Ministry for Labour and Social Affairs.

Part III

Social divisions

Chapter 8

Women and social policy

Prue Chamberlayne

One puzzle and disappointment for women from East and West since 1989 has been the difficulty in achieving any sense of feminist unity. This chapter explores both structural and cultural dimensions of this disjuncture – the legislation, social policies and political discourse which have framed women's roles in the two societies, but also the responses of women themselves, in the way they pattern their lives as well as through women's movements. Structural and cultural dimensions in social policy intertwine and cannot easily be disentangled. In order to explore differences in social policies concerning women in the 1970s and 1980s, the chapter proceeds in three parts. First, it will contrast the position of women in East and West Germany in that period with regard to employment, training, childcare and pensions. This will be followed by an outline of key policy developments concerning women in those two decades, and the reactions of women themselves. Finally, it will address the issues, problems and prospects posed by unification, for women, for feminists and policy-makers.

In both East and West Germany, the family was seen as central to post-war reconstruction, but whereas 'the family for socialism' embraced the socialist perspective of female emancipation through labour, with state provisions to relieve domestic burdens, West Germany's quest for social 'normalisation' centred on the restoration of the patriarchal, breadwinner model of the family, which cast women's roles firmly in the domestic sphere. So German unification brought two of Europe's most counterposed welfare systems face to face, and the contrast was particularly marked in social policies concerning women. For whereas equality between men and women was upheld as a goal of the East German system, backed by comprehensive social provisions to enable women to work, in West Germany male and female roles were cast

173

as emphatically different and complementary. In East German social policy the lead female figure was the working woman, who was also a mother; in West Germany marriage and the housewife were placed centre-stage. Thus the two systems exemplified what has been characterised as public and private patriarchy (Hernes, 1984). Law in 1950s West Germany subordinated wives to their husbands; they could not, for instance, take employment without their husband's permission. Women in East Germany were free of such personal control, but their lives were tightly constrained by the 'guardian' state.

The clause in the West German constitution (1949) proclaiming equal rights between women and men is one of the best in the world, though it was not lightly won (Gerhard, 1990). Its insertion was only achieved after three attempts in parliament and a herculean campaign by women, led by Elisabeth Selbert, a Social Democrat. In practice it was largely ignored in the 1950s and 1960s in favour of the clause giving state protection to marriage and the family. This clause originated among the Social Catholics of the CDU/CSU fraction, and was used as the foundation stone for Family Minister Wuermeling's policies in the 1950s (Joosten, 1990). This conflict between goals of 'equality' and 'difference' for women, which was exemplified in these 1949 debates on the constitution, as well as in antagonisms between East and West German policies, had long roots in conflicts between bourgeois and socialist feminist movements in Germany. Federal policy on the family in 1949 claimed to uphold traditional values of gender 'difference', against their violation by both Nazism and communism. But this claim to represent German heritage denied the existence of the longstanding German social democratic tradition, which had always emphasised 'equality'.

If the dominant models of womanhood were in strong contrast in East and West Germany, so were the institutional structures of welfare by which women's life-courses were shaped. The 'unity of economic and social policy', introduced in East Germany by Erich Honecker in 1971, entailed a tight coordination of employment and family policy, organised through centralised state structures (Adams, 1990). Organisations of civil society had already been eradicated, as had space for the development of independent political mobilisation or public discourse. The West German system, by contrast, was Janus-faced (Leibfried and Ostner, 1991, p. 176). On one side lay the strong, equivalence-based, employment-centred insurance system, dominated by the corporatist interests of male breadwinners; on the other were weak and fragmented social services, based on principles of subsidiarity. This dualism in the West German system reflected the sharp division between public and private, male and female worlds, a separation which was insisted on by Family Minister Wuermeling in the 1950s as the hallmark of the West German system. Freedom from state interference was meant to be paramount. Marriage and the family were to be institutionalised 'in their own logic, as unregulated private spheres far from the state in their inner core' (Bast and Ostner, 1992, p. 251). Internal regulation of the household was to be the prerogative and responsibility of the husband and father. This 'hands-off' approach in West Germany implied minimal state services connected with the family. But while public services to relieve families were inadequate and patchy, they did allow scope for alternative pluralised initiatives. Such opportunities were taken up by feminists throughout the 1970s and 1980s, initially along 'autonomous' or 'separatist' lines, giving rise to alternative institutional structures, from childcare and safe houses to equal rights offices (Kulawik, 1992). The strong gender division within federal public policy and its apparatuses doubtless played a part in catalysing a forceful and autonomous feminist discourse and field of action in West Germany. Thus structural and cultural factors were intertwined in the shaping of West German feminism.

The position of women East and West

By the 1970s and 1980s, the impact on women's lives of thirty and more years of the social market in the West and of state socialism in the East was clear to see. On a series of indices such as employment levels and hours, training levels, childbearing patterns, divorce and illegitimacy, women in East and West Germany stood at opposite ends of the European spectrum. Employment levels of 90 per cent, a figure reached by the mid-1970s, placed East German women at the top of the European league. Only 25 per cent of them, mostly middle-aged, worked part-time, and often for thirty hours, which in West Germany would be classed as full-time. It may be that many more East German women would have liked to work part-time (Kolinsky, 1993, p. 282), but the pattern does show that part-time work was not necessary to combine motherhood and employment, as is so common in Britain. Combining motherhood and full-time employment was virtually universal among younger East German women, since 90 per cent of them bore children. It was facilitated by full state provision of childcare, at crèche and kindergarten levels, after school and in the holidays.

Female employment in Germany had been extraordinarily constant at about 35 per cent from the 1880s through to the 1930s, and West Germany continued this stable pattern in the post-war period, though with a steady rise after 1975 (Frevert, 1989, p. 333). Within that constancy, however, came an enormous rise in the employment of married women, and, in the 1980s, of working women with small children (Bertram and Borrmann-Müller, 1988). Few of these worked full-time: about 20 per cent in 1989. But whereas in 1972 only a quarter of women with children up to the age of 6 were in employment, by 1982 this figure had risen to over a third (Vogelheim, 1988). By contrast, three-quarters of unmarried mothers were working, often full-time, even though half of them were below the poverty line (Ostner, 1993). This makes an interesting comparison with Britain, where the social security system and high childcare costs result in very few single mothers working, with something like 80 per cent in poverty.

The life-course for women in East Germany was remarkably standardised, in that nearly 90 per cent had at least one child, usually in their early 20s, often while they were still studying (Ostner, 1993). Single parenthood and divorce, usually initiated by women, were common. Employment, high levels of qualification, full childcare provisions, subsidies for basic living expenses and special benefits for single parents all facilitated an independent life. In West Germany, the privileging of marriage through tax and advantageous pensions for widows, the exclusion of girls from skilled apprenticeships and consequent labour market segmentation, together with the lack of childcare and the pattern of halfday schooling all acted as impediments to the combination of employment and childrearing. The post-war system emphasised a housewife role for women. Even in 1961, a well-known study of working mothers by Elisabeth Pfeil, which acknowledged the positive effect of employment on the female personality, also regretted the 'reduced patience, a diminishing capacity for personal devotion and self-denial, a loss of ability to wait, to let mature, of calm, grace and tenderness' (Pfeil in Schütze, 1988, p. 385). This view exemplified a widespread belief in 'motherliness', a discourse much strengthened through the influence of Social Catholicism in the 1950s and 1960s, but with long roots in bourgeois feminism in Germany (Moeller, 1989; Chamberlayne, 1990; Joosten, 1990; Münch, 1990).

The impediments in West German social policy to the combining of employment and motherhood produced a curious polarisation between women with and without children. In a perverse manner it encouraged both careerist childlessness and traditional housewife roles. In the 1980s, 26 per cent of West German women were childless (Ostner, 1993, p. 106), for while the welfare system favoured the unemployed married housewife, an alternative remained the pursuit of an independent career within which the privileges of the (usually male) 'standard working life' could be secured. Since interruptions in earnings reduced pension levels dramatically, two 'rational' options faced the working woman: to maintain earnings at all cost, or to abandon employment. In addition to pressures on women arising from the pensions system, the 'opportunity costs' of childrearing were higher in West Germany than in other, lower wage societies. Childless working wives stood to benefit from their own full pension and from generous widows' benefits. Moreover, the opportunity costs of parenthood were high even within marriage, for it was marriage rather than childbearing which the system sought to promote. In 1988, it was calculated that one child reduced per capita income by 38 per cent, two children by 52 per cent (Hinrichs, 1990). In the GDR, various forms of family assistance covered about 70 per cent of childrearing costs; in West Germany they covered only 25 per cent (Gerhard, 1992). Occupational position, marital status and childbearing, therefore, influenced women's choices. As Leibfried and Ostner conclude, 'the average married *un*employed woman is often much better off over the whole lifecourse than any other average female category' (1991, p. 176).

The numbers of children in households were remarkably similar in East and West Germany in 1971, but by 1981 significant differences had appeared (Rosenberg, 1993). The West saw a growth in the proportion of households with no children and, despite a decline, the maintenance of a higher proportion of households with three or more children than East Germany. East Germany showed no increase in households without children, a considerable growth in households with one child, and a fall in households with more than three children (Rosenberg, 1993, p. 133). Here again is evidence of the West German polarisation between childlessness and traditional roles. The East German figures show the success of pro-natalist policies introduced in the East in 1971, despite abortion becoming freely available in that year.

Higher qualifications for women were prioritised earlier in East Germany, though in the West, too, levels increased markedly in the 1970s and 1980s. Nevertheless, by the late 1980s only 3 per cent of East German women had no qualifications at all, as against 30 per cent in West Germany (Kolinsky, 1993, p. 276). In both societies there was strong vertical as well as horizontal segregation in the labour market, though whereas 90 per cent of women were restricted to thirteen occupations in East Germany, the range was a narrower eight occupations in the West.

Pay and pension differentials were marked in both societies. Women's earnings were only 75 per cent of men's in East Germany, largely because of bonuses for heavy physical work and overtime done by men. In West Germany, due to the favouring of men by corporatist mechanisms, the differential was 70 per cent (Ostner, 1993, p. 113). In both countries, lower and interrupted earnings resulted in huge gender divisions in pensions and marked poverty among women in old age. However, in making gender comparisons in pensions it must be borne in mind that women aged 60–80 in 1970 were of working age between 1910 and 1970 and that women aged between 60–80 in 1990 were of working age between 1930 and 1990. They suffered the interruptions of war and much of their life-course was spent as housewives. Thus pension differentials reflect historical policies and life-patterns, although they can be rectified by later legislation, as in 1930 and 1990 (see Chapter 3).

In East Germany, women's pensions averaged 77 per cent of men's, compared with 46 per cent and 53 per cent for blue- and white-collar workers respectively in West Germany. However, the greater inequality in the West would be modified for many elderly women by the higher widows' pensions there: these were calculated at 60 per cent of the husband's pension, compared with 25 per cent in the GDR (Ostner, 1993). East Germany laid no claim to pre-eminence in pensions policy or care of the elderly – children and young people were the preferred age groups (Bast and Ostner, 1992) – whereas in West Germany pensions occupied a strategic position in state policy and legitimation. Nevertheless, poverty among elderly women was severe in West Germany as well as in the GDR, as became highlighted in poverty reports in the 1970s and 1980s.

Such research exposed the 'underside' of the allegedly generous West German welfare system and the gendered nature of its 'Janus-faced' divide. The emphasis on the protection of women by their breadwinner husbands, both in life and after their deaths, hid from view the plight of widows whose husbands had a low or short earnings record, and of the growing numbers of women outside assumed family structures, through single parenthood or divorce. In East Germany, older people suffered neglect through the misfortune of having predated the revolutionary, younger generation in whom the future was invested, and, unless they had anti-fascist credentials, of being tainted with Nazism and the old order (Chamberlayne, 1992a).

To summarise, both societies were highly gendered in employment and earnings patterns, but the gendering took different forms. For West German women the combining of family and employment remained a dilemma, which a large minority solved by opting against childbearing. This minority struck out for 'equality', and the spoils of the employment-centred welfare system encouraged this choice, as we have seen, despite official emphasis on family roles for women and thereby 'difference'. East German women were likely to be locked into a standardised pattern of 'equality' consisting of full-time employment and early childbearing. Here, despite the formal espousal of equality and public provisions to ease domestic roles, the remaining but officially disregarded domestic responsibilities ensured an unequal position, notably in employment and in political life.

The 1970s in West Germany saw a marked break in the strongly patriarchal character of federal family law, stress on the individual rights of family members, and a turn to the labour market role of women. To some degree this brought a stronger alignment between the position of women East and West, modified by the development of strongly autonomous feminist politics in the West in that period. In the 1980s, however, stronger attention in the West to the sphere of reproduction, to choices for women and to consideration of feminine subjectivities only strengthened the divergence between East and West. Meanwhile, the GDR saw a continuation of policies to support women in combining home and work, a continued neglect of fatherhood and the lack of any discourse on subjective experience and gender issues in the private sphere. Informally, meanwhile, in the eastern 'niche' society of weekend house and garden, a rather traditional and close-knit family life flourished, in which women assumed domestic roles in antithesis to their public image as gender-neutral 'productive forces'. Perhaps it would not be too fanciful to characterise the two situations as public progressivism and private traditionalism in the East, and public traditionalism and private radicalism in the West.

Policy developments in West Germany

In West Germany, family policy under Christian Democrat Family Minister Wuermeling in the 1950s and early 1960s aimed to strengthen the family unit, foster self-sufficiency and protect family privacy. Housing subsidies, family tax allowances and a tightening of divorce law were the main instruments of policy, backed by an outpouring of prescriptive rhetoric (Joosten, 1990; Münch, 1990). The mid-1960s coalition between Christian and Social Democrats and the Social–Liberal era from 1969 brought a more critical view of the family as an obstacle to social equality and to the emancipation of both women and children. Extra-familial pre-school education was advocated as a means of equalising children's life-chances. As social research gained prominence in political discourse, much debate centred on the family reports of 1975 and 1979. Social equality was to be achieved by communication and information. The aim was to facilitate better parenting, awareness of rights and opportunities for women, confidence and personal effectivity (Münch, 1990). There was a shift beyond the mother–child relationship to consideration of the father's role, social networks, the quality of outside care, and stress on children's sociability with others (Schütze, 1988).

Post-war West German family law had been extraordinarily patriarchal. There might be all kinds of psycho-social explanations for this, such as compensation for military defeat, overzealous efforts by men to find a place in the family from which they had been excluded for so long and to assert control over wives who had become resourceful and self-sufficient and over children they had never known. Kuhn (1991) depicts the vigour of political activity and thinking among women in 1945–7 in Germany: the countless journals, the ubiquitous women's committees, the independent Women's Party, the determination to transform the ethics of politics, primarily by a closer integration of public and private concerns. All this was overridden in the preparations for elections and the new constitution in 1949 and became eclipsed in constructions of women as 'exhausted' and 'heroic but a-political' (Kuhn, 1991). The official reason for strengthening male authority was the need to restore the role of the *pater familias* which had been expropriated by Nazism, and thereby re-establish an appropriate independence of the family from the state. In the Federal Legal Code (*Bundesgesetzbuch*) all decision-making was vested in the husband; this clause was not annulled until 1957, after vehement discussion. The more definite watershed in family law came in the 1977 Marriage and Family Rights reform, which introduced the notion of partnership in the sense of joint responsibility between husband and wife, and equal worth between the wife's employment outside the home and her family roles, with recognition of family caring in pension law. The 1977 law abolished an earlier clause which subordinated a woman's employment to her home duties, but obliged her to take a job if the husband's income was insufficient. However, the law giving the father overriding power of decision over children was not abolished until 1980 (Bast and Ostner, 1992). The new respect for women's rights remained severely negated in abortion law. In 1974, after a dramatic campaign by prominent women, a more liberal reform was accepted, only to be overturned through the influence of the Bavarian CSU in 1975. Thus West German abortion policy remained one of the most restrictive in Europe throughout the 1980s, allowing terminations only for 'indicated reasons' such as medical, criminal, eugenic or economic need.

The new emphasis on women's rights formed part of the cultural liberal-isation which permeated West German society in the aftermath of 1968. But it was also prompted by shifts in the labour market and employer interest in 'unused' female labour. The early 1970s saw a spate of employer reports and statements advocating full childcare, training for older women, protection for part-time workers, the coordination of school and work schedules, meals provision at work and at school, the development of the service sector to lighten housework, and even men's participation in housework (Vogelheim, 1988). Subsequently, in the deepening ecomomic crisis of 1979, women came to be portrayed by employers less as a group with unrealised potential and more as a problem group to be blamed for their own disadvantages. The family was once again pathologised as a source of problems for the state, economy and society (Vogelheim, 1988). This was the context in which the newly returned Conservative–Liberal coalition of 1982 advocated 'new motherliness', a new valuing of women's domestic roles and a convenient return from the labour market to the home. The reaction of women as expressed in polls then caused a hasty turnabout in favour of an emphasis on combining home and employment and shared roles between men and women, the Family Minister himself producing a pamphlet entitled 'The End of Male-Dominated Society' (Geissler, 1986; Chamberlayne, 1990).

Childrearing allowances (*Erziehungsgeld*) and parental leave (*Erzieh-ungsurlaub*) were introduced with a fanfare by the Christian Democrats in 1986 as part of a 'DM 10 billion family package'. It provided a universal flat rate DM 600 monthly payment for the first six months of a child's life, to be taken by either parent, with one change allowed. *Erziehungsurlaub* could be taken for up to three years, with job security and a means-tested benefit of up to DM 600 (for two years) (see Chapter 3). Since the DM 600 was equivalent to a half-time job and it was permissible to work up to nineteen hours a week in addition, which would entail childcare costs, the whole arrangement was on a par with a low female wage. It was open to either parent, but the opportunity costs would be greater for the higher-earning partner, usually the man, and thus it seemed likely that the policy would reinforce gender divisions. At first the reform seemed to make it advantageous for women to leave work; only later did they realise the cost to their career opportunities (Münch, 1990). It was pro-natalist, while accommodating to the fact of women's employment; the CDU had been forced to realise that otherwise voluntary childlessness would increase further. As critics pointed out, the DM 10 billion only just made up for cuts in family benefits and tax allowances which had been made in the period 1982–5 (Grottian, 1988). The spending increase was really the result of demography, the number of children under 18 having fallen from 14 million in 1981 to 11.4 million in 1986. By the mid-1980s, a return had been made to the 'self-responsible' indirect benefits of the 1960s, in place of the cash benefits which had become more common in the 1970s (Münch, 1990).

The 1980s thus became a period of intense argument about women's roles and fierce debate within and between all parties, with women being more prominent and vocal in German politics than they had been since the 1920s. Through the Green Party and its ability to bring together a range of social movements, the previously autonomous women's movement moved into formal but innovative and non-hierarchical politics. Quotas rapidly became the order of the day and by 1987 equality offices had been established in all the *Länder* and in some 300 local authorities. These focused on the gender-specific needs of women in such policy areas as domestic violence, city planning, cultural activities, support for networking, job training and advice (Ferree, 1992).

Legislation in the Federal Republic carried no thrust for equality, but did repeal laws which seemed to predetermine women's roles; it made space for alternative structures and values (Hoskyns, 1988). Likewise, in tracing West German responses to EC policies on women, Hoskyns (1988) argues that there was a lack of mobilisation among women for equality measures, which she attributes to their concern for 'difference', 'equality' seeming positively damaging to their concerns. Thus the central concerns of feminists in West Germany have either lain outside the orbit of the EC, such as abortion and violence, or have involved anti-discrimination rather than equality measures. At a conference supported by the EC's Women's Information Bureau in Berlin in 1977, women argued not for equality measures but for a special 'law for women' to support positive action and self-help. Gerhard (1990), a prominent German professor, argues against a false dichotomy between equality and difference, claiming that equality only makes sense on the basis of difference, and that difference can only be lived out on the basis of equality. The goal is not complete equality, which would be identity, and certainly not equal rights to imitate all the errors, destructiveness and arrogance which have threatened the world under male rule. It is rather a question of a search for a feasible measure of freedom, male and female. The state has a positive obligation to facilitate and secure equal rights for women in different aspects of their lives and to guarantee their social participation (Gerhard, 1990).

Feminists were not alone in their scepticism about the nature of the male-dominated public world. The 1980s was a dynamic period in West German politics, accompanying rapid technological restructuring and jobless growth. Its early and middle years produced widespread debate on the anachronism of the welfare system's premiss of 'standard working lives' and proposals for a guaranteed or basic income independent of an individual's labour market 'record'. This was accompanied by a broader cultural critique of 'employment-centred' society, in which feminist voices were prominent. Through such debates as well as those concerning shifts in family policy, the 1980s brought greater attention to the informal sphere of reproduction, with considerable overlap and ambiguity between radical 'alternative' and new conservative perspectives. Both were concerned with combining home and work roles, while giving greater space to personal lives. Some radical feminists, like those involved in the Mothers' Manifesto, argued for difference to the point of a separation of roles between men and women, whereas the Christian Democrats maintained they were promoting shared roles, and equality between housewives and employed women. But many feminists saw policies such as the *Erziehungsgeld* and *Erziehungsurlaub* as deft footwork, playing with a rhetoric of equality while promoting flexible labour in accordance with labour market needs, and reinforcing inequalities.

Social policies concerning women in West Germany in the 1970s and 1980s were therefore vibrant, diverse and hotly debated, involving not just industrial and distributional relations, but cultural spaces and the forging of new subjectivities (Kulawik, 1992). Concern to draw women into the workforce in the 1970s was followed by greater recognition of home roles in the 1980s, supposedly in a fashion to enhance choices for women. Schütze (1988) characterises the 1980s as being concerned less with mother–child relations and more with the 'life-situation' of women. The polarisation between women with and without children, between careerists and 'mothers', was reflected in political polarisations within the West German women's movement. But the lines of fracturing were complex, radicals and conservatives counting themselves on either side of the equality/difference debate, although in a sense most were for difference. As we have seen, the modernisation of marriage and family law was extraordinarily delayed, but in the eyes of Erler, 'the time lag in the "modernisation" of female biographies in Germany may turn out to have been a great opportunity for alternative modernisation, corresponding to the needs of the emerging post-industrial society' (1988, p. 238). The explicitly patriarchal nature of the system facilitated the politicisation of public–private relations. As Kulawik puts it: 'The linkage between the private and the public was probably more visible and therefore accessible to politicisation than in any other Western country' (1992, p. 79).

Policy developments in East Germany

By contrast, issues of public–private relations in the family in East Germany were obscured from view. Far from there being a conscious policy of retaining family privacy, the family was part of the seamless web of socialist society. All studies of the family and of micro-level social relations were conducted in the functionalist framework of the 'socialist way of life' (Kahl *et al.*, 1984). Penrose (1990) distinguishes three periods in policies concerning women: 1946–65 as a period of integrating women into the labour-force and protecting mothers; 1963–72 as a period emphasising higher education and professional qualifications; 1971–89 as a period focusing on combining career and family. Thus, whereas in West Germany there were major breaks in policies towards women in the 1970s and 1980s, in the Democratic Republic there was marked continuity through the two decades, and a relative absence of debate, until 1989.

The 1970s began dramatically enough. Women's responses to the availability of free contraception and abortion and the burden of combining full employment with home roles were expressed by a drastic drop in birth rates and by high divorce rates. In 1973 and 1974, the birth rate was down to 1.1 per cent, well below the 2.2 per cent necessary to reproduce the population, given some measure of infertility. In 1971, Erich Honecker had declared that equal rights between men and women had been achieved due to progressive legislation and the high participation rate of women in the workforce. However, it has been argued that this only 'freed the backs' of the SED leaders for a pro-natalist offensive, which became designated as 'women's politics' (Penrose, 1990, p. 69).

By the early 1970s, women had already been granted a monthly 'household day' and comprehensive childcare provision. Increased maternity allowances, credits for young couples up to the age of 25, allowances for students with children, lengthening of maternity leave and reduction of the working week to forty hours for mothers with three or more children were then introduced. In 1976, maternity leave was increased further from twelve to twenty weeks. Mothers with two children became entitled to the forty-hour week and also to the new 'baby year', which comprised a year's leave from work with allowances, and entitlements to paid sick leave on account of children were extended from single parents to parents of three children. From 1984 the baby year was extended to eighteen months for mothers of three children, and from 1986 one year's leave was made available after the first child. Meanwhile a subtle media campaign purveyed the wish to have children as 'natural'. Indeed, between 1975 and 1982 attitude surveys concerning the 'ideal' number of children showed a marked fall in the number of men and women who favoured one child, and an increase in the number favouring two and then three. Public portrayals of 'leading women' invariably featured married career women with several children – the childless career woman slipped from view (Penrose, 1990).

Just as measures designed to give greater recognition to home roles in West Germany may have increased gender divisions and inequalities, so mother-oriented policies in East Germany became deleterious to women's equality. The scale of maternity leave soon caused serious labour shortages and discontinuities in female-dominated industries and, in the absence of any discourse laying responsibilities for childcare with fathers, to resentment against female labour. Employees without childcare responsibilities and jealous of mothers' 'privileges', which included men, allocated domestic roles even more firmly to them. There was no public discussion of men's roles in the domestic sphere, or of the bearing of inequalities in the private sphere on inequalities in the public arena. Thus 'the personal' was not seen as 'political', except in the growing alternative cultures grouped around the churches. Fathers were officially treated 'like grandparents' (Ferree, 1993, p. 94) – to be called on in emergency, even though in practice, with both parents working, fathers may have habitually done more than average fathers in the West. There was no public discourse on alternative life-styles, household forms or sexual orientations. Throughout the 1980s, standardised, heterosexual life-courses and life-styles were the public 'norm'.

Dölling (1991) argues that the public patriarchy of state socialism gave rise to a tutelary mentality, and that the evident progressivism of the system obscured from women themselves the nature and extent of their subordination and oppression. The fact that the niche society of weekend house and garden served as a retreat from the meaninglessness of public society into a greater meaningfulness in personal and family relations also impeded the addressing of gender conflicts and the politicisation of personal life which has been at the heart of western feminism (Dölling, 1991). The author highlights the 'multiple devaluation' suffered by women in the GDR, not just the manifest inequalities in the public sphere, but the lack of any celebration or recognition of domestic roles and of their centrality in female identity.

The fact that women erupted so passionately on to the political scene in 1989 showed the discord between official GDR 'women's politics' and women's own political subjectivities. Among such organisations as the *Unabhängiger Frauenverband* (UFV, Independent Women's Association), immediate objection was made to the paternalism of the 'guardian state', the public patriarchy of state socialism and the anomaly of 'women's politics' never having been shaped or defined by women themselves. The replacement of administrative bureaucratic politics by a radical democracy based on self-determination became a key theme in the new burgeoning of civil society and social movements which formed part of the process of unification.

Nevertheless, it must be stressed that, from its inception, the GDR had granted women the kind of legal independence which West German women only achieved in the 1977 legislation. Although women carried an undue proportion of domestic roles, they were not subject to private patriarchy in the West German sense of legal subordination to and financial dependence on men. By the 1980s, three generations of children had been brought up by working mothers, and the greater independence of women was evident in the frequency of single parenthood and divorce.

The focus of reform in the East in the 1970s and 1980s was on pronatalist material benefits to facilitate the combining of work and home roles. It led to highly standardised life-courses and a 'normalised' life-style, and precluded discussion of relations between the productive and reproductive spheres as well as issues of gender and subjectivity. Reforms in the East concerned legislation and subsidies, whereas in the West there 'has been a cultural change, a revolution in our minds, our consciousness, and in gender relations in everyday life' (Gerhard, 1992, p. 31). Thus the situation of women in East Germany was at great odds with that of women in West Germany, who, as we have seen, were themselves deeply divided. One might perhaps speak of a three-way division, between 'mothers' and 'careerists' in the West and 'working mothers' in the East, with considerable mutual hostility. For women from the West, the unproblematised GDR policies of 'equality' exemplified how 'sameness' produces inequality by ignoring feminine specificities. On the other hand, women from the East had little time for western dilemmas over combining home and work. Moreover, only 3 per cent of East German women espoused a full-time housewife role, as against 25 per cent in West Germany (Gerhard, 1992, p. 23). They thus vehemently rejected the West German 'housewife' model, but felt equally alienated from the 25 per cent of West German women who opted for childlessness.

Unification

Ina Merkel, a leading figure in the Independent Women's Association, described unification as 'three steps back' for East German women. Many writers, from both East and West, consider that women in East Germany are bearing the brunt of unification, through higher unemployment, the loss of social rights and provisions and a more fundamental change in their habitual social relations. Single mothers and older women are worst placed, but women with children or the prospect of having children are also strongly affected. Wild fluctuations in general social indicators following unification bore witness to the social trauma. The birth rate fell by 62 per cent between 1989 and 1992 (*Guardian*, 12 August 1993), marriages dropped by 60 per cent, divorces by 80 per cent (though divorce figures could be affected by new legal procedures) (*Guardian*, 25 May 1993), and in 1992 a huge increase in demand for sterilisations to enhance job prospects was reported.

In 1992, three-quarters of the unemployed in the new *Länder* were women and they were greatly disadvantaged because of the need for mobility in many jobs – car, driving licence, phone, childcare, availability for long hours, and training and even employment away from home. The effect of federal protective legislation was to remove women wholesale from certain jobs such as those in the building and electrical trades. Many women worked in job creation schemes, but these were of limited duration. There were fewer training opportunities for them than for men, and least of all for older women. Older women were least likely to find work, and those who were single or divorced could not look forward to protection through husbands' and widows' pensions. Pension differentials trebled in East Germany through unification, one reason being the loss of credits for childrearing. Women pensioners in East Germany used to gain on average nine years' pension credit for childrearing, whereas until 1992 the federal system allowed only one year per child (Gerhard, 1992). Since then three years per child have been allowed. The change from being a fully employed woman with publicly provided childcare to being a 'housewife' with children in a typically small flat with few neighbourhood playplaces is dramatic. With job loss went the loss of workplace-based social networks, through which much sociability was organised in the GDR, much more than in the neighbourhood. Being more dependent on social contacts than men, women were more affected by the destruction of social relations and ways of behaving which were firmly embedded in enterprises, and by the replacement of communality by egoistic competition (Bertram, 1993).

Abortion rights was one of the slowest issues to be resolved in the process of unification. Eventually it was agreed to continue the respective systems for two years, and a provisional compromise was reached in 1993. This allowed abortions up to twelve weeks, subject to obligatory counselling, on which notes must be kept, 'with a view to protecting the unborn child' and 'emphasising alternatives to abortion'. The counselling is delegated to particular organisations such as *Pro Familia* and *Caritas*, and is chargeable to the individual, not the sickness insurance funds (*Die Zeit*, 16 July 1993; *Guardian*, 12 August 1993).

Many commentators have been struck by the relative quiescence with which women have suffered these losses, following their prominent and active role in the events of the political 'spring' of 1989–90. Not that all has been lost from that creative period. By 1991 an astonishing 272 women's equality offices had been established in the former GDR (Ferree, 1993), notably more oriented to 'equality' than to 'special treatment' as in the case of their West German counterparts. A great number of local initiatives continued into 1992 and 1993, often as self-help groups, though relying on temporary posts. Nursery cutbacks were successfully fought in many places, more nurseries remaining open for longer hours than had been projected. And the proposals from the Round Table's Social Charter, to which women had contributed a great deal, continued to be actively discussed, as in the Frankfurt Forum 'Women for a New Constitution', organised by western feminists (Feministische Studien, 1991).

Unification in the context of recession also resulted in cut-backs in social spending and in federal reform programmes. One reform of great significance to older women, now jeopardised, is the much debated new care insurance (*Pflegeversicherung*). This was designed to reduce poverty arising from costs of care in old age, and would disproportionately benefit women, since they live longer and are poorer. It has been the subject of much political controversy, even holding up the formation of the government in 1991, because of CDU/FDP disputes over the structure of contributions. Controversy continued in 1993 over proposals to fund it by sacrificing a public holiday or by removing payments from the first two days of sickness (see Chapter 3).

Most feminists have been bitterly disappointed by the outcomes of unification, seeing a strengthening of patriarchy in both East and West. 'Much of what has been accomplished in the past decades in the interests of dismantling patriarchal gender roles and the emancipation of women, laborious and inadequate though it has been, is now endangered' (Dölling, 1991, p. 14). Rather than blaming women from the East, Rosenberg castigates western feminists for a failure to fight for the preservation of entitlements and legal guarantees of the GDR. She derisively argues that West German feminists have only ever been 'passive and secondhand beneficiaries' of East German pro-natalist policies, since improvements in West Germany resulted not from feminist-led campaigns but from the pressure of East German decrees (Rosenberg, 1993).

Analogies have been drawn between the restrengthening of patriarchy in the 1990s and patriarchal resurgences following the French Revolution and both world wars. Yet again the 'fraternal contract' seems to have operated, the pact between otherwise rivalrous men against womankind (Pateman, 1988), in this case to privilege the position of western and eastern men in the labour market, to the disadvantage of women. Women's rights have once more been sacrificed to alleged economic 'imperatives'. Indeed it seems likely that in the context of the recession women themselves consider men's breadwinner roles as primary, though there is little evidence that eastern women accept housewife roles enthusiastically – numerous attitude surveys have shown the contrary. It may well be, too, that the general sense of 'defeat' in East Germany not only fuels racism and nationalism, but increases patriarchal, even violent, behaviour in the home, as after the Second World War. The resurgence of patriarchy in the old *Länder* is associated partly with the reassertion of nationalism and the sense of superiority and victory over the GDR, and partly with the 'new realism', the pragmatism which ended the radical and theoretical rethinking of 'employment-centredness' and gender relations in the mid-1980s. Hopes that unification would provide a golden opportunity for 'modernisation' of the 'Janus-faced' West German welfare system and the gender relations which it frames were dashed.

Summary

This chapter has explored differences in the position of women in East and West Germany in the 1970s and 1980s, disjunctures in legislation and social policies concerning women, and counter-positions in the standpoint of women themselves, especially feminists, towards issues of equality. Broadly speaking, the West German system can be characterised as reinforcing private patriarchy and the East German system as operating public patriarchy. But contradictions in each situation have also been noted – the way employment-centred West German policies, with the emphasis on marriage rather than children, paradoxically encourage childless careerism among women; the private radicalism arising from twenty years of cultural challenge and change; and the complexities of West German understandings of 'equality' underpinned and enhanced by 'difference'. In the East, the traditionalism in family life underlying East German 'equality' has been pointed to, as have the 'submerged networks' of oppositional consciousness prior to 1989, the social independence of East German women, and the brevity of the period of radical and creative renewal in the 'spring' of 1989–90. The emphasis in West Germany on gender difference appears in many guises: in Social Catholic thinking, dominant after the war; in the movement of autonomous feminism in the 1970s; in predominantly SPD and Green proposals for special measures to realise women's interests in the 1980s; and in 1980s Christian Democrat thinking, which gave more recognition to household roles. Virtually all these West German approaches clash dramatically with the GDR orientation towards equality and support for working mothers, and its neglect of issues of female subjectivity. So far the common interests of women in East and West Germany in combating patriarchy have not produced unity, and neither side feels it has much to gain from the ideas and situation of the other.

Guide to further reading

The ability to read German is a great asset in this field, since there is rather little on women and social policy in Germany in English. Perhaps this is because West German approaches to women have not been seen in the English-speaking world as worthy of emulation. In fact there has been rather more in English on East Germany, given a strong research community in North America oriented to social policy in the GDR.

There are a number of fairly recent and comprehensive texts in German on women and social policy in West Germany. Examples would be Kickbusch and Riedmüller (1984), Gerhard *et al.* (1987) and Münch (1990). There are also chapters in more general books on social policy, such as those by Bender, Gerhard and Ridder-Melchers respectively in Heinze *et al.* (1987) and by Sachße and Tennstedt (1982). For a more general profile of the changing situation of women, Gerhard and Schütze (1988) is useful, together with the volumes on the family in West and East Germany by H. Bertram (1991, 1992), and the chapter by Glatzer and Herget (1984). Perhaps the only book to date giving an overview of the position of women in East and West Germany since 1945 is the volume by Helwig and Nickel (1993), in which several articles pertain to social policy. A more theoretical approach with an emphasis on changing subjectivities among women in West Germany can be found in Müller and Schmidt-Waldherr (1989), and literature on conflicts between home and work provides a useful contextualisation for social policy, as in Beck-Gernsheim (1980), Becker-Schmidt *et al.* (1985) and the chapter by Schultheis (1988). More attention has been paid to elderly women in recent times including Gather *et al.* (1991) and Veil *et al.* (1992). The *Deutsches Zentrum für Altersfragen* has produced a great deal of material and books. Riedmüller (1985) has a chapter on poverty among women.

Material in English on women and social policy in West Germany is scant. Leibfried and Ostner (1991) give a broad consideration to social security issues, and there are several texts on employment issues, mostly focusing on relations between family and work, such as Hinrichs (1990), Scarlett Epstein *et al.* (1986) and chapters by Vogelheim (1988) and Nave-Herz (1989). More general consideration to the position of women in West Germany is given in Kolinsky (1989, rev. edn 1993). On East Germany there are articles in English by Ecklein (1982), Ecklein and Giele (1981), Lane (1983) and Chamberlayne (forthcoming). In German, Penrose (1990) gives an overview of social policy change over time, and Winkler (1990) gives a useful statistical profile. On social policy and unification, literature in English and German is more evenly balanced. In German, Bast and Ostner (1992) make a historical comparison of social policies concerning women in East and West Germany, Nickel (1991) looks at changing gender relations, Süssmuth and Schubert (1992) conduct a debate about the situation of women in East Germany, and Schwarz and Zenner (1990) give voice to the scepticism of East German women themselves in the face of unification. In English, a chapter by Ostner (1993) discusses social policy developments in East and West Germany. A greater focus on the impact of changes in the East is found in articles by Dölling (1991), Ferree (1993), Rosenberg (1993), as well as in the special issue of *German Politics and Society* (1991/2), published by Harvard University.

Journals such as *Blätter der Wohlfahrtspflege, Sozialer Fortschritt, WSI-Mitteilungen* and *Zeitschrift für Sozialreform* reflect the prominence of issues concerning women in social policy in the 1980s in Germany. *Feministische Studien* occasionally carries articles relevant to social policy. These are all in German. Another source in English would be the German sections from EC studies, such as those on single women, single parents, childcare and family policies.

Acknowledgements

Warm thanks to a wide range of people for discussions and for help with collecting literature, and especially Kerstin Bast, Ilona Ostner, Mechthild Veil, Claudia Neusüß, Eva Mädje, Irene Dölling, Hildegaard Nickel, Katrin Leonhart and Annette King.

Chapter 9

Ethnic minorities and social policy

Norman Ginsburg

Migration and settlement

The position of ethnic minority groups in Germany has much in common with other capitalist welfare states, but it is also quite distinctive in a number of ways. The post-war pattern of immigration has not been shaped directly by colonialism, unlike the processes in Britain and France. During the immediate post-war years, quite unlike any other state, West Germany received about fourteen million refugees, almost all ethnic Germans, from Eastern Europe. By the late 1950s, shortages of unskilled labour followed by the construction of the Berlin Wall led the federal government to promote the recruitment of single male workers from Southern Europe, who became known as *Gastarbeiter* or guestworkers. The Federal Labour Office established recruitment agencies in Italy, Spain, Greece, Morocco, Turkey, Yugoslavia and Portugal, and also concluded bilateral recruitment agreements with these countries' governments. The term 'guestworker' suggested, intentionally, that they were recruited on a temporary basis. Indeed the government's stated policy was that they should be rotated on a three-year 'tour of duty'. In recessions in the mid-1960s, early 1970s and early 1980s, many hundreds of thousands of guestworkers returned home, often with financial encouragement from the federal government.

In 1973, active recruitment of guestworkers was ended and tough immigration controls were introduced in a major policy U-turn. This was prompted by a number of factors, including increasing industrial militancy amongst the guestworkers, rising unemployment and falling labour demand, growing racist politics and violence, and concern about the alleged costs of

191

access to the welfare state by settled guestworkers. Partly in response to the firm immigration control after 1973, many of the already established guestworkers brought over their wives and children. Several million former guestworkers and their families have now settled permanently, if never too securely, into German society. It is a clear paradox that in West Germany, as elsewhere, the tightening of immigration control increased the level of permanent settlement. Federal governments have tried many measures to discourage permanent settlement, including financial inducements to leave and at one point withdrawal of child benefit. The reality of permanent settlement is still not accepted by many German people.

Over the past two decades, West Germany has been comparatively open in allowing entry to people seeking asylum from civil war and political oppression around the world. In the 1980s 700,000 people entered the country as asylum seekers, and in the 1990s the numbers increased dramatically, reaching 438,000 for the year 1992 alone. Strongly represented among the asylum seekers in recent years have been Kurdish refugees from Turkey and refugees from former Yugoslavia, Romania, Iran, Lebanon and Afghanistan. It is not clear from the official statistics precisely how many asylum seekers have been able to settle permanently in Germany, but according to Marshall (1992a) at least half of the applicants achieve some form of residence in Germany.

Finally, from the mid-1970s onward the numbers of ethnic Germans from Eastern Europe (beyond the former GDR) migrating to West Germany began to rise. In the mid-1980s, with perestroika, these numbers rose very sharply reaching a peak of almost 400,000 in 1990. In the post-war period, therefore, there have been two very distinct categories of immigrants to Germany, the ethnic Germans and the foreigners (largely former guestworkers and non-German asylum seekers).

German citizenship: the ethnic German identity

German citizenship law dates back to 1913 and is based on *ius sanguinis* (literally 'blood law'). This means that German identity and citizenship are inherited by descent through the father, by being able to trace one's roots to the homeland. A national 'ethnic German' identity was constructed by the Nazis in the 1930s on the mythical idea of the German *Volk*. Article 116 of West Germany's Basic Law (the written constitution adopted in 1949) bestows German citizenship on spouses and descendants of people settled in the German Reich on 31 December 1937, and also on refugees and deportees with German ethnicity (Wilpert, 1991). One of the purposes of Article 116 was to preserve the rights of German people deported under Stalin to various parts of the Soviet Union. During the Cold War, Article 116 symbolised the openness of the West to refugees from the East and of West

Germany as the inheritor of the German homeland. The ethnic Germans, the *Volksdeutsche* or *Aussiedler*, have full rights of citizenship upon entry. Between 1950 and 1991, 2.6 million ethnic Germans from Eastern Europe became citizens of West Germany under this legislation, more than half of them coming from Poland. Just under half of these migrants arrived in the years 1988–91. It has been estimated that there may be another 2 to 3.5 million ethnic Germans hoping to move to Germany from Eastern Europe.

With the very rapid increase in the number of ethnic Germans seeking entry in recent years, the federal government has made strenuous efforts to stem the flow by assisting ethnic Germans abroad and through publicity campaigns in countries of emigration (Marshall, 1992b). In 1991, new legislation significantly tightened the criteria required for proof of German identity. At the same time, the new *Länder* of the former GDR, where benefits, housing and social conditions are inferior to those in the West, were required to take their fair share of newly arrived *Aussiedler*. Newly arrived ethnic Germans now have to stay for at least three years in the place to which they are allocated. If they move, they lose their special status and are treated as foreigners. Nevertheless the welfare benefits available to the ethnic German immigrants are still substantial, including an arrival grant, access to cheap loans, full social insurance rights, the right to paid employment and training, and access to special needs education and skilled trades.

An overall assessment of the status of the newly arrived ethnic Germans in the welfare state is difficult. There are no statistics, for example, on the level of unemployment they experience. They appear to be competing for jobs and housing with foreigners and resettled East Germans rather than with West Germans. Ethnic Germans are much more likely to be employed in manufacturing industry than ordinary Germans. They do not appear to be significantly racialised as a social group and have experienced relatively little hostility compared to foreigners. Hence 'today the ethnic Germans have to prove their Germanity and right to citizenship by presenting papers – which derive directly from the fascist period – in which they are defined as Germans' (Räthzel, 1991, p. 42). This means that the ideological constructions of 'race' and 'nation' embodied in German state policy are almost coterminous, and exclusionary on an ethnic basis. Within this ideology, it is therefore clear that non-Germans are considered outsiders, the Other. As Räthzel puts it,

> there existed a racialized picture of this Other, dark-haired, from the poor
> South, underdeveloped, doing the dirty jobs, of Muslim religion. In short, the
> Other was Turkish, and all other migrants could be constructed as more or less
> Turkish. (1991, p. 46)

The explicitly racist concept of citizenship incorporated in Article 116 is arguably an ideological cornerstone which reinforces the inferior status of foreigners in Germany. In the context of reunification and mass unemployment in the early 1990s, it also provides a form of legitimation for the recent epidemic of racist violence against ethnic minorities. In turn there have been growing pressures for a reform of Article 116. The Editor of the major weekly *Die Zeit* recently called for Germany 'to throw open the door of citizenship to our non-German residents . . . mere "fellow citizen" status is not enough. It is a status that condemns non-German residents to a system of apartheid' (Sommer, 1993, p. 22). The Green Party, the Social Democratic Party (SPD) and the Free Democratic Party (FDP) have all expressed their support for the repeal of Article 116, but Helmut Kohl's Christian Democrat-dominated government is hesitant. His coalition partners in the right-wing Bavarian Christian Social Union (CSU) are resolutely opposed to reform. Both Chancellor Kohl and Foreign Minister Kinkel floated the idea of temporary double citizenship for long-term immigrants in the aftermath of the Solingen tragedy (below) in June 1993. The government-appointed Commissioner for Foreigners is supporting a campaign for all children of foreigners to gain German citizenship, for naturalisation after eight years residence and for dual nationality (Tomforde, 1993a).

From guestworkers to foreigners

With the shift to permanent settlement and immigration control after 1973, the term 'guestworker' was replaced in popular and official discourses by the term 'foreigner' (*Ausländer*). This is a

> seemingly neutral term [which] is becoming pejorative, just as the word 'immigrant' did in Britain two decades ago . . . the legal, socioeconomic and cultural status of 'foreigner' is the distinguishing mark of the minorities in West Germany, just as being black is the clearest sign of minority status in Britain. (Castles, 1984, pp. 98–9)

In practice the term 'foreigner' is rarely applied in ordinary discourse to white people of Northern European or North American origin. It has come to denote the families and descendants of the former guestworkers from Southern Europe and of the asylum seekers from Southern Europe, Asia and Africa. The great majority of the foreigners in Germany are people of colour, visibly identifiable as 'the Other'. They have been the targets for the racist terror of the recent past.

There are also hidden groups of foreigners without work or residence permits, including people whose asylum applications have failed. They may be illegally employed, often on sub-contracts by large corporations. They are especially vulnerable to exploitation and brutality because of their status. This was revealed in the work of Günther Wallraff (1988), who disguised himself as a Turkish worker and experienced at first hand highly dangerous and exploitative working conditions, and overt racism from German bosses and workers. The use of illegal migrant workers as highly exploitable cheap labour is of course common in many advanced capitalist economies, including Britain and the United States, but it has been particularly significant in West Germany.

In 1990, 'foreigners' officially comprised 8.2 per cent of the population of West Germany, living mostly in ethnically segregated inner areas of the big cities, particularly in the Rhineland, the Munich area and West Berlin. They are most commonly accommodated in privately rented tenement flats, while more recent asylum seekers are accommodated in hostels. More than a quarter of the residents of Frankfurt are foreigners. The reality is that, as in Britain and France, many cities are now multi-racial and multi-cultural in their social composition with permanently settled ethnic minority communities. Around 60 per cent of foreigners have been resident for more than ten years and 70 per cent of foreign children under 16 were born in Germany.

By far the largest ethnic group are the 1.7 million people of Turkish origin, around one-third of the foreign population. Most of the Turkish community has been settled for at least two decades and is particularly heterogeneous. There are very significant cultural and political divisions among them, for example between Kurdish refugees and former guestworkers. A Turkish middle class is emerging in professions such as medicine, social work and school teaching, though career opportunities in the professions have been severely limited by nationality laws and qualification regulations. There are 35,000 self-employed Turkish business people. The Turkish community is comparatively youthful, with 36 per cent under the age of 18. Although young Turkish people are entering higher education, they are three times more likely to leave school without qualifications than German young people (Gow, 1993a; see also Chapter 6). Around 15 per cent of Turkish homes are owner-occupied as compared with 40 per cent of all homes in Germany (see Chapter 5). It has been estimated that the Turkish community contributes 9 per cent of GNP and 7 per cent of the total tax revenue. Turkish people pay 8 per cent of contributions to the pension funds, but receive only 2.5 per cent of payments, because of their comparative youth (Tomforde, 1993a). Indeed, the leader of the SPD recently suggested that 'Germany will soon need an annual influx of about 300,000 immigrants, simply to be able to pay the pensions of its rapidly ageing population' (Gow, 1993b). The importance of foreigners' contributions has given a new twist to the tough political debate about the fiscal crisis of the German social insurance schemes.

Only about 1,000 Turkish people a year were successful in achieving naturalisation before 1991, but applications increased fivefold in 1991 when regulations were eased slightly under the new Aliens Act (below). Surveys suggest that 83 per cent want to settle permanently (Tomforde, 1993a) and that 90 per cent of young Turkish people would apply for dual citizenship if it were possible (Gow, 1993a). Less than 1 per cent of the Turkish community have German citizenship. This is not only due to Article 116 but also because dual citizenship is not permitted. Also, Turkish law only permits Turkish nationals to own property in Turkey, and people of Turkish origin in Germany are understandably unwilling to renounce their property rights. In 1992, an estimated 140,000 people living in Turkey applied for German visas, most of them trying to join relatives in Germany. About 30 per cent of applications were rejected (O'Toole, 1993). Annually around 25,000 Turkish people, particularly Kurdish refugees, apply for political asylum in Germany.

Asylum seekers

In the early 1990s, the attention of the policy-makers and the media was not focused on the established ethnic minority communities, nor on the question of Article 116. The concern of the political establishment focused predominantly on the increasing number of people seeking asylum in Germany. After the war, in an effort to distance itself from the fascist past, West Germany adopted a comparatively liberal asylum law in Article 16 of the Basic Law which says that 'every politically persecuted individual has a right to asylum' (quoted by Marshall, 1992b, p. 124). Asylum seekers could remain in the country while their applications were evaluated. From 1980 onward, the federal government introduced a series of measures designed to make West Germany less attractive and less accessible to asylum seekers, including a ban on employment for the first five years (rescinded in 1991), no child benefit while applications were considered and access only to benefits in kind (Marshall, 1992b). New visa regulations made access to asylum for non-Europeans much more difficult from the mid-1980s. Nevertheless, by the early 1990s Germany was allowing entry to many more asylum seekers than ever before and ten times more than any other European country. In 1992, 78 per cent of those arriving at immigration control in EC countries and gaining entry as refugees went to Germany. Untold numbers were rejected at the border. Most of those entering came from former Yugoslavia, Romania and Bulgaria. Around 30 per cent came from Africa and Asia. It has been estimated that the cost of caring for these people in 1992 in Germany was about £4 billion (Tomforde, 1993b). During the refugee crisis of the early 1990s and in the context of resettling former East Germans and ethnic Germans, the German government received little or no support from other EC members in coping with the asylum seekers. In 1992, while Germany accepted applications from 437,996 people, Britain accepted them from only 24,610 and France from 26,825 (Carvel, 1993a). In the words of Martin Kettle, the lack of sympathy and understanding for Germany's predicament is truly shocking. Unlike Britain, which has barely been affected by it, Germany has had to take the full weight of post-1989 European destabilisation . . . what do we do? We remain indifferent. We check the locks on our own doors. We look the other way. And we even say it serves them right. (1993, p. 26)

This indifference to the asylum question and the relentless bolstering of Fortress Europe by EC immigration ministers in recent years may come back to haunt governments in a much more destructive way in the future as the crisis in Central and Eastern Europe unfolds. Given the indifference of other EC countries and growing public hostility to the refugees, the German parliament voted in May 1993 to amend Article 16 drastically. Article 16 was being blamed for the rise in racist attacks. As Sivanandan has said, 'instead of Germany getting rid of that clause . . . the rest of Europe should rise up to Germany's example' (1993, p. 72). The vote, however, was carried by 521–132 with the support of the SPD leadership, although it had been previous SPD policy to insist on reform of Article 116 alongside Article 16. The new policy came into force on 1 July 1993. Asylum seekers who are already refugees in allegedly safe third countries are now refused entry and their application is considered while they remain outside Germany. Over 80 per cent of asylum seekers had travelled from such 'safe' countries, particularly the Czech Republic and Poland. The July 1993 restrictions led to a drop of 25 per cent in the number of refugees entering Germany in 1993 as a whole, suggesting that the new rules have cut the flow by over 50 per cent on an annual basis (Carvel, 1994a). This new policy in Germany coincided with an EC immigration ministers' meeting at which it was agreed to introduce 'rigorous checks to identify and expel foreign students and residents who take jobs without authorisation . . . [and] stricter monitoring of short-stay visitors and people allowed in to be reunited with their families or to marry a Community resident' (Carvel, 1993b).

Once admitted to the country, asylum seekers face months or years awaiting the outcome of their applications. Asylum seekers have to remain resident where they are allocated accommodation by the authorities while their applications are considered. They are distributed across all the *Länder* according to a formula. Within a few weeks of reunification, the East German *Länder* were obliged to accept 20 per cent of asylum seekers, despite a dearth of support services for them (Marshall, 1992b). Their reception in East Germany has been particularly inhospitable. According to Marshall they 'receive no help with language classes as integration into German society is not intended, but basic health care is provided. While children of asylum seekers can attend a school in some *Länder*, there is no federal mandatory provision' (1992a, p. 254). Under the 1990 Aliens Act, asylum seekers can get a permit to work for a particular firm 'provided that no other workers are available to do this work and/or can be placed there by the employment office' (Heinelt, 1993, p. 88). In recent years, only about

6 per cent of applications for asylum have been successful. An analysis of unsuccessful asylum seekers in 1989 showed that 6 per cent were returned to their home country, 15 per cent left West Germany voluntarily, 6 per cent put in another appeal, 34 per cent were allowed to stay on humanitarian grounds, 17 per cent were 'tolerated temporarily' and the fate of the other 18 per cent was unknown (Marshall, 1992b). In other words, more than half of the unsuccessful asylum seekers were allowed to stay.

Legal status of foreigners

Despite the reality of permanent settlement in the last two or three decades, state policy continues to treat the ethnic minorities in ways which reflect their status not merely as foreigners but perhaps as an underclass. The fundamental policy principle has always been that West Germany 'is not nor should ever become a "country of immigration"' (Edye, 1987, p. 13). This principle has been reasserted regularly since the 1960s by politicians from all the major parties except the Greens. It was emphatically restated in a report commissioned by the SPD/FDP coalition government in 1977, which said that it was 'necessary to restrict the employment of foreigners and to maintain an awareness of the possibility of returning home' (Edye, 1987, p. 35). Thus the legal and policy status of foreigners is very distinct at a formal level and extremely ambiguous at a day-to-day level. The Foreigners Act of 1965 denied them the right to vote, although this was conceded by some local authorities and by some *Länder* for local and regional elections in the 1980s. In 1990, however, the Federal Constitutional Court decreed these concessions unconstitutional. Ironically, the 1965 Act states clearly that 'Foreigners enjoy all basic rights, except the basic rights of freedom of assembly, freedom of association, freedom of movement, and free choice of occupation, place of work and place of education, and protection from extradition abroad' (Castles, 1984, p. 77).

Legislation in 1969 prescribed that German citizens must always be given preference over a foreigner when a job vacancy is filled. In effect this legislation, refined by several other subsequent measures and enforced by specialist local foreigner departments and police forces, has established unusually explicit forms of institutional racism. It bestows the privilege of residence in Germany, which can be rescinded in the event of unemployment, differences with an employer, brushes with the law and so on, so that 'deportation is a permanent Damocles' sword' (Castles, 1984, p. 77). Only a tiny proportion of foreigners have become naturalised citizens of Germany and the children of foreigners remain foreigners under the 'blood law'. The barriers to naturalisation and citizenship are much higher in Germany than in other European countries for reasons discussed above.

In 1990 a new double-edged Aliens Act was passed, which came into effect on 1 January 1991. On the positive side, it has improved the legal right of abode for long-settled foreigners, making it easier for close relatives to rejoin their families and a little easier to achieve naturalisation. However, the new legislation also gave the authorities further repressive powers, for example to eject 'undesirables', including people with AIDS, to establish a computerised register of foreigners and to limit the right of abode for separated and divorced foreign women. Also, foreigners who want to apply for a permanent residence permit have to be resident for eight years rather than five previously, to have made at least sixty months social insurance contributions and to prove they have 'sufficient living space' (Marshall, 1992a, pp. 251–2). Under the new Act, according to Räthzel,

> foreign workers, except for a very small minority [EC citizens], can be treated
> even more absolutely as disposable units of labour; they can be repatriated
> or 'rotated' at will – a demand hitherto voiced in public only by the extremist
> right-wing Republican Party. (1991, p. 43)

The Minister of the Interior commented that 'the main aim is to take steps to ensure that hostility to foreigners is not allowed to grow . . . [but] Third World problems cannot be solved by unrestricted access' (*Guardian*, 13 April 1990, p. 15). Nevertheless, the hostility to ethnic minorities has very little to do with their legal status, nor was the recruitment of foreign labour anything to do with solving Third World problems. The new Aliens Act was strongly opposed by churches, trade unions, pressure groups and ethnic minority organisations.

Germany has no legislation explicitly addressing the question of racial discrimination comparable to the US Civil Rights Acts or the Race Relations Act in Britain. In common with most other European countries, questions about the rights of ethnic minorities are subsumed under constitutional and other legal rights of individuals in general. Hence there is a clause in the Basic Law covering all public bodies which says that 'no one may be prejudiced or favoured because of his sex, his parentage, his race, his language, his homeland and origin, his faith or his religious or political opinions' (Forbes and Mead, 1992, p. 40). For the private sector, the Works Constitution Act imposes a similar obligation on employers and works councils. Legally resident foreigners are covered by these statutes but it is unclear to what extent they are actually invoked, if at all, in cases of alleged racial discrimination, whether direct or indirect. It appears that cases are normally dealt with informally by the trade unions and/or by the regional and federal officials responsible for the integration of foreign workers. According to Forbes and Mead,

> at present, foreigners feel discrimination more keenly in the public arena
> generally than in the employment sector. The main problem for ethnic
> minorities concerns the right to gain permission to work at all (this is in the
> hands of the government and the operation of its offices dealing with residence

permits) . . . Even if an individual is discriminated against in the employment situation, it is unlikely that a complaint will be brought. (1992, p. 42)

The nationality laws and regulations on non-German qualifications make it very difficult for a non-German doctor, dentist or pharmacist to establish his or her own office or for non-German teachers or lawyers to gain the all important civil servant status. A foreigner has to have permanent residence status and official approval before becoming self-employed. The trade union federation (DGB) and the Federal Commissioner for the Integration of Foreign Workers and Their Dependants have called for the introduction of anti-discrimination legislation to protect ethnic minorities, but for the moment this seems a distant prospect.

Ethnic minority employment and social welfare

Official statistics for the western *Länder* for 1991 give some insight into the distribution of foreigners in the labour market (Statistisches Bundesamt, 1992, Table 6.10). Foreigners are significantly over-represented in the manufacturing and construction industries, particularly the plastics, rubber, metal and textile industries, as well as in hotel, catering and cleaning services. In the latter, predictably perhaps, ethnic minority women predominate over men. Foreigners are significantly under-represented in trade, commerce and communications, particularly among the self-employed and in the postal service. They are also particularly under-represented in some services including banking and insurance, science and the arts, education, advertising, health care, legal and consultancy services, voluntary organisations and in local and regional authorities. In comparison with Britain, the ethnic minorities in Germany have clearly gained significantly less access to self-employment and employment in public sector services. It is generally true to say that both these sectors have traditionally enjoyed a higher status and greater exclusivity in Germany than in Britain.

Unemployment has differentially affected the ethnic minorities very clearly over the past two decades. Fluctuations in the overall level of registered unemployment in the 1960s and 1970s were commonly considered to be cyclical, though after the 1973 recession the level remained around 4 per cent for the rest of the decade. The figure was kept down by the departure of over half a million guestworkers in the mid-1970s. The more severe 1981 recession raised the level for the rest of the 1980s to between 8 and 10 per cent. Women and foreign workers have borne more of the burden of registered unemployment than German men. According to an April 1990 mini-census (Statistisches Bundesamt, 1992, Table 6.5), 11.5 per cent of foreigners were unemployed but seeking paid employment, compared with 5.8 per cent of Germans. Of foreign women, 14.3 per cent were unemployed and seeking paid employment, compared to 7.6 per cent of German women. Clearly unemployment continues to affect women and foreigners differentially, and ethnic minority women in particular. In the decade 1978–88, the registered unemployment rate for foreigners rose relatively modestly from 10.4 per cent to 12.0 per cent, while doubling from 4.3 per cent to 8.7 per cent for the population as a whole. On the other hand, the fall in registered unemployment in the late 1980s was greater for German workers than for foreign workers. On the basis of these statistics, it can tentatively be suggested that the level of unemployment amongst foreign workers is more immune to the effects of recession than for German workers. However, the level of unemployment amongst foreign workers varies between one and a half times and double that for German workers. This is a marginally better situation than that in Britain where the ethnic minority unemployment rate in the 1980s remained at twice the level for the workforce as a whole, whether the economy was booming or in recession. Foreigners who have been unemployed for more than a year, have insufficient social insurance contributions and do not have a special work permit are in a particularly difficult situation. If they

> cannot be found work by the employment office . . . they are then considered to be 'non-placeable' and thus they no longer have any right to payments in lieu of wages [unemployment assistance] . . . when the employment offices are placing people, [such individuals] are to be considered only *after* local people, citizens of member states of the EC and foreigners with a special work permit. (Heinelt, 1993, p. 91)

Aussiedler, on the other hand, have a relatively privileged position within the welfare state, as mentioned already. They have been given a special positive status within the social insurance system: the contribution principle has been suspended, giving them full access to benefits with credited contributions (Heinelt, 1993, p. 92).

Ethnic minorities have, as we have seen, enjoyed limited political rights under the law, but since the early 1970s they have received some of the benefits and services of the welfare state, including unemployment benefit and social assistance. The number of social assistance claimants from the 'foreign' communities has risen very significantly in recent years, from 9.1 per cent of the total number of claimants in 1984 to 21.7 per cent in 1990 (Statistisches Bundesamt, 1992, Table 19.12). In part this is a result of pressure from ethnic minorities themselves, making the point that they have always been net contributors to the welfare state through social insurance contributions and taxation over the past two or three decades. There were two obvious reasons for the relatively low level of claims by the 'foreign' community prior to the 1980s. First, before the settlement of dependants since the early 1970s, single guestworkers made very few demands on the welfare state. They were either employed or returned home. Second, the number of ethnic minority elderly people is very small, when compared to the number of German state pensioners. Subsequently, however, the picture has changed somewhat. In 1990, the proportion of foreigners in paid employment was 43 per cent, exactly the same proportion as for the population as a whole. The proportion of foreigners receiving pensions was 12 per cent, compared to 22 per cent of the population as a whole. The proportion of foreigners described as dependants was 42 per cent compared to 34 per cent for the population as a whole (Statistisches Bundesamt, 1992, Table 6.1). These statistics indicate the considerable level of potential and actual demand for social welfare from the foreigner communities. Nevertheless, the settled ethnic minorities remain net contributors to, rather than net beneficiaries of, the social security system.

Eligibility for welfare benefits, of course, depends on the particular status of a foreigner seeking to claim. As Heinelt (1993, p. 87) puts it, 'asylum seekers, people entitled to asylum, foreigners seeking work and *Aussiedler* enter a selection corridor' in which each group has a different legal status. Asylum seekers who breach the regulations regarding employment, length of stay, accommodation and so on cannot claim benefit. There are a considerable number in this position. Asylum seekers are only eligible for a restricted form of social assistance, which typically just provides hostel accommodation and pocket money. Successful applicants for asylum are eligible for the full range of welfare benefits. Migrant workers are eligible for social insurance benefits covering sickness, old age and unemployment. However, the level of benefits is strictly earnings-related and related to the number of insurance contributions (see Chapter 3). Inevitably, therefore, most foreigners do not benefit from social insurance as fully as the indigenous population. This is another contributory factor to the relatively high level of social assistance claims from the ethnic minorities. Migrant workers from outside the EC can claim full social assistance benefit, but such a claim can be used as evidence for deportation.

Politics, policy and racist violence

The position of the ethnic minorities has not of course gone unquestioned in German politics. Since the official end of the guestworker policy in the early 1970s, liberals have advocated integrationist or multiculturalist policies. The most important example of this at federal government level was the Kühn report of 1979, commissioned by the SPD/FDP coalition. The report recognised the reality of permanent settlement and advocated a more secure legal standing for foreigners. Specific proposals included the right to employment and to naturalisation for foreigners' children, and the right to vote in local elections after ten years' residence. The Kühn report reflected political pressure exerted by foreigners through the trade union movement and their own community political organisations. Foreigners are about 10 per cent of trade union membership; around 50 per cent of Turkish workers are unionised. The biggest trade union, the engineering workers of *IG Metall*, supported the Kühn report, but the trade union federation, the DGB, did not. The SPD/FDP government did not implement any of Kühn's proposals. The government's support of the status quo was indicated by the introduction of tougher immigration rules in 1981.

The election of the conservative federal government in 1982 prompted an immediate commitment from Chancellor Kohl to cut the foreign population by a million by the end of the decade. This was to be achieved by voluntary repatriation. The Ministry of the Interior, rather than the Ministry of Labour and Social Affairs, became responsible for foreigners. This, according to Castles 'symbolised a change in the perception of migrants: they were no longer useful labour, but rather a problem of public order' (1992, p. 49). In 1983, parliament passed a law to encourage voluntary repatriation, offering a cash sum to unemployed migrant workers who were prepared to leave the country immediately and for good. Only 16,883 workers took up the offer. Castles suggests that 'the real impact of this law was ideological: it led people to think that the government was doing something about "the foreigner problem"' (1992, p. 51). In 1983, a government commission proposed over eighty changes to foreigner policies, including summary deportation of the long-term unemployed, social assistance claimants, people convicted of a criminal offence, political 'extremists' and people failing to carry an identity card. However, although some restrictions on asylum seekers and foreigners were subsequently tightened, the new Foreigners Act never emerged. The proposals were successfully opposed by a broad coalition of ethnic minority organisations, liberals and anti-racists, including trade unions, the Green Party, the SPD and liberal churches. Under these latter pressures, regional and local government and some progressive employers have invested substantially in education, welfare, housing and health care projects for the ethnic minority communities.

With the sharp increase in unemployment in the early 1980s, local citizens' action groups began to campaign for '*Ausländer raus*' ('foreigners out') (Derbyshire, 1987). The Republican Party (REP) was formed in 1984 as a breakaway from the CSU, advocating forced repatriation of foreigners and reunification within Germany's 1937 frontiers, which include large tracts of Polish territory. The REP has been able to 'establish a firm and broad base of support, particularly amongst young working-class men, and also inside sections of the state apparatus like the police and armed forces' (Atkinson, 1993, p. 156). The REP and the more overtly fascist *Deutsche Volksunion* (DVU) have gained increasing support at local and regional elections since the late 1980s. In March 1993, the REP and DVU won more than 13 per cent of the vote in regional elections in Frankfurt, achieving over a third of the vote in some working-class districts.

Racial attacks and harassment of ethnic minorities in Germany increased steadily during the 1980s. Since the sudden incorporation of East Germany into the Federal Republic in the autumn of 1990, a great increase in racist activity and violence directed largely at non-European refugees and former guestworkers has occurred. From reunification up to mid-June 1993 there had been 7,555 attacks on foreigners officially recorded in Germany. The number of people killed by racists increased from 25 in 1992 to 52 in 1993 (Doyle, 1994, p. 16). Three incidents in particular have focused the attention of the world. In August 1992 in the East German city of Rostock, neo-Nazis attacked and destroyed a hostel housing Vietnamese people, encouraged by a large crowd of local people and ignored by the police. In November 1992, a Turkish woman and two Turkish girls died in an arson attack on their home in Mölln in the far north of West Germany. In May 1993, in the Ruhr steel town of Solingen, two Turkish women and three Turkish girls died when their house was set on fire. Twenty people were asleep in the house at the time. This was followed by several days of angry demonstrations by the Turkish community and supporters. The events of 1992–3 have prompted large anti-racist demonstrations across the country, notably the largest demonstration ever seen in Berlin in November 1992. According to Habermas,

> on the streets of big German cities resistance is obviously stirring. Resolute and credible opposition to xenophobia and anti-semitism is . . . [coming from] the left-wing and liberal grassroots . . . defending the standards of civic intercourse which were acquired and partly taken for granted in the old Federal Republic. (1993, p. 65)

Of course, racist terrorism is not confined to Germany. In the EC as a whole there were fifty-four officially recorded racist murders in 1992. Racist murders have occurred regularly in Britain over recent years, only some of which have attracted national media attention. Currently the problem appears to be significantly worse in Germany, where neo-Nazi groups have been able to motivate and mobilise some young people. The racial violence in Germany inevitably attracts media attention nationally and internationally because of Germany's past. The official denial of permanent settlement, the blood law of citizenship and the general emphasis on the 'otherness' of ethnic minorities, as described above, have unquestionably helped to create a context in which racism and neo-Nazism can flourish. The amendment of Article 16 must be seen as a victory for the far right and, moreover, one for which all the West European nations must accept responsibility.

Habermas suggests that German conservatives are 'undergoing a split, now that the unifying bonds of anticommunism have dissolved' (1993, p. 66). On the one hand, conservatives of the right are embracing a 'historically-laden Deutschmark nationalism' which shelters in concepts of nationhood and citizenship defined by ethnicity and the blood law. On the other hand, conservatives of the left are more openly supporting more modern, more republican notions of citizenship and nationhood based upon ethnic pluralism and a social contract. In their characteristically hesitant and arm's-length approach to recent events, Helmut Kohl and his cabinet have tended towards the former position. Former cabinet members such as Rita Süssmuth and Heiner Geissler have occupied the latter ground. Süssmuth, now the president of the German parliament, has urged the government to 'go on the offensive' against the far right by considering reform of the citizenship laws and the legal status of foreigners (Crawshaw, 1993).

Conclusion

Racialised ethnic minorities in Germany, mostly recruited by the state as guestworkers, have now settled permanently. They have a more insecure and inferior status within the labour market and within the welfare state than in most other European states. This is enforced by comparatively explicit racist immigration and citizenship laws, and by institutional racism. It is also being reinforced by racist intimidation and violence. These processes are, of course, being stoutly resisted by the ethnic minority communities themselves, supported by German liberals and anti-racists. However, it remains the case that Germany and Switzerland are the only western states which continue to adhere formally to an 'exclusionary' model of immigration in which 'the dominant definition of the nation is that of a community of birth and descent . . . unwilling to accept immigrants and their children as members of the nation' (Castles and Miller, 1993, p. 223). The exclusionary model, as symbolised in the present citizenship law, appears to have considerable popular support, but it seems unlikely that it can be sustained in the long term if reasonable social harmony is to be maintained. On the far right, fascists and racists are gathering support for more extreme policies, nurtured by the revival of German nationalism in the wake of reunification, the model of ethnic cleansing in former Yugoslavia, and the rise in unemployment. In December 1993, official German unemployment reached 3.7 million, a post-war record.

The only immediately feasible alternative to the exclusionary model and to fascism is some variant on the mix of the multiculturalist and assimilationist models adopted in states such as Australia, Holland, Sweden and Britain (see Castles and Miller, 1993). It almost goes without saying that racism and racial inequalities are prominent in all these states, but anti-racism, racial tolerance and multiculturalism appear to be more securely founded. Post-war migration into the advanced capitalist states has undermined to some extent the discourse of national, cultural homogeneity which developed alongside capitalism in the eighteenth and nineteenth centuries (see Miles, 1993). This process has progressed least in Germany, for a host of historical reasons.

An important vehicle for helping to deliver positive policy change in Germany may be the European Union, which is currently considering proposals from the European Commission on immigration and asylum policy following the Maastricht Treaty. The Commission proposes strengthening immigration controls at the border of the European Union and tougher measures against illegal immigrants. To legitimise these controls, it has proposed harmonisation of asylum policies and measures against racial discrimination, and an easing of restrictions on the movement of third-country nationals within the EU. Europe-wide asylum policies could relieve Germany of its unfair burden in this respect. Europe-wide anti-discrimination measures could ease the reform of Article 116 (the blood law) and to legitimate positive multicultural and/or assimilationist developments. Nevertheless, there are obvious strict limits to what can be achieved by European policy delivered from Brussels. At the time of writing (April 1994) the Commission seems to have gone into retreat on some of the more liberal aspects of the above proposals by reasserting member states' right to fix their own nationality laws (Carvel, 1994b, p. 14). Convincing enough of the German and other European electorates that a non-racial basis for nationhood and immigration policy and the adoption of multiculturalism and/or assimilationism is in their interests remains only a long-term prospect.

Guide to further reading

See Marshall (1992a, 1992b) for a discussion of German migration policies, asylum seekers and ethnic minorities. Räthzel (1991) and Wilpert (1991) cover similar topics and problems in unified Germany. A recent publication concerning the issue of migration in Germany and other countries is Castles and Miller (1993).

References

Abelshauser, W. (1983) *Wirtschaftsgeschichte der Bundesrepublik Deutschland 1945–1980*, Frankfurt a.M.: Suhrkamp.

Abelshauser, W. (ed.) (1987) *Die Weimarer Republik als Wohlfahrtsstaat*, Stuttgart: Steiner.

Adams, P. (1990) 'The unity of economic and social policy in the GDR', in B. Deacon and J. Szalai (eds.), *Social Policy in the New Eastern Europe*, Aldershot: Avebury.

Adler, M., Bell, C., Clasen, J. and Sinfield, A. (eds.) (1991) *The Sociology of Social Security*, Edinburgh: Edinburgh University Press.

Alber, J. (1986a) 'Germany', in P. Flora (ed.), *Growth to Limits: The West European welfare states*, vol. II, Berlin: de Gruyter.

Alber, J. (1986b) 'Der Wohlfahrtsstaat in der Wirtschaftskrise – eine Bilanz der Sozialpolitik in der Bundesrepublik seit den frühen siebziger Jahren', *Politische Vierteljahresschrift*, 27 (1), pp. 28–60.

Alber, J. (1987) *Vom Armenhaus zum Wohlfahrtsstaat*, Frankfurt a.M.: Campus.

Alber, J. (1988a) 'The West German welfare state in transition', in R. Morris (ed.), *Testing the Limits of Social Welfare*, Hanover: Brandeis University Press.

Alber, J. (1988b) 'Die Gesundheitssysteme der OECD-Länder im Vergleich', in M. G. Schmidt (ed.), *Staatstätigkeit: International und historisch vergleichende Analysen*, Opladen: Westdeutscher Verlag.

Alber, J. (1989) *Der Sozialstaat in der Bundesrepublik 1950–1983*, Frankfurt a.M.: Campus.

Alber, J. (1991) 'The West German health care system in comparative perspective', in E. Kolinsky (ed.), *The Federal Republic of Germany: The end of an era*, New York: Berg.

Allen, A. T. (1991) *Feminism and Motherhood in Germany 1800–1914*, New Brunswick, NJ: Rutgers University Press.

Anheier, H. K. (1990) 'A profile of the third sector in West Germany', in H. K. Anheier and W. Seibel (eds.), *The Third Sector: Comparative studies of nonprofit organizations*, Berlin: de Gruyter.

Atkinson, G. (1993) 'Germany: nationalism, nazism and violence', in T. Björgo and R. Witte (eds.), *Racist Violence in Europe*, Basingstoke: Macmillan.

Bäcker, G. (1991) 'Sozialpolitik im vereinigten Deutschland', *Aus Politik und Zeitgeschichte*, 3–4, pp. 3–15.

Bäcker, G. (1993) 'Solidarische Bewältigung der Einigungsfolgen: Sozialpolitische

Herausforderungen im vereinten Deutschland', in R. Hickel, E.-U. Huster and H. Kohl (eds.), *Umverteilen*, Cologne: Bund Verlag.

Bäcker, G., Bispink, R., Hofemann, K. and Naegele, G. (1989) *Sozialpolitik und soziale Lage in der Bundesrepublik Deutschland*, vols. I and II, Cologne: Bund Verlag.

Backhaus-Maul, H. and Olk, T. (1992) 'Intermediäre Organisationen als Gegenstand sozialwissenschaftlicher Forschung', in W. Schmähl (ed.), *Sozialpolitik im Prozeß der deutschen Vereinigung*, Frankfurt a.M.: Campus.

Baldwin, P. (1990) *The Politics of Social Solidarity: Class bases of the European welfare state 1875–1975*, Cambridge: Cambridge University Press.

Ball, M., Harloe, M. and Martens, M. (1988) *Housing and Social Change in Europe and the USA*, London: Routledge.

Bargel, T. (1985) 'Studium – hohe Schule, hohe Hürden', in W. Gaiser, S. Hübner-Funk, W. Krüger and R. Rathgeber (eds.), *Immer diese Jugend!*, Munich: Koesel Verlag.

Bast, K. and Ostner, I. (1992) 'Ehe und Familie in der Sozialpolitik der DDR und BRD – ein Vergleich', in W. Schmähl (ed.), *Sozialpolitik im Prozeß der deutschen Vereinigung*, Frankfurt a.M.: Campus.

Baumann, U. (1992) *Protestantismus und Frauenemanzipation in Deutschland 1850 bis 1920*, Frankfurt a.M.: Campus.

Beck, U. (1992) *Risk Society: Towards a new modernity*, trans. Mark Ritter, London: Sage (first published as *Risikogesellschaft: Auf den Weg in eine andere Moderne*, Frankfurt a.M.: Suhrkamp, 1986).

Beck-Gernsheim, E. (1980) *Das halbierte Leben: Männerwelt Beruf – Frauenwelt Familie*, Frankfurt a.M.: Fischer.

Becker-Schmidt, R., Knapp, G. A. and Schmidt, B. (1985) *Eines ist zuwenig – beides ist zuviel: Erfahrungen von Arbeiterfrauen zwischen Familie und Fabrik*, Bonn: Verlag Neue Gesellschaft.

Bendit, R. (1985) 'Bestimmungsfaktoren von Lebenslagen ausländischer Jugendliche in der Bundesrepublik Deutschland oder die gesellschaftliche Reproduktion einer marginalisierten Unterschicht', in R. Bendit, *Lebenslage Jugend*, Munich: DJI Materialen.

Bendit, R., Gaiser, W. and Nissen, U. (1993) 'Growing up in the Federal Republic of Germany: chance and risk in a modern Sozialstaat', in L. Chisholm and E. Leibau (eds.), *Youth, Social Change and Education: Issues, problems, policies in post-1992 Europe, Journal of Education Policy*, 8 (1), special issue, pp. 43–59.

Berger, H., Hinrichs, W. and Priller, E. (1993) 'Entwicklung der Wohlfahrt in Ost und West', *WZB Mitteilungen*, 61, pp. 41–5.

Bertram, B. (1992) 'Aufbruch in Umbruch: Berufliche Orientierung von Jugendlichen in den neuen Bundesländern', *Diskurs*, 912, pp. 40–2.

Bertram, B. (1993) 'Zurück an den Herd?', *Spiegel Spezial*, 1, pp. 62–6.

Bertram, H. (1991) *Die Familie in Westdeutschland: Stabilität und Wandel familialer Lebensformen*, Opladen: Leske und Budrich.

Bertram, H. (1992) *Die Familie in den neuen Bundesländern: Stabilität und Wandel in der gesellschaftlichen Umbruchsituation*, Opladen: Leske und Budrich.

Bertram, H. and Borrmann-Müller, R. (1988) 'Der Einfluß struktureller Wandlungen des Frauseins auf familiales Zusammenleben', in U. Gerhard and Y. Schütze (eds.), *Frauensituation, Veränderungen in den letzten zwanzig Jahren*, Frankfurt a.M.: Suhrkamp.

Bessel, R. (1990) 'State and society in Germany in the aftermath of the First World War', in W. R. Lee and E. Rosenhaft (eds.), *The State and Social Change in Germany 1880–1980*, Oxford: Berg.

von Beyme, K. (1985) 'Policy making in the Federal Republic of Germany: a systematic introduction', in K. von Beyme and M. G. Schmidt (eds.), *Policy and Politics in the Federal Republic of Germany*, Aldershot: Gower.

von Beyme, K. (1992) 'The effects of reunification on German democracy: a preliminary evaluation', *Government and Opposition*, 27, pp. 158–76.

von Beyme, K. and Schmidt, M. G. (eds.) (1985) *Policy and Politics in the Federal Republic of Germany*, Aldershot: Gower.

Bialas, C. and Ettl, W. (1993) 'Wirtschaftliche Lage, soziale Differenzierung und Probleme der Interessenorganisationen in den neuen Bundesländern', *Soziale Welt*, 44, pp. 52–74.

Bieback, K.-J. (ed.) (1986) *Die Sozialversicherung und ihre Finanzierung*, Frankfurt a.M.: Campus.

Blackwell, J. (1992) 'Changing work patterns and their implications for social protection', paper given at *Social Security: 50 Years after Beveridge*, International Conference, University of York, 27–30 September.

Blanc, M. (1991) 'Du logement insalubre a l'habitat social devalorisé: les minorités ethniques en Allemagne, France et Grande-Bretagne', *Les Annales de la Recherche Urbaine*, 49.

Blandow, J. and Tangemann, M. (1992) 'Von christlicher Liebestätigkeit zum Wohlfahrtsverband: Caritas und Diakonie der ehemaligen DDR in der Transformation', in R. Bauer (ed.), *Sozialpolitik in deutscher und europäischer Sicht*, Weinheim: Deutscher Studien Verlag.

Blanke, B., Benzler, S. and Heinelt, H. (1992) 'Explaining different approaches to local labour market policy in the Federal Republic of Germany', *Policy and Politics*, 20, pp. 15–28.

BMAS (Bundesministerium für Arbeit und Sozialordnung) (1990) *Sozialbericht 1990*, Bonn.

BMAS (1991) *Übersicht über die Soziale Sicherheit*, Bonn.

BMAS (1993) *Soziale Sicherheit*, Bonn.

Bock, G. (1984) 'Racism and sexism in Nazi Germany', in R. Bridenthal, A. Grossmann and M. Kaplan (eds.), *When Biology Became Destiny: Women in Weimar and Nazi Germany*, New York: Monthly Review Press.

Boelhouwer, P. and van der Heijden, H. (1992) *Housing Systems in Europe*, Part 1, Delft: Delft University Press.

Borkenstein, H.-J. (1993) 'Ausgabenschwerpunkte im Haushalt 1993 des Bundesbauministeriums', *BundesBauBlatt*, 2 (February), pp. 84–92.

Bradshaw, J., Ditch, J., Holmes, H. and Whiteford, P. (1993) *A Comparative Study of Child Support in Fifteen Countries*, DSS Research Report No. 21, London: HMSO.

Braun, H. and Niehaus, M. (eds.) (1990) *Sozialstaat Bundesrepublik Deutschland auf dem Weg nach Europa*, Frankfurt a.M.: Campus.

Brauns, H.-J. and Kramer, D. (1989) 'West Germany – the break-up of consensus and the demographic threat', in B. Munday (ed.), *The Crisis in Welfare*, Hemel Hempstead: Harvester Wheatsheaf.

Britton, A. (1993) 'Two routes to full employment', *National Institute Economic Review*, 2 (93), pp. 5–11.

vom Bruch, R. (1985) 'Bürgerliche Sozialreform im deutschen Kaiserreich', in R. vom Bruch (ed.), *Weder Kommunismus noch Kapitalismus: Bürgerliche Sozialreform in Deutschland vom Vormärz bis zur Ära Adenauer*, Munich: Beck.

Brühl, A. (1989) *Mein Recht auf Sozialhilfe*, Munich: DTV.

Büchtemann, C. F. (1985) 'Soziale Sicherung bei Arbeitslosigkeit und Sozialhilfebedürftigkeit: Datenlage und neue Befunde', *Mitteilungen aus der Arbeitsmarkt- und Berufsforschung*, 4, pp. 450–66.

Buck, G. (1983) 'Die Entwicklung der freien Wohlfahrtspflege von den ersten Zusammenschlüssen der freien Verbände im 19. Jahrhundert bis zur Durchsetzung des Subsidiaritätsprinzips in der Weimarer Fürsorgegesetzgebung', in R. Landwehr and R. Baron (eds.), *Geschichte der Sozialarbeit: Hauptlinien ihrer Entwicklung im 19. und 20. Jahrhundert*, Weinheim/Basle: Beltz.

Burkhardt, D. (1992) 'Berufsbildung Made in Germany-West und -Ost: Schwierigkeiten bei der Übertragung des dualen Systems', *Diskurs*, 91/2, pp. 14–17.

Burleigh, M. and Wippermann, W. (1991) *The Racial State: Germany 1933–1945*, Cambridge: Cambridge University Press.

Buskase, H. (1992) 'Wohnen in den neuen Bundesländern – Erblasten und Perspektiven', *Der langfristige Kredit*, 21 and 22 November, pp. 734–6.

Bynner, J. and Roberts, K. (eds.) (1991) *Youth and Work: Transition to Employment in England and Wales*, London: Anglo-German Foundation.

Cannan, C., Berry, L. and Lyons, K. (1992) *Social Work and Europe*, London: Macmillan.

Carvel, J. (1993a) 'EC cracks down on migrants', *Guardian*, 26 May, p. 1.

Carvel, J. (1993b) 'Changing face of EC refugees', *Guardian*, 1 June, p. 6.

Carvel, J. (1994a) 'EU is "tough and tender" on migrants', *Guardian*, 6 January, p. 10.

Carvel, J. (1994b) 'EU acts to help ethnic minorities', *Guardian*, 24 February, p. 14.

Casey, B. (1983) 'Integrating young persons into work', *Policy Studies*, 3 (3), pp. 170–83.

Castles, S. (1984) *Here for Good: Western Europe's new ethnic minorities*, London: Pluto Press.

Castles, S. (1992) 'Migrants and minorities in post-Keynesian capitalism: the German case', in M. Cross (ed.), *Ethnic Minorities and Industrial Change in Europe and North America*, Cambridge: Cambridge University Press.

Castles, S. and Miller, M. (1993) *The Age of Migration*, Basingstoke: Macmillan.

Chamberlayne, P. (1990) 'The Mother's Manifesto and the concept of "Mütterlichkeit"', *Feminist Review*, 35, pp. 9–23.

Chamberlayne, P. (1992a) 'Focus on Volkssolidarität (VS)', *Community Development Journal*, 27 (2), pp. 149–55.

Chamberlayne, P. (1992b) 'Income maintenance and institutional forms: a comparison of France, West Germany, Italy and Britain, 1945–1990', *Policy and Politics*, 20, pp. 299–318.

Chamberlayne, P. (forthcoming) 'Transitions in the private sphere in Eastern Germany', in W. R. Lee and E. Rosenhaft (eds.), *The State and Social Change in Germany 1880–1990*, 2nd edn, Oxford: Berg.

Chandler, E. J. and Wallace, C. D. (1990) 'Some alternatives in youth training: franchise and corporatist models compared', in D. Gleeson (ed.), *Training and its Alternatives*, Milton Keynes: Open University Press.

Chisholm, L. (1992) 'A crazy quilt: education, training and social change in Europe', in J. Bailey (ed.), *Social Europe*, Harlow: Longman.

Chisholm, L., Büchner, P., Krüger, H. H. and Brown, P. (eds.) (1990) *Childhood, Youth and Social Change*, Basingstoke: Falmer.

Christa, H. and Halfar, B. (1992) 'Wohlfahrtsverbände im Wettbewerb: Empirische Ergebnisse zum Spendenmarketing', in T. Bock (ed.), *Sozialpolitik und Wissenschaft – Positionen zur Theorie und Praxis der sozialen Hilfen*, Frankfurt a.M.: Eigenverlag des Deutschen Vereins für öffentliche und private Fürsorge.

Clasen, J. (1992) 'Unemployment Insurance in two countries: a comparative analysis of Great Britain and West Germany in the 1980s', *Journal of European Social Policy*, 2 (4), pp. 279–300.

Clasen, J. (1994) *Paying the Jobless: A comparison of unemployment benefit policies in Great Britain and Germany*, Aldershot: Avebury.

Conradt, D. P. (1993) *The German Polity*, 5th edn, New York: Longman.

Council of Mortgage Lenders (1990) *Housing Finance in Europe*, London: Council of Mortgage Lenders.

Crawshaw, S. (1993) 'Kohl urged to strike back against far right', *Independent*, 12 June, p. 12.

Czarnowski, G. (1991) *Das kontrollierte Paar: Ehe- und Sexualpolitik im National-sozialismus*, Weinheim: Deutscher Studien Verlag.

Dangschat, J. (1990) 'Economic improvement divides the city – the case of Hamburg', paper to International Housing Conference Workshop F, Paris, June.

Dangschat, J. (1993) 'Berlin and the German systems of cities', *Urban Studies*, 30 (6), pp. 1025–51.

Dehnbostel, P. and Rau, E. (1986) 'Youth unemployment in the Federal Republic of Germany: are the West Germans better off?', in R. Rist (ed.), *Finding Work: Cross-national perspectives in employment and training*, Lewes: Falmer.

Dennis, M. (1985) 'Youth in the German Democratic Republic', in E. Kolinsky (ed.), *Youth in East and West Germany*, Modern German Studies, Aston: University of Aston.

Dennis, M. (1988) *The German Democratic Republic: Politics, economics and society*, London: Pinter.

Derbyshire, I. (1987) *Politics in West Germany*, London: Chambers.

Derbyshire, I. (1991) *Politics in Germany: From division to unification*, Edinburgh: Chambers.

Deutsche Bundesbank (1991) 'Recent trends in the finances of the statutory health insurance institutions', *Monthly Report*, January, pp. 25–36.

Dick, E. (1993) 'Mietenreform und Wohngeldsondergesetz in den neuen Bundes-ländern', *BundesBauBlatt*, 4 (April), pp. 242–52.

DIW (Deutsches Institut für Wirtschaftsforschung) (1993a) 'Einkommensverteilung und Einkommenszufriedenheit in ostdeutschen Privathaushalten', *DIW Wochenbericht*, 6, pp. 55–9.

DIW (1993b) 'Sinkende Beschäftigung und steigende Arbeitslosigkeit in Deutschland', *DIW Wochenbericht*, 4, pp. 35–41.

DIW (1993c) 'Beschäftigungsabbau setzt sich fort', *DIW Wochenbericht*, 28, pp. 377–84.

DIW (1993d) 'Zur Entwicklung der Finanzlage der ostdeutschen Kommunen', *DIW Wochenbericht*, 30, pp. 405–11.

Döhler, M. (1991) 'Policy networks, opportunity structures and neo-conservative reform strategies in health policy', in B. Marin and R. Mayntz (eds.), *Policy Networks: Empirical evidence and theoretical considerations*, Frankfurt a.M.: Campus.

von Dohnanyi, K. (1991) *Das deutsche Wagnis*, Berlin: Knaur.

Dölling, I. (1991) 'Between hope and hopelessness – women in the GDR after the turning point', *Feminist Review*, 39, pp. 3–36.

Döring, D., Hauser, R., Rolf, G. and Tibitanzi, F. (1992) 'Old age security of women in the twelve EC-countries: to what extent are Beveridge's two main principles of universality and guaranteed minimum fulfilled?', paper given at *Social Security: 50 Years after Beveridge*, International Conference, University of York, 27–30 September.

Dorwart, R. A. (1971) *The Prussian Welfare State before 1740*, Cambridge, MA: Harvard University Press.

Doyle, L. (1994) 'Racism: West Europe's mounting death toll', *Independent*, 13 January, p. 16.

Dumon, W. (1992) *National Family Policies in EC-Countries in 1991: European observatory of national family policies*, Brussels: Commission of the European Communities, DG V – Employment, Industrial Relations and Social Affairs.

Duvigneau, H. J. and Schonefeldt, L. (1989) *Social Housing Policy, Federal Republic of Germany*, Brussels: COFACE.

Ecklein, J. (1982) 'Women in the GDR: impact of culture and social policy', in J. Giele (ed.), *Women in the Middle Years: Current knowledge and directions for research and policy*, New York: Wiley.

Ecklein, J. and Giele, J. Z. (1981) 'Women's lives and social policy in East Germany and the US', *Studies in Comparative Communism*, 14 (2–3), pp. 191–207.

Edinger, L. J. (1986) *West German Politics*, New York: Columbia University Press.

Edye, D. (1987) *Immigrant Labour and Government Policy*, Aldershot: Gower.

Eifert, C. (1993) *Frauenpolitik und Wohlfahrtspflege: Zur Geschichte der sozial-demokratischen 'Arbeiterwohlfahrt'*, Frankfurt a.M.: Campus.

Einhorn, B. (1992) 'German Democratic Republic', in C. Corrin (ed.), *Superwomen and the Double Burden: Women's experience of change in Central and Eastern Europe and the former Soviet Union*, London: Scarlet Press.

Emms, P. (1990) *Social Housing – a European Dilemma*, Bristol: SAUS.

Employment Observatory (1993) *East Germany. Labour Market Developments and Policies in the new German Länder*, no. 9, November, Brussels: Commission of the European Communities, DG V/A/2 – Employment, Industrial Relations and Social Affairs.

Erler, G. (1988) 'The German paradox – non-feminisation of the labour force and post-industrial social policies', in J. Jenson, E. Hagen and C. Reddy (eds.), *Feminisation of the Labour Force: Paradoxes and promises*, Cambridge: Polity Press.

Esping-Anderson, G. (1990) *The Three Worlds of Welfare Capitalism*, Cambridge: Polity Press.

Eurostat (1993) *Basic Statistics of the Community*, Brussels: CEC.

Evans, K. and Heinz, W. (1994) 'Introduction', in K. Evans and W. Heinz (eds.), *Becoming Adults in England and Germany*, London: Anglo-German Foundation.

Evans, R. J. and Geary, D. (eds.) (1987) *The German Unemployed: Experiences and consequences of mass unemployment from the Weimar Republic to the Third Reich*, London: Croom Helm.

Evers, A. and Wintersberger, H. (eds.) (1988) *Shifts in the Welfare Mix: Their impact on work, social services and welfare policies*, Vienna: European Centre for Social Welfare Training and Research.

Federal Government (1993) 'Medical Studies', Federal Embassy, London, 12 January, mimeo.

Federal Ministry of Education and Science (1993) *Basic and Structural Data 1992/3*, Bonn.

Federal Ministry of Youth, Family Affairs, Women and Health (1984) *Jugendbericht 7*, Bonn.

Federal Ministry of Youth, Family Affairs, Women and Health (1990) *Jugendbericht 8*, Bonn.

Feldmann, U. and Kahler, B. (eds.) (1992) *Die Zusammenarbeit öffentlicher und freier Träger der sozialen Arbeit in den neuen Bundesländern*, Frankfurt a.M.: Eigenverlag des Deutschen Vereins für offentliche und private Fürsorge.

Feministische Studien (1991) *Frauen für eine neue Verfassung*, Extra.

Ferree, M. (1992) 'Institutionalising gender equality: feminist politics and equality offices', *German Politics and Society*, 24–5, pp. 53–65.

Ferree, M. (1993) 'The rise and fall of "mommy politics": feminism and unification in (East) Germany', *Feminist Studies*, 19 (1), pp. 89–115.

Ferris, J. and Page, R. (eds.) (1994) *Social Policy in Transition: Anglo-German perspectives in the new European Community*, Aldershot: Avebury.

Flamm, F. (1983) *The Social System and Welfare Work in the Federal Republic of Germany*, 2nd edn, Frankfurt: Eigenverlag des Deutschen Vereins für öffentliche und private Fürsorge.

Flora, P. and Heidenheimer, A. (eds.) (1981) *The Development of Welfare States in Europe and America*, New Brunswick, NJ: Rutgers University Press.

Forbes, I. and Mead, G. (1992) *Measure for Measure: A comparative analysis of measures to combat racial discrimination in the member countries of the EC*, London: Employment Department.

Ford, R. (1987a) 'Social welfare provision in the Federal Republic of Germany', in R. Ford and M. Chakrabarti (eds.), *Welfare Abroad*, Edinburgh: Scottish Academic Press.

Ford, R. (1987b) 'Social welfare provision in the German Democratic Republic', in R. Ford and M. Chakrabarti (eds.), *Welfare Abroad*, Edinburgh: Scottish Academic Press.

Förster, A. (1991) 'Vergleich und Analyse der Frauenerwerbsarbeit im Deutschland der Nachkriegszeit', in M. Assenmacher (ed.), *Frauen am Arbeitsmarkt*, Probleme der Einheit, Band 4, Marburg: Metropolis.

Freeman, R. (1994) 'Prevention in health policy in the Federal Republic of Germany', *Policy and Politics*, 22 (1), pp. 3–16.

Freudenstein, U. (1992) 'After the wall came down', *Health Matters*, 12, p. 19.

Frevert, U. (1989) *Women in German History: From bourgeois emancipation to sexual liberation*, Oxford: Berg.

Fricke, D. (1976) *Die deutsche Arbeiterbewegung 1869 bis 1914*, Berlin: Dietz.

Gaiser, W. (1991) 'Prolongation of the youth phase in the Federal Republic of Germany: life situation and coping strategies of young people and consequences for youth policy', *Youth and Policy*, 32, pp. 33–8.

Gaiser, W., Hübner-Funk, S., Kruger, W. and Rathgeber, R. (eds.) (1985) *Immer diese Jugend!*, Munich: Koesel Verlag.

Gallagher, M., Laver, M. and Mair, P. (1992) *Representative Government in Western Europe*, New York: McGraw-Hill.

Ganssmann, H. (1993) 'After unification: problems facing the German welfare state', *Journal of European Social Policy*, 3 (2), pp. 79–90.

Gather, C., Gerhard, U., Prinz, K. and Veil, M. (eds.) (1991) *Frauen-Alterssicherung – Lebensläufe von Frauen und ihre Benachteiligung im Alter*, Berlin: Sigma.

Geissler, H. (ed.) (1986) *Abschied von der Männergesellschaft*, Frankfurt a.M.: Ullstein.

Gerhard, U. (1990) 'Gleichberechtigung Heute? 40 Jahre nach Elisabeth Selbert', *Frauenforschung*, 8 (4), pp. 87–94.

Gerhard, U. (1992) 'German women and the costs of unification', *German Politics and Society*, 24/5, pp. 16–33.

Gerhard, U. and Schütze, Y. (1988) *Frauensituation – Veränderungen in den letzten zwanzig Jahren*, Frankfurt a.M.: Suhrkamp.

Gerhard, U., Schwarzer, A. and Slupik, V. (eds.) (1987) *Auf Kosten der Frauen – Frauenrechte im Sozialstaat*, Weinheim: Beltz.

Ghekiere, L. (1991) *Marches et politiques du logement dans la CEE*, Paris: La Documentation Française.

Ghekiere, L. (1992) *Les politiques du logement dans l'Europe de demain*, Paris: La Documentation Française.

Gilbert, M. (1986) *Inflation and Social Conflict*, Brighton: Wheatsheaf.

Ginsburg, G. (1992) *Divisions of Welfare*, London: Sage.

Gladen, A. (1974) *Geschichte der Sozialpolitik in Deutschland*, Stuttgart: Steiner.

Glaessner, G.-J. (1992) *The Unification Process in Germany*, London: Pinter.

Glatzer, W. and Herget, H. (1984) 'Ehe, Familie und Haushalt', in W. Glatzer and W. Zapf (eds.), *Lebensqualität in der BRD – Objektive Lebensbedingungen und subjektives Wohlbefinden*, Frankfurt a.M.: Campus.

Glendinning, C. and McLaughlin, E. (1993) *Paying for Care: Lessons from Europe*, Social Security Advisory Committee, Research Paper 5, London: HMSO.

Göckenjan, G. (1985) *Kurieren und Staat machen: Gesundheit und Medizin in der bürgerlichen Welt*, Frankfurt a.M.: Suhrkamp.

Gow, D. (1993a) 'Kohl threatens Turk extremists', *Guardian*, 2 June, p. 8.

Gow, D. (1993b) 'Old Germans need young migrants' pay', *Guardian*, 1 September, p. 9.

Grottian, P. (1988) *Die Wohlfahrtswende – Der Zauber konservativer Sozialpolitik*, Munich: Beck.

Grünen, Die (1986) 'Umbau der Industriegesellschaft: Schritte zur Überwindung von Erwerbslosigkeit, Armut und Umweltzerstörung', resolution at the Federal Conference, Nuremberg, 26–8 September.

Grunow, D. (1986) 'Debureaucratisation and the self-help movement: towards a restructuring of the welfare state in the FRG?', in E. Øyen (ed.), *Comparing Welfare States and Their Futures*, Aldershot: Gower.

Gude, S. (1991) 'Discrimination problems in the housing market', in A. Norton and K. Novy (eds.), *Low-Income Housing in Britain and Germany*, London: Anglo-German Foundation.

Gutschick, D. (1992) 'Freie Wohlfahrtspflege in den neuen Bundesländern', *Soziale Arbeit*, 41 (1), pp. 9–18.

Habermas, J. (1993) 'The second life fiction of the Federal Republic: we have become "normal" again', *New Left Review*, 197 (February), pp. 58–66.

Haffner, M. (1991) 'Fiscal treatment of owner-occupiers in the EC: a description', paper to conference *Housing Policy as a Strategy for Change*, 24–7 June 1991, Oslo.

Hamm, H. (1993a) 'Wohnungsbautätigkeit 1992: Wohnungsbauexpansion als Motor der Wirtschaftsentwicklung', *BundesBauBlatt*, 7 (July), pp. 498–509.

Hamm, H. (1993b) 'Der soziale Wohnungsbau im Jahre 1992', *BundesBauBlatt*, 5 (May), pp. 340–8.

Hansen, E. (1991) *Wohlfahrtspolitik im NS-Staat*, Augsburg: Maro.

Harloe, M. and Martens, M. (1983) 'Comparative housing research', *Journal of Social Policy*, 13, pp. 255–77.

Hartmann, H. (1985) 'Armut trotz Sozialhilfe: Zur Nichtinanspruchnahme von Sozialhilfe in der Bundesrepublik', in S. Leibfried and F. Tennstedt (eds.), *Politik der Armut und die Spaltung des Sozialstaats*, Frankfurt a.M.: Suhrkamp.

Harvey, E. (1993) *Youth and the Welfare State in Weimar Germany*, Oxford: Oxford University Press.

Hass-Klau, C. (1986) 'Berlin: "soft" urban renewal in Kreuzberg', *Built Environment*, 12 (3), pp. 165–75.

Hausen, K. (1987) 'The German nation's obligation to the heroes' widows of World War I', in M. R. Higonnet, J. Jenson, S. Michel and M. C. Weitz (eds.), *Behind the Lines: Gender and the two world wars*, New Haven, CT: Yale University Press.

Heidenheimer, A. (1980) 'Organised medicine and physician specialisation in Scandinavia', *West European Politics*, 3 (3), pp. 373–87.

Heidenheimer, A. J., Heclo, H. and Teich-Adams, C. (1990) *Comparative Public Policy*, 3rd edn, New York: St Martin's Press.

Heier, D. (1991) 'Arbeitslosigkeit in den neuen Bundesländern', *Sozialer Fortschritt*, 4, pp. 83–95.

Heimann, E. (1980) *Soziale Theorie des Kapitalismus: Theorie der Sozialpolitik*, Frankfurt a.M.: Suhrkamp.

Heinelt, H. (1993) 'Immigration and the welfare state in Germany', *German Politics*, 2 (1), pp. 78–96.

Heinz, W. (1991) 'The role of local authorities in meeting housing need', in A. Norton and K. Novy (eds.), *Low-Income Housing in Britain and Germany*, London: Anglo-German Foundation.

Heinz, W., Krüger, H., Rette, U., Wacht, Veitl, E. and Witzel, A. (1987) *Hauptsache eine Lehrstelle: Jugendliche vor den Hürden des Arbeitsmarkts*, Weinheim: Deutscher Studien Verlag.

Heinze, R. G., Hinrichs, K. and Olk, T. (1986) 'The institutional crisis of a welfare state: the case of Germany', in E. Øyen (ed.), *Comparing Welfare States and Their Futures*, Aldershot: Gower.

Heinze, R. G., Hombach, B. and Scherf, H. (eds.) (1987) *Sozialstaat 2000*, Bonn: Neue Gesellschaft.

Heinze, R. G. and Olk, T. (1991) 'Die Wohlfahrtsverbände im System sozialer Dienstleistungsproduktion', *Kölner Zeitschrift für Soziologie und Sozialpsychologie*, 33 (1), pp. 94–114.

Helm, J. (1981) 'Citizen initiatives and the growth of voluntary action in West Germany', *Journal of Voluntary Action Research*, 10 (2), pp. 49–61.

Helwig, G. and Nickel, H. (1993) *Frauen in Deutschland 1945–1992*, Bonn: Bundeszentrale für Politische Bildung.

Henke, K.-D. (1991) 'Fiscal problems of German unity – the case of health care', *Staatswissenschaft und Staatspraxis*, 2, pp. 170–8.

Hennock, E. P. (1987) *British Social Reforms and German Precedents: The case of social insurance 1880–1914*, Oxford: Clarendon Press.

Hentschel, V. (1983) *Geschichte der deutschen Sozialpolitik 1880–1980: Soziale Sicherung und kollektives Arbeitsrecht*, Frankfurt a.M.: Suhrkamp.

Herbert, U. (1983) 'Apartheid nebenan: Erinnerungen an die Fremdarbeiter im Ruhrgebiet', in L. Niethammer (ed.), *Die Jahre weiß man nicht, wo man die heute hinsetzen soll: Faschismuserfahrungen im Ruhrgebiet*, Berlin/Bonn: Dietz.

Herbert, U. (1990) *A History of Foreign Labour in Germany, 1880–1980*, Ann Arbor: University of Michigan Press.

Herder-Dorneich, P. (1991) 'Theorie der Wende', in G. Kleinhenz (ed.), *Sozialpolitik im vereinten Deutschland*, vol. I, Berlin: Duncker und Humblot.

Hernes, H. M. (1984) 'Women and the welfare state: the transition from private to public dependence', in H. Holter (ed.), *Patriarchy in a Welfare State*, Oslo: Norwegian University Press.

Hernes, H. M. (1986) 'Die zweigeteilte Sozialpolitik: Eine Polemik', in K. Hausen and H. Nowotny (eds.), *Wie männlich ist die Wissenschaft?*, Frankfurt a.M.: Suhrkamp.

Hills, J., Hubert, F., Tomann, H. and Whitehead, C. (1990) 'Shifting subsidy from bricks and mortar to people', *Housing Studies*, 5, pp. 147–67.

Hinrichs, K. (1990) 'Structural change in the family and in the labour market: consequences for the German public pension system', paper presented at the Anglo-German Conference, University of Nottingham, 11 April.

Hinrichs, K. (1991) 'Irregular employment patterns and the loose net of social security: some findings within the West German development', in M. Adler, C. Bell, J. Clasen and A. Sinfield (eds.), *The Sociology of Social Security*, Edinburgh: Edinburgh University Press.

Hockerts, H. G. (1980) *Sozialpolitische Entscheidungen im Nachkriegsdeutschland: Alliierte und deutsche Sozialversicherungspolitik 1945–1959*, Stuttgart: Steiner Verlag.

Hockerts, H. G. (1981) 'German post-war social policies against the background of the Beveridge Plan: some observations preparatory to a comparative analysis', in W. J. Mommsen and W. Mock (eds.), *The Emergence of the Welfare State in Britain and Germany*, London: German Historical Institute/Croom Helm.

Hockerts, H. G. (1983) 'Die Entwicklung vom Zweiten Weltkrieg bis zur Gegenwart', in P. A. Köhler and H. F. Zacher (eds.), *Beiträge zu Geschichte und aktueller Situation der Sozialversicherung*, Berlin: Duncker und Humblot.

Hofemann, K. (1992) 'Aktuelle Sozialhilfeentwicklung in West- und Ostdeutschland', *Sozialer Fortschritt*, 12, pp. 293–8.

Hong, Y.-S. (1990) 'Femininity as a vocation: gender and class conflict in the professionalization of German social work', in G. Cocks and K. Jarausch (eds.), *German Professions 1800–1950*, Oxford: Oxford University Press.

Hong, Y.-S. (1992) 'The contradictions of modernization in the German welfare state: gender and the politics of welfare reform in First World War Germany', *Social History*, 17, pp. 251–70.

Hoskyns, C. (1988) '"Give us equal pay and we'll open our own doors" – a study of the impact in the FRG and the Republic of Ireland of the EC's policy on women's rights', in M. Anderson and M. Buckley (eds.), *Women, Equality and Europe*, London: Macmillan.

Hubert, F. (1992) 'Risks and incentives in German social housing', Free University Berlin (mimeo).

Hubert, F. (1993) 'Germany's housing policy at the crossroads', Free University Berlin, Institut für Wirtschaftspolitik und Wirtschaftsgeschichte, discussion paper (November).

Huster, E.-U. (1993) 'Schroffe Segmentierung in Ost und West: Die doppelt gespaltene Entwicklung in Deutschland', in R. Hickel, E.-U. Huster and H. Kohl (eds.), *Umverteilen*, Cologne: Bund Verlag.

Jacobs, K., Kohli, M. and Rein, M. (1991) 'Germany: the diversity of pathways', in M. Kohli, M. Rein, A.-M. Guillemard and A.-M. Gunsteren (eds.), *Time for Retirement*, Cambridge: Cambridge University Press.

Jarré, D. (1991) 'Subsidiarity in social services in Germany', *Social Policy and Administration*, 25 (3), pp. 211–17.

Jones, G. and Wallace, C. (1990) 'Beyond individualisation: what sort of social change?', in L. Chisholm, P. Büchner, H.-H. Krüger and P. Brown (eds.), *Childhood, Youth and Social Change: A comparative perspective*, London: Falmer.

Joosten, A. (1990) *Die Frau, das 'segenspendende Herz der Familie' – Familienpolitik als Frauenpolitik in der 'Ära Adenauer'*, Pfaffenweiler: Centaurus.

Kahl, A., Wildsorf, S. and Wolf, H. (1984) *Kollektivbeziehungen und Lebensweise*, Berlin: Dietz.

Karcher, H. (1992) 'Doctors furious with German government's health reforms', *British Medical Journal*, 17 October, p. 909.

Katzenstein, P. J. (1987) *Policy and Politics in West Germany: The growth of a semisovereign state*, Philadelphia: Temple University Press.

Kettle, M. (1993) 'Dumping problems on Germany', *Guardian*, 29 May, p. 26.

Kickbusch, I. and Riedmüller, B. (eds.) (1984) *Die Armen Frauen – Frauen und Sozialpolitik*, Frankfurt a.M.: Suhrkamp.

Kirchner, E. J. (1992) 'The European Community: seeds of ambivalence', in G. Smith, W. E. Paterson, P. H. Merkl and S. Padgett (eds.), *Developments in German Politics*, Basingstoke: Macmillan.

Kittner, M. (1989) *Arbeit und Sozialordnung: Ausgewählte und eingeleitete Gesetzestexte*, Cologne: Bund Verlag.

Klee, E. (1985) *'Euthanasie' im NS-Staat; die 'Vernichtung lebensunwerten Lebens'*, Frankfurt a.M.: Fischer.

Kleinhenz, G. (ed.) (1991) *Sozialpolitik im vereinten Deutschland*, vol. I, Berlin: Duncker und Humblot.

Kleinhenz, G. (ed.) (1992) *Sozialpolitik im vereinten Deutschland*, vol. II, Berlin: Duncker und Humblot.

Kleinman, M. (1992) *Policy Responses to Changing Housing Markets: Towards a European housing policy?*, LSE Welfare State Programme, Discussion Paper WSP/73, London School of Economics.

Kleinman, M. (1993) 'Large-scale transfers of council housing to new landlords: is British social housing becoming more "European"?', *Housing Studies*, 8 (3), pp. 163–78.

Koditz, V. (1985) 'The German Federal Republic: how the state copes with the crisis – a guide through the tangle of schemes', in R. Fiddy (ed.), *Youth, Unemployment and Training: A collection of national perspectives*, Lewes: Falmer.

Kohl, J. (1992) 'The public/private mix in the income package of the elderly: a comparative study', paper given at *Social Security: 50 Years after Beveridge*, International Conference, University of York, 27–30 September.

Kohli, J. (1993) 'Wohnungspolitik und Wohnungswirtschaft in den neuen Ländern', *Geographische Rundschau*, 3, (March), pp. 140–5.

Köhnen, H. (1992) *German–English Glossary of Youth Services: A comparative handbook*, Weinheim/Munich: Juventa.

Kolinsky, E. (1989) *Women in West Germany: Life, work and politics*, Oxford: Berg.

Kolinsky, E. (1991) 'Socio-economic change and political culture in West Germany', in J. Gaffney and E. Kolinsky (eds.), *Political Culture in France and Germany*, London: Routledge.

Kolinsky, E. (1993) *Women in Contemporary Germany: Life, work and politics*, rev. edn, Oxford: Berg.

Krätke, M. (1985) 'Klassen und Sozialstaat', *Prokla*, 58, pp. 89–108.

Kreibich, V. (1991) 'Housing needs now and in the 1990s', in A. Norton and K. Novy (eds.), *Low-Income Housing in Britain and Germany*, London: Anglo-German Foundation.

Krisch, H. (1985) *The German Democratic Republic*, Boulder, CO: Westview Press.

Krüger, H. (1989) 'Gesellschaft als Strukturkategorie im Bildungssystem: Alter und neue Konturen geschlechtspezifischer Diskriminierung', Paderborn: Arbeitskreis Sozialwissenschaftliche Arbeitsmarktforschung (SAMF).

Krüger, H. (1990) 'The shifting sands of a social contract: young people in the transition between school and work', in L. Chisholm, P. Büchner, H.-H. Krüger and P. Brown (eds.), *Childhood, Youth and Social Change: A comparative perspective*, London: Falmer.

Krüger, M. and Pfaller, A. (1991) 'The Federal Republic of Germany', in A. Pfaller, I. Gough and G. Therborn (eds.), *Can the Welfare State Compete?*, Basingstoke: Macmillan.

Krüger, R. and Zimmermann, G. (1991) 'Die Erziehungshilfen nach dem KJHG im Spannungsfeld zwischen Jugendamt und freien Trägern', *Soziale Arbeit*, 40 (8), pp. 359–66.

Kühl, J. (1993) 'Arbeitslosigkeit in der vereinigten Bundesrepublik Deutschland', *Aus Politik und Zeitgeschichte*, 35 (93), pp. 3–15.

Kuhn, A. (1991) '1945 – versäumte Emanzipationschancen?', in *Frauen in den neuen Bundesländern: Rückzug in die Familie oder Aufbruch zur Gleichstellung in Beruf und Familie?*, Gesprächskreis Frauenpolitik 2, Bonn: Friedrich Ebert Stiftung.

Kühn, D. (1986) 'Entwicklung des Jugend- und Gesundheitsamts im National-sozialismus', *Neue Praxis*, 16 (4), pp. 322–32.

Kulawik, T. (1992) 'Autonomous mothers? West German feminism reconsidered', *German Politics and Society*, 24/5, pp. 67–85.

Kurbjuweit, D. (1991) 'Kranke zweiter Klasse', *Die Zeit*, 1 March, p. 30.

Lampert, H. (1990) 'Die soziale Komponente im vereinten Deutschland', *Zeitschrift für Bevölkerungswissenschaft*, 16, pp. 397–405.

Lampert, H. (1991) *Lehrbuch der Sozialpolitik*, 2nd rev. edn, Berlin: Springer Verlag.

Landua, D. (1993) 'The social aspects of German unification', in A. Ghanie Ghanssy and W. Schäffer (eds.), *The Economics of German Unification*, London: Routledge.

Landwehr, R. and Baron, R. (eds.) (1983) *Geschichte der Sozialarbeit: Hauptlinien ihrer Entwicklung im 19. und 20. Jahrhundert*, Weinheim/Basle: Beltz.

Lane, C. (1983) 'Women in socialist society with special reference to the GDR', *Sociology*, 17 (4), pp. 489–505.

Langan, M. and Ostner, I. (1991) 'Gender and welfare', in G. Room (ed.), *Towards a European Welfare State?*, Bristol: University of Bristol/SAUS.

Lawson, R. (1980) 'Poverty and inequality in West Germany', in V. George and R. Lawson (eds.), *Poverty and Inequality in Common Market Countries*, London: Routledge & Kegan Paul.

Leibfried, S. (1992) 'Welfare state trajectories of the European Community', in H.-U. Otto and G. Flössner (eds.), *How to Organize Prevention*, Berlin: de Gruyter.

Leibfried, S. and Ostner, I. (1991) 'The particularism of West German welfare capitalism', in M. Adler, C. Bell, J. Clasen and A. Sinfield (eds.), *The Sociology of Social Security*, Edinburgh: Edinburgh University Press.

Leibfried, S. and Tennstedt, F. (eds.) (1985) *Politik der Armut und die Spaltung des Sozialstaats*, Frankfurt a.M.: Suhrkamp.

Leisering, L. (1992) *Sozialstaat und demographischer Wandel: Wechselwirkungen, Generationenverhältnisse, politisch-institutionelle Steuerung*, Frankfurt a.M.: Campus.

Lepsius, M. R. (1979) 'Soziale Ungleichheiten und Klassenstrukturen in der Bundes-republik Deutschland', in H.-U. Wehler (ed.), *Klassen in der europäischen Sozialgeschichte*, Göttingen: Vandenhoek und Ruprecht.

Lex, T. (1990) *Precarious Occupational Careers of Juveniles and Young Adults in the Federal Republic of Germany*, DJI Arbeitspapier 1-017, Munich: Deutsches Jugendinstitut.

Light, D. and Schuller, A. (eds.) (1986) *Political Values and Health Care: The German experience*, Cambridge, MA: MIT Press.

Linton, D. S. (1991) *'Who Has Youth Has the Future': The campaign to save young workers in imperial Germany*, Cambridge: Cambridge University Press.

Lødemel, I. and Schulte, B. (1992) 'Social Assistance – a part of social security or the Poor Law in disguise?', paper delivered to international conference *Social Security, 50 Years after Beveridge*, University of York, 27–30 September.

Lorenz, W. (1991) 'The new German Children and Young People Act', *British Journal of Social Work*, 21, pp. 329–39.

Lorenz, W. (1994) *Social Work in a Changing Europe*, London: Routledge.

Lötsch, M. (1991) 'Ungleichheit – materielle, politische und soziale Differenzierung und ihre gesellschaftpolitischen Konsequenzen', in J. Glaessner (ed.), *Eine*

Deutsche Revolution, Berliner Schriften zur Politik und Gesellschaft 4, Frankfurt a.m.: Verlag Peter Lang.

Lötsch, M. (1992) 'Systemtransformationen und soziale Strukturbrüche in der ehemaligen DDR', in W. Schmähl (ed.), *Sozialpolitik im Prozeß der deutschen Vereinigung*, Frankfurt a.m.: Campus.

Lüdtke, A. (1993) *Eigen-Sinn: Fabrikalltag, Arbeitererfahrungen und Politik vom Kaiserreich bis in den Faschismus*, Hamburg: Ergebnisse Verlag.

Lukas, H. (1991) 'Jugendämter im Umbruch? Verändertes Handeln in traditionellen Arbeitsbereichen und Etablierung neuer Handlungsfelder', *Soziale Arbeit*, 40 (4), pp. 110–17.

McCauley, M. (1983) *The German Democratic Republic since 1945*, Basingstoke: Macmillan.

McKeown, T. (1976) *The Role of Medicine: Dream, mirage or nemesis?*, London: Nuffield Provincial Hospitals Trust.

Mangen, S. (1989) 'The politics of welfare', in G. Smith, W. E. Paterson and P. H. Merkl (eds.), *Developments in West German Politics*, Basingstoke: Macmillan.

Mangen, S. (1991a) 'Social policy, the radical right and the German welfare state', in H. Glennerster and J. Midgley (eds.), *The Radical Right and the Welfare State: An international assessment*, Hemel Hempstead: Harvester Wheatsheaf.

Mangen, S. (1991b) 'The German social state, 1949–1989: a selective audit', in E. Kolinsky (ed.), *The Federal Republic of Germany: The end of an era*, New York: Berg.

Mangen, S. (1992) 'Social policy: one state, two-tier welfare', in G. Smith, W. E. Paterson, P. H. Merkl and S. Padgett (eds.), *Developments in German Politics*, Basingstoke: Macmillan.

Marshall, B. (1992a) 'German migration policies', in G. Smith, W. E. Paterson, P. H. Merkl and S. Padgett (eds.), *Developments in German Politics*, Basingstoke: Macmillan.

Marshall, B. (1992b) 'Migration into Germany: asylum seekers and ethnic Germans', *German Politics*, 1 (1), pp. 124–34.

Mason, T. (1993) *Social Policy in the Third Reich: The working class and the Volksgemeinschaft*, Providence, RI/Oxford: Berg.

Matz, K.-J. (1980) *Pauperismus und Bevölkerung*, Stuttgart: Klett-Cotta.

Mayer, C., Krüger, H., Rabe-Kleberg, U. and Schütte, I. (eds.) (1983) *Mädchen und Frauen: Beruf und Biographie*, Munich: DJI Materialen Verlag.

Meyer-Renschhausen, E. (1989) *Weibliche Kultur und soziale Arbeit*, Cologne: Böhlau.

Michalsky, H. (1985) 'The politics of social policy', in K. von Beyme and M. G. Schmidt (eds.), *Policy and Politics in the Federal Republic of Germany*, Aldershot: Gower.

Miles, R. (1993) *Racism after 'Race Relations'*, London: Routledge.

Milles, D. (1990) 'Industrial hygiene: a state obligation?', in W. R. Lee and E. Rosenhaft (eds.), *A State and Social Change in Germany 1880–1980*, Oxford: Berg.

Mishra, R. (1984) *The Welfare State in Crisis: Social thought and social change*, Brighton: Wheatsheaf.

MISSOC (1993) *Social Protection in the Member States of the Community*, Brussels: Commission of the European Communities, DG V – Employment, Industrial Relations and Social Affairs.

Mitchell, D. (1992) 'Welfare states and welfare outcomes in the 1980s', *International Social Security Review*, 45 (1–2), pp. 73–90.

Moeller, R. G. (1989) 'Reconstructing the family in reconstruction Germany – women and social policy in the Federal Republic, 1949–55', *Feminist Studies*, 15 (1), pp. 137–69.

Moeller, R. G. (1993) *Protecting Motherhood: Women and the family in the politics of postwar West Germany*, Berkeley: University of California Press.

Mommsen, W. J. and Mock, W. (eds.) (1981) *The Emergence of the Welfare State in Britain and Germany 1850–1950*, London: Croom Helm.

Moran, M. (1990) *Distributional Struggles in the German Health Care System: The cases of cost containment and the doctor glut*, Working Paper 2/90, Manchester: University of Manchester European Policy Research Unit.

Moran, M. (1994) 'Reshaping the health-care state', *Government and Opposition*, 29 (1), pp. 48–63.

Moran, M. and Wood, B. (1993) *States, Regulation and the Medical Profession*, Buckingham: Open University Press.

Muller, C. W. (1989) 'Germany, West', in J. Dixon and R. P. Scheurell (eds.), *Social Welfare in Developed Market Countries*, London: Routledge.

Müller, K. (1991) 'Nachholende Modernisierung', *Leviathan*, 2, pp. 261–91.

Müller, U. and Schmidt-Waldherr, H. (eds.) (1989) *FrauenSozialKunde: Wandel und Differenzierung von Lebensformen und Bewußtsein*, Bielefeld: AJZ Verlag.

Münch, U. (1990) *Familienpolitik in der BRD*, Freiburg: Lambertus.

Munday, B. (ed.) (1992) *Social Services in the Member States of the European Community: A handbook of information and data*, Canterbury: University of Kent.

Murswieck, A. (1985) 'Health policy-making', in K. von Beyme and M. G. Schmidt (eds.), *Policy and Politics in the Federal Republic of Germany*, Aldershot: Gower.

Nave-Herz, R. (1989) 'Tensions between paid work in hours and family life', in K. Boh, M. Bak, C. Clason, M. Pakratova, J. Qvortrup, G. Sigritta and K. Waerness (eds.), *Changing Patterns of European Family Life: A comparative analysis of 14 European countries*, London: Routledge.

Nickel, H. M. (1990) 'Frauen in der DDR', *Das Parlament*, 16–17, 13 April.

Nickel, H. M. (1991) 'Geschlechterverhältnis in der Wende?', in *Frauen in den neuen Bundesländern: Rückzug in die Familie oder Aufbruch zur Gleichstellung in Beruf und Familie?*, Gesprächskreis Frauenpolitik 2, Bonn: Friedrich Ebert Stiftung.

Nippert, R. (1992) 'The development and practice of social dentistry in Germany', *Journal of Public Health Dentistry*, 52 (5), pp. 312–16.

Nissen, S. (1988) 'Jenseits des Arbeitsverhältnisses: Sozialpolitische Positionen der Tarifparteien zwischen Mitglieder- und Verbandsinteressen', *Zeitschrift für Sozialreform*, 11/12, pp. 695–709.

Nissen, S. (1990) 'Zwischen lohnarbeitszentrierter Sozialpolitik und sozialer Grundsicherung: Sozialpolitische Reformvorschläge in der parteipolitischen Diskussion', in G. Vobruba (ed.), *Strukturwandel der Sozialpolitik*, Frankfurt a.M.: Suhrkamp.

Nootbaar, H. (1983) 'Sozialarbeit und Sozialpädagogik in der Bundesrepublik 1949–1962', in R. Landwehr and R. Baron (eds.), *Geschichte der Sozialarbeit: Hauptlinien ihrer Entwicklung im 19. und 20. Jahrhundert*, Weinheim/Basle: Beltz.

Norton, A. and Novy, K. (eds.) (1991) *Low-income Housing in Britain and Germany*, London: Anglo-German Foundation.

Nowak, J. (1988) *Soziale Probleme und soziale Bewegungen*, Weinheim/Basle: Beltz.

OECD (1988) *Reforming Public Pensions*, Paris: OECD.

OECD (1992a) *US Health Care at the Cross-roads*, Paris: OECD.

OECD (1992b) *The Reform Of Health Care: A comparative analysis of seven OECD countries*, Paris: OECD.

OECD (1992c) *Economic Surveys: Germany*, Paris: OECD.

OECD (1993) *Health Facts*, Paris: OECD.

Offe, C. (1991) 'Smooth consolidation in the West German welfare state: structural changes, fiscal policies, and populist politics', in F. F. Piven (ed.), *Labor Parties in Postindustrial Societies*, Cambridge: Polity Press.

Ogus, A. (1990) *The Federal Republic of Germany as a Sozialstaat: A British perspective*, Working Paper 3, Manchester: University of Manchester Faculty of Law.

Oldiges, D. (1991) 'Krankenversicherung: Arbeitsministerium nicht mehr zuständig', *Die Ortskrankenkasse*, 4–5, pp. 158–9.

Olk, T. (1987) 'Zwischen Verbandsmacht und Selbstorganisation', in F. Boll and T. Olk (eds.), *Selbsthilfe und Wohlfahrtsverbände*, Freiburg: Lambertus.

Opielka, M. and Ostner, I. (eds.) (1987) *Umbau des Sozialstaats*, Essen: Klartext.

Oppl, H. (1992a) 'Zur "Marktposition" der freien Wohlfahrtspflege', *Soziale Arbeit*, 41 (5), pp. 152–8.

Oppl, H. (1992b) 'Der europäische Binnenmarkt: freie Wohlfahrtspflege auf dem Prüfstand', *Soziale Arbeit*, 41 (10–11), pp. 357–64.

Orthbandt, E. (1980) *Der Deutsche Verein in der Geschichte der deutschen Fürsorge*, Frankfurt a.M.: Eigenverlag des Deutschen Vereins für öffentliche und private Fürsorge.

Osenberg, H. (1993) 'Rehousing the homeless: new model projects in Germany, East and West', paper delivered to International Housing Conference *Transformation in the East, Transition from the West*, Budapest, September.

Ostner, I. (1993) 'Slow motion: women, work and the family in Germany', in J. Lewis (ed.), *Women and Social Policies in Europe: Work, family and the state*, Cheltenham: Edward Elgar.

O'Toole, P. (1993) 'Germany remains the goal', *Guardian*, 9 June, p. 10.

Otto, H.-U. and Sünker, H. (eds.) (1989) *Soziale Arbeit und Faschismus*, Frankfurt a.M.: Suhrkamp.

Oxley, M. and Smith, J. (1993) *Private Rented Housing in the European Community*, European Housing Research Working Paper 3, Milton Keynes: De Montfort University.

Padgett, S. (1992) 'The new German economy', in G. Smith, W. E. Paterson, P. H. Merkl and S. Padgett (eds.), *Developments in German Politics*, Basingstoke: Macmillan.

Pankoke, E. (1986) 'Von "guter Policey" zu "socialer Politik": "Wohlfahrt", "Glückseligkeit" und "Freiheit" als Wertbindung aktiver Sozialstaatlichkeit', in C. Sachße and F. Tennstedt (eds.), *Soziale Sicherheit und soziale Disziplinierung*, Frankfurt a.M.: Suhrkamp.

Paqué, K. and Soltwedel, R. (1993) 'Germany: shaping factors', in A. Jacquemin and D. Wright (eds.), *The European Challenge Post-1992*, Aldershot: Edward Elgar.

Parkes, C. (1992) 'Rebuilding from the ruins', *Financial Times*, Financial Times Survey, 26 October, p. 7.

Pateman, C. (1988) 'The fraternal contract', in J. Keane (ed.), *Civil Society and the State: New European perspectives*, London: Verso.

Penrose, V. (1990) 'Vierzig Jahre SED-Frauenpolitik: Ziele, Strategien und Ergebnisse', *Frauenforschung*, 8 (4), pp. 60–77.

Peukert, D. (1986) *Grenzen der Sozialdisziplinierung: Aufstieg und Krise der deutschen Jugendfürsorge 1878–1932*, Cologne: Bund Verlag.

Pfaff, A. B. and Roloff, J. (1990) 'Familienpolitik in der Bundesrepublik Deutschland: Gewinn oder Verlust für die neuen Bundesländer?', *Frauenforschung*, 8 (4), pp. 29–44.

Pfaller, A., with Gough, I. and Therborn, G. (1991) 'Welfare statism and international competition: the lesson of the case studies', in A. Pfaller, I. Gough and G. Therborn (eds.), *Can the Welfare State Compete?*, Basingstoke: Macmillan.

Potter, P. and Drevermann, M. (1988) 'Home ownership, foreclosure and compulsory auction in the Federal Republic of Germany', *Housing Studies*, 3 (2), pp. 94–104.

Power, A. (1993) *Hovels to High-Rise*, London: Routledge.

Prelinger, C. M. (1986) 'The nineteenth-century deaconessate in Germany: the efficacy of a family model', in R.-E. B. Joeres and M. J. Maynes (eds.), *German Women in the Eighteenth and Nineteenth Centuries*, Bloomington: Indiana University Press.

Preller, L. (1949) *Sozialpolitik in der Weimarer Republik*, Kronberg/Ts.: Athenäum (reprinted 1978).

Priemus, H., Kleinman, M., Maclennan, D. and Turner, B. (1993) *European Economic, Monetary and Political Union: Consequences for national housing policies*, Delft: Delft University Press.

Priemus, H., Kleinman, M., Maclennan, D. and Turner, B. (1994) 'Maastricht Treaty: consequences for national housing policies', *Housing Studies*, forthcoming.

Prinz, M. (1986) *Vom neuen Mittelstand zum Volksgenossen: Die Entwicklung des sozialen Status der Angestellten von der Weimarer Republik bis zum Ende der NS-Zeit*, Munich: Oldenbourg.

Quataert, J. (1984) 'Workers' reactions to social insurance: the case of homeweavers in the Saxon Oberlausitz in the late nineteenth century', *Internationale Wissenschaftliche Korrespondenz zur Geschichte der deutschen Arbeiterbewegung*, 20, pp. 17–35.

Raeff, M. (1975) 'The well-ordered police state and the development of modernity in seventeenth- and eighteenth-century Europe: an attempt at a comparative approach', *American Historical Review*, 80, pp. 1221–43.

Räthzel, N. (1991) 'Germany: one race, one nation?', *Race and Class*, 32 (3), pp. 31–48.

Rauschenbach, T. (1990) 'Jugendhilfe als Arbeitsmarkt – Expertise zum Achten Jugendbericht', in Sachverständigenkommission des Achten Jugendberichts (ed.), *Jugendhilfe - historischer Rückblick und neuere Entwicklungen*, vol. 1, Munich: Verlag Deutsches Jugendinstitut.

Rauschenbach, T. (1991) 'Sozialpädagogik – eine akademische Disziplin ohne Vorbild?', *Neue Praxis*, 21 (1), pp. 1–11.

Rauschenbach, T. (1993) 'Soziale Berufe im Umbruch', *Sozialmagazin*, 18 (4), pp. 18–29.

Recker, M.-L. (1985) *Nationalsozialistische Sozialpolitik im zweiten Weltkrieg*, Munich: Oldenbourg.

Riedmüller, B. (1985) 'Armutspolitik und Familienpolitik. Die Armut der Familie ist die Armut der Frau', in S. Leibfried and F. Tennstedt (eds.), *Politik der Armut und die Spaltung des Sozialstaates*, Frankfurt a.M.: Suhrkamp.

Ritter, G. A. (1986) *Social Welfare in Germany and Britain*, Leamington Spa: Berg.

Ritter, G. A. (1991) *Der Sozialstaat: Entstehung und Entwicklung im internationalen Vergleich*, 2nd edn, Munich: Oldenbourg.

Roesler, J. (1991) 'Mass unemployment in Eastern Germany', *Journal of European Social Policy*, 1 (2), pp. 129–36.

Rohde, B. (1993) 'Umbruch, Armutsentwicklung und Sozialverwaltung – ein Situationsbericht aus den neuen Bundesländern', *Nachrichtendienst des deutschen Vereins für öffentliche und private Fürsorge*, 73 (10), pp. 370–4.

Room, G. (1992) *Observatory on National Policies to Combat Social Exclusion*, 2nd annual report, Brussels: Commission of the European Communities DG V – Employment, Industrial Relations and Social Affairs.

Rose, R. and Wignanek, G. (1990) *Training without Trainers? How Germany avoids Britain's supply-side bottleneck*, London: Anglo-German Foundation.

Rosenberg, D. (1993) 'The new home economics: women in the united Germany', *Debatte*, 1, pp. 111–34.

Rowland, D. (1991) 'Health status in East European countries', *Health Affairs*, 10 (3), pp. 203–15.

Sachße, C. (1986) *Mütterlichkeit als Beruf: Sozialarbeit, Sozialreform und Frauen-bewegung*, Frankfurt a.M.: Suhrkamp.

Sachße, C. and Tennstedt, F. (1980) *Geschichte der Armenfürsorge in Deutschland – vom Spätmittelalter bis zum 1. Weltkrieg*, Stuttgart: Kohlhammer.

Sachße, C. and Tennstedt, F. (1982) 'Familienpolitik durch Gesetzgebung: die juristische Regulierung der Familie', in F.-X. Kaufmann (ed.), *Staatliche Sozial-politik und Familie*, Munich: Oldenbourg.

Sachße, C. and Tennstedt, F. (1988) *Geschichte der Armenfürsorge in Deutschland Fürsorge und Wohlfahrtspflege 1871 bis 1929*, Stuttgart: Kohlhammer.

Scarlett Epstein, T., Crehan, K., Gerzer, A. and Sass, J. (1986) *Women, Work and Family in Britain and Germany*, London: Croom Helm.

Scharf, C. B. (1984) *Politics and Change in East Germany: An evaluation of socialist democracy*, London: Pinter.

Scharf, C. Bradley (1987) 'Social policy and social conditions in the GDR', in M. Rueschemayer and C. Lemke (eds.), *The Quality of Life in the German Democratic Republic*, Armonck, New York: Sharpe.

Schieber, G., Poullier, J.-P. and Greenwald, L. (1993) 'Health spending, delivery, and outcomes in OECD countries', *Health Affairs*, 12 (2), pp. 120–9.

Schmähl, W. (1992a) 'Sozialpolitik und Systemtransformation', in W. Schmähl (ed.), *Sozialpolitik im Prozeß der deutschen Vereinigung*, Frankfurt a.M.: Campus.

Schmähl, W. (ed.) (1992b) *Sozialpolitik im Prozeß der deutschen Vereinigung*, Frankfurt a.M.: Campus.

Schmähl, W. (1993) 'The "1992 reform" of public pensions in Germany: main elements and some effects', *Journal of European Social Policy*, 3 (1), pp. 39–51.

Schmid, G., Reissert, B. and Bruche, G. (1992) *Unemployment Insurance and Active Labor Market Policy: An international comparison of financing systems*, Detroit: Wayne State University Press.

Schmidt, M. G. (1988) *Sozialpolitik: Historische Entwicklung und internationaler Vergleich*, Opladen: Leske und Budrich.

Schmidt, M. G. (1989) 'Learning from catastrophes: West Germany's public policy', in F. G. Castles (ed.), *The Comparative History of Public Policy*, Cambridge: Polity Press.

Schmidt, M. G. (1992) 'Political consequences of German unification', *West European Politics*, 15, pp. 1–15.

Schneider, U. (1993) *Solidarpakt gegen die Schwachen: Der Rückzug des Staates aus der Sozialpolitik*, Munich: Knaur Verlag.

Schober, K. (1992) 'Probleme des Berufstarts im geeinten Deutschland', *Diskurs*, 91/2, pp. 5–13.

Schulte, B. (1991) 'Die Folgen der EG-Integration für die wohlfartsstaatlichen Regimes', *Zeitschrift für Sozialreform*, 37, pp. 548–78.

Schulte, B. and Trenk-Hinterberger, P. (1988) *Bundessozialhilfegesetz (BSHG)*, 2nd edn, Munich: C. H. Beck.

Schultheis, F. (1988) 'Fatale Strategien und ungeplante Konsequenzen beim Aushandeln "familiärer Risiken" zwischen Mutter, Kind und "Vater Staat"', in K. Lüscher, F. Schultheis and M. Wehrspaun (eds.), *Die postmoderne Familie*, Konstanz: Universitätsverlag.

Schütze, Y. (1988) 'Mütterliche Erwerbsarbeit und wissenschaftliche Forschung', in U. Gerhard and Y. Schütze (eds.), *Frauensituation – Veränderungen in den letzten 20 Jahren*, Frankfurt a.M.: Suhrkamp.

Schwarz, G. and Zenner, C. (eds.) (1990) *Wir wollen mehr als ein 'Vaterland' – DDR-Frauen im Aufbruch*, Hamburg: Rowohlt.

Sivanandan, A. (1991) 'Editorial', *Race and Class*, 32 (3), pp. v–vi.

Sivanandan, A. (1993) 'Racism: the road from Germany', *Race and Class*, 34 (3), pp. 67–75.

Smith, G. (1986) *Democracy in Western Germany: Parties and politics in the Federal Republic*, 3rd edn, Aldershot: Dartmouth.

Smith, G. (1992a) 'The nature of the unified state', in G. Smith, W. E. Patterson, P. H. Merkl and S. Padgett (eds.), *Developments in German Politics*, Basingstoke: Macmillan.

Smith, G. (1992b) 'The "new" party system', in G. Smith, W. E. Paterson, P. H. Merkl and S. Padgett (eds.), *Developments in German Politics*, Basingstoke: Macmillan.

Smith, G., Paterson, W. E., Merkl, P. H. and Padgett, S. (eds.) (1992) *Developments in German Politics*, Basingstoke: Macmillan.

Sommer, T. (1993) 'Darkness that breaks the chain of light', *Guardian*, 4 June, p. 22.

SPD (Sozialdemokratische Partei Deutschlands) (1988) 'Die Zukunft sozial gestalten – sozialpolitisches Programm der SPD', resolution at Annual Conference, Münster.

Spicker, P. (1991) 'The principle of subsidiarity and the social policy of the European Community', *Journal of European Social Policy*, 1 (1), pp. 3–14.

Spiegel, Der (1993) 'Arm an Wissen über Armut', *Der Spiegel*, 31, pp. 26–8.

Statistisches Bundesamt (1992) *Statistisches Jahrbuch für die Bundesrepublik Deutschland*, Stuttgart: Metzler-Poeschel.

Steinmetz, G. (1993) *Regulating the Social: The welfare state and local politics in imperial Germany*, Princeton: Princeton University Press.

Stone, D. (1980) *The Limits of Professional Power: National health care in the Federal Republic of Germany*, Chicago: University of Chicago Press.

Sturm, R. (1992) 'The changing territorial balance', in G. Smith, W. E. Paterson, P. H. Merkl and S. Padgett (eds.), *Developments in German Politics*, Basingstoke: Macmillan.

Süssmuth, R. and Schubert, H. (1992) *Bezahlen die Frauen die Wiedervereinigung?*, Munich: Piper.

Tampke, J. (1981) 'Bismarck's social legislation: a genuine breakthrough?', in W. J. Mommsen and W. Mock (eds.), *The Emergence of the Welfare State in Britain and Germany 1850–1950*, London: Croom Helm.

Tennstedt, F. (1977) *Soziale Selbstverwaltung: Geschichte der Selbstverwaltung in der Krankenversicherung*, Bonn: Verlag der Ortskrankenkassen.

Tennstedt, F. (1981) *Sozialgeschichte der Sozialpolitik in Deutschland*, Göttingen: Vandenhoeck und Ruprecht.

Tennstedt, F. (1992) 'Die Spitzenverbände der freien Wohlfahrtspflege im dualen Wohlfahrtsstaat', *Soziale Arbeit*, 41 (10–11), pp. 342–56.

Titmuss, R. M. (1974) *Social Policy*, London: George Allen & Unwin.

Tomann, H. (1990) 'Housing in Germany', in D. Maclennan and R. Williams (eds.), *Affordable Housing in Europe*, York: Joseph Rowntree Foundation.

Tomann, H. (1993) 'Developments in German housing finance', in B. Turner and C. Whitehead (eds.), *Housing Finance in the 1990s*, Research Report SB53, Gavle, Sweden: National Swedish Institute for Building Research.

Tomforde, A. (1993a) 'Where the law of blood still rules', *Guardian Europe*, 2 March, p. 15.

Tomforde, A. (1993b) 'Bonn defies protestors to curb asylum rights', *Guardian*, 27 May, p. 24.

Trojan, A., Halves, E. and Wetendorf, H. W. (1986) 'Self-help groups and consumer participation: a look at the German health care self-help movement', *Journal of Voluntary Action Research*, 15 (2), pp. 14–23.

Tufts, A. (1992) 'Germany: new health care law agreed', *The Lancet*, 14 November, pp. 1216–17.

Turner, B., Hegedus, J. and Tosics, I. (1992) *The Reform of Housing in Eastern Europe and the Soviet Union*, London: Routledge.

Ullmann, H.-P. (1981) 'German industry and Bismarck's social security system', in W. J. Mommsen and W. Mock (eds.), *The Emergence of the Welfare State in Britain and Germany 1850–1950*, London: Croom Helm.

Usborne, C. (1992) *The Politics of the Body in Weimar Germany*, London: Macmillan.

van Vliet, W. (1990) *International Handbook of Housing Policies and Practices*, New York: Greenwood Press.

Veil, M., Prinz, K. and Gerhard, U. (eds.) (1992) *Am modernen Frauenleben vorbei*, Berlin: Sigma.

Vobruba, G. (ed.) (1990) *Strukturwandel der Sozialpolitik*, Frankfurt a.M.: Suhrkamp.

Vogelheim, E. (1988) 'Women in a changing workplace – the case of the FRG', in J. Jenson, E. Hagen and C. Reddy (eds.), *Feminisation of the Labour Force: Paradoxes and promises*, Cambridge: Polity Press.

Wagner, W. (1984) *Die nützliche Armut: Eine Einführung in die Sozialpolitik*, Berlin: Rotbuch Verlag.

Walker, A., Alber, J. and Guillemard, A.-M. (1993) *Older People in Europe: Social and economic policies. The 1993 Report of the European Observatory*, Brussels: Commission of the European Communities, DG V – Employment, Industrial Relations and Social Affairs.

Wall, R. and Winter, J. (eds.) (1988) *The Upheaval of War: Family, work and welfare in Europe 1914–1918*, Cambridge: Cambridge University Press.

Wallace, C. (1994) 'Young women', in K. Evans and W. Heinz (eds.), *Becoming Adults in England and Germany*, London: Anglo-German Foundation.

Wallraff, G. (1988) *Lowest of the Low*, London: Methuen.

Webber, D. (1988) 'Krankheit, Geld und Politik: zur Geschichte der Gesundheitsreformen in Deutschland', *Leviathan*, 16 (2), pp. 156–203.

Webber, D. (1989) 'Zur Geschichte der Gesundheitsreformen in Deutschland – II. Norbert Blüms Gesundheitsreform und die Lobby', *Leviathan*, 17 (2), pp. 262–300.

Webber, D. (1991) 'Health policy and the Christian–liberal coalition in West Germany: the conflicts over the health insurance reform, 1987–8', in C. Altenstetter and S. Haywood (eds.), *Comparative Health Policy and the New Right*, London: Macmillan.

Weindling, P. (1993) *Health, Race and German Politics between National Unification and Nazism 1870–1945*, 2nd edn, Cambridge: Cambridge University Press.

Weisbrod, B. (1981) 'The crisis of German unemployment insurance in 1928/1929 and its political repercussions', in W. J. Mommsen and W. Mock (eds.), *The Emergence of the Welfare State in Britain and Germany 1850–1950*, London: Croom Helm.

Weiss, O., Schönebeck, M. and Köhler, P. (1990) 'Sozialwesen und Sozialfürsorgeausbildung in der DDR', *Soziale Arbeit*, 39 (6), pp. 80–5.

Welzmüller, R. (1989) 'Kräftige Gewinnsteigerungen durch unerwarteten Wachstumsschub: Zur Entwicklung der Einkommensverteilung im Jahre 1988', *WSI-Mitteilungen*, 7, pp. 361–75.

Whalen, R. W. (1984) *Bitter Wounds: German victims of the Great War, 1914–1939*, Ithaca, NY: Cornell University Press.

Whitehead, C., Cross, D., Kleinman, M. and Connolly, V. (1992) *Housing the Nation: Choice, access and priorities*, vol. 2, London: Royal Institution of Chartered Surveyors.

Wilderer, H. (1993) 'Der deutsche Wohnungsmarkt – nicht nur in Ballungszentren ein Problemfall ohne Ende', *Der langfristige Kredit*, August, pp. 221–4.

Wilpert, C. (1991) 'Migration and ethnicity in a non-immigration country: foreigners in a united Germany', *New Community*, 18 (1), pp. 49–62.

Wilson, M. (1993) 'The German welfare state: a conservative regime in crisis', in A. Cochrane and J. Clarke (eds.), *Comparing Welfare States: Britain in international context*, London: Sage/Open University Press.

Winkler, G. (1989) *Geschichte der Sozialpolitik der DDR 1945–1985*, Berlin: Akademie Verlag.

Winkler, G. (1990) *Frauenreport 1990*, Berlin: Die Wirtschaft.

Wolf, J. (1991) 'Die Vergesellschaftungslücke: der Vorruhestand in den neuen Bundesländern', *Zeitschrift für Sozialreform*, 11, pp. 723–35.

Zapf, W. (1986) 'Development, structure and prospects of the German social state', in R. Rose and R. Shiratori (eds.), *The Welfare State East and West*, Oxford: Oxford University Press.

Zapf, W. (1991) 'Der Untergang der DDR und die soziologische Theorie der Modernisierung', in B. Giesen and C. Leggewie (eds.), *Experiment Vereinigung*, Berlin: Rotbuch Verlag.

Index

Abelshauser, W., 33, 39
abortion, 177, 180, 183, 186
accident insurance, 67, 71
accountability, 94, 165
Adams, P., 174
Alber, J., 8, 9, 12, 63–4, 65, 73–4, 75, 91, 93
Aliens Act (1990), 195, 197, 198–9
Allen, A.T., 30
apprenticeships, 131, 136–8, 139
  young women, 144
Article 16 *see* citizenship law
asylum seekers, 16, 69, 196–8, 202
  and Article 16, 196, 197
  and EC indifference, 196–7
  educational disadvantage, 145–6
  numbers, 196
  reception of, 197–8
Atkinson, G., 203

baby years, 66, 183
Bäcker, G., 66, 72, 75, 79–80
Backhaus-Maul, H., 54, 55, 166, 167
Baldwin, P., 63, 76
Bargel, T., 134, 135
Baron, R., 151
Bast, K., 175, 178, 180
Bendit, R., 145–6
Berger, H., 45
Bertram, B., 142, 143, 186
Bertram, H., 175
Bessel, R., 33
Beyme, K. von, 3, 4, 5, 6, 7, 12, 16, 54
Bialas, C., 55
Bismarck, Otto von, 26–30, 62–3
Blackwell, J., 74
Blanc, M., 47, 122

Blandow, J., 154
Bock, G., 36
Boelhouwer, P., 103, 106, 107, 108–9, 118, 119
Borkenstein, H.–J., 111
Borrmann-Müller, R., 175
Braun, H., 10
Britton, A., 118
Bruch, R. vom, 28
Brühl, A., 68
Buchtemann, C.F., 74
Buck, G., 152
Bumer, Gertrud, 152
Burkhardt, D., 142
Burleigh, M., 36
Buskase, H., 125

Cannan, C., 169
care insurance, 67, 70, 71, 74, 78–9, 187
Caritas, 55, 149, 154, 160
Carvel, J., 196, 197, 206
Casey, B., 138
Castles, S., 194, 198, 203, 205
CDU, 4, 38, 55, 76
Chamberlayne, Prue, 16, 45, 173–90
Chandler, E.J., 137
child benefit, 39–40, 63, 64, 69, 70
child labour, 24, 26
childbearing/childrearing, 185
  allowances, 66, 71, 180
  effect on income, 176–7
  and employment, 175–7, 178, 180–1
  media campaign, GDR, 183–4
  patterns, 175, 177
  rejection of, 176–7, 178, 182, 188